Re-Enacting the Past

What is re-enactment and how does it relate to heritage? Re-enactments are a ubiquitous part of popular and memory culture and are of growing importance to heritage studies. As concept and practice, re-enactments encompass a wide range of forms: from the annual 'Viking Moot' festival in Denmark drawing thousands of participants and spectators, to the (re)staged war photography of An-My Lê, to the Titanic Memorial Cruise commemorating the centennial of the ill-fated voyage, to the symbolic retracing of the Berlin Wall across the city on 9 November 2014 to mark the 25th anniversary of its toppling.

Re-enactments involve the sensuousness of bodily experience and engagement, the exhilarating yet precarious combination of imagination with 'historical fact', in-the-moment negotiations between and within temporalities, and the compelling drive to re-make, or re-presence, the past. As such, re-enactments present a number of challenges to traditional understandings of heritage, including taken-for-granted assumptions regarding fixity, conservation, originality, ownership and authenticity. Using a variety of international, cross-disciplinary case studies, this volume explores re-enactment as practice, problem, and/or potential, in order to widen the scope of heritage thinking and analysis toward impermanence, performance, flux, innovation and creativity.

This book was originally published as a special issue of the *International Journal of Heritage Studies*.

Mads Daugbjerg is Associate Professor of Anthropology at Aarhus University, Denmark.

Rivka Syd Eisner is a postdoctoral research fellow with the UFSP Asien und Europa at the University of Zurich, Switzerland.

Britta Timm Knudsen is Associate Professor of Aesthetics and Communication at Aarhus University, Denmark.

Re-Enacting the Past

Heritage, materiality and performance

Edited by
Mads Daugbjerg, Rivka Syd Eisner
and Britta Timm Knudsen

LONDON AND NEW YORK

First published 2016
by Routledge
2 Park Square, Milton Park, Abingdon, Oxon, OX14 4RN, UK

and by Routledge
711 Third Avenue, New York, NY 10017, USA

First issued in paperback 2017

Routledge is an imprint of the Taylor & Francis Group, an informa business

British Library Cataloguing in Publication Data
A catalogue record for this book is available from the British Library

ISBN 13: 978-1-138-29484-4 (pbk)
ISBN 13: 978-1-138-94186-1 (hbk)

Typeset in Times New Roman
by RefineCatch Limited, Bungay, Soffolk

Publisher's Note
The publisher accepts responsibility for any inconsistencies that may have
arisen during the conversion of this book from journal articles to book chapters,
namely the possible inclusion of journal terminology.

Disclaimer
Every effort has been made to contact copyright holders for their permission to
reprint material in this book. The publishers would be grateful to hear from any
copyright holder who is not here acknowledged and will undertake to rectify
any errors or omissions in future editions of this book.

Contents

Citation Information

The chapters in this book were originally published in the *International Journal of Heritage Studies*, volume 20, issues 7–8 (September – November 2014). When citing this material, please use the original page numbering for each article, as follows:

Chapter 1
Re-enacting the past: vivifying heritage 'again'
Mads Daugbjerg, Rivka Syd Eisner and Britta Timm Knudsen
International Journal of Heritage Studies, volume 20, issues 7–8 (September – November 2014) pp. 681–687

Chapter 2
Re-enacting process: temporality, historicity and the Women's Liberation Music Archive
Deborah Withers
International Journal of Heritage Studies, volume 20, issues 7–8 (September – November 2014) pp. 688–701

Chapter 3
From a colonial reinvention to postcolonial heritage and a global commodity: performing and re-enacting Angkor Wat and the Royal Khmer Ballet
Michael S. Falser
International Journal of Heritage Studies, volume 20, issues 7–8 (September – November 2014) pp. 702–723

Chapter 4
Patchworking the past: materiality, touch and the assembling of 'experience' in American Civil War re-enactment
Mads Daugbjerg
International Journal of Heritage Studies, volume 20, issues 7–8 (September – November 2014) pp. 724–741

Chapter 5
Between narratives and lists: performing digital intangible heritage through global media
Sheenagh Pietrobruno
International Journal of Heritage Studies, volume 20, issues 7–8 (September – November 2014) pp. 742–759

Chapter 6

Performing heritage (studies) at the Lord Mayor's Show
Duncan Grewcock
International Journal of Heritage Studies, volume 20, issues 7–8 (September –
November 2014) pp. 760–781

Chapter 7

The time travellers' tools of the trade: some trends at Lejre
Cornelius Holtorf
International Journal of Heritage Studies, volume 20, issues 7–8 (September –
November 2014) pp. 782–797

Chapter 8

Drought and Rain: *re-creations in Vietnamese, cross-border heritage*
Rivka Syd Eisner
International Journal of Heritage Studies, volume 20, issues 7–8 (September –
November 2014) pp. 798–817

For any permission-related enquiries please visit:
http://www.tandfonline.com/page/help/permissions

Notes on Contributors

Mads Daugbjerg is an associate professor of Anthropology at Aarhus University, Denmark. His main research concerns the intersections of heritage and museology, experience-based tourism and practices of memory and belonging. His publications include articles in *The International Journal of Heritage Studies*, in *History and Anthropology* (co-edited special issue with Thomas Fibiger on 'Globalized Heritage', 2011), and in *Museum and Society*. His first book, entitled *Borders of Belonging: Experiencing History, War and Nation at a Danish Heritage Site*, was published in 2014.

Rivka Syd Eisner is a postdoctoral research fellow at the UFSP Asien und Europa at the University of Zurich. Her current research engages the lives and works of contemporary artists in Vietnam, exploring relationships between performance, politics, memory, transnationality and the body. Her work has appeared in journals such as *TDR: The Drama Review, Performance Research, Cultural Studies*, and in various edited volumes.

Michael S. Falser is an architect and art historian, and currently postdoctoral project leader at the Chair of Global Art History within the Cluster of Excellence, 'Asia and Europe in a Global Context', at the University of Heidelberg, Germany. Since 2009, his research has focused on 'heritage as a transcultural concept' with the case study of the Cambodian temple of Angkor Wat in the 19th to 21st centuries (forthcoming, 2016). His latest edited volume was entitled *Cultural Heritage as Civilizing Mission. From Decay to Recovery* (2015). Currently he works on architectural style building processes in late-colonial empires, including the Dutch East Indies, French Indochina and British India (1900–1950).

Duncan Grewcock is a principal lecturer in Museum and Heritage Studies at Nottingham Trent University, where he teaches on the MA Museum and Heritage Development programme. An academic and museum and heritage planner, his research interests lie in the relationships between museums, heritage and place and in the critical-creative academic practices of the field. His recent book, *Doing Museology Differently* (2014) challenges conventional approaches to museum study.

Cornelius Holtorf is professor of Archaeology at Linnaeus University in Kalmar, Sweden. His current research interests include the future of cultural heritage in society, the archaeology of time travelling, contemporary zoos and long-term communication regarding final depositories of nuclear waste. He is the author of numerous works on theoretical issues relating to cultural heritage. He is also associate editor of the journals *Heritage & Society* and the *Journal of Contemporary Archaeology*.

Britta Timm Knudsen is associate professor of Aesthetics and Communication at Aarhus University, Denmark.

Sheenagh Pietrobruno is an assistant professor of English at Fatih University in Istanbul, Turkey. Her research combines digital heritage, new media, performing arts and intangible heritage. She is the author of *Salsa and Its Transnational Moves* (2006). Her forthcoming book is entitled *Digital Legacies: The Global Archiving of Intangible Heritage*.

Deborah Withers is a writer, researcher, curator and publisher. She is the curator of two exhibitions about the cultural history of the Women's Liberation Movement, Sistershow Revisited (2011) and Music & Liberation (2012), both funded by the Heritage Lottery Fund. Her academic work has been published in the *Journal of Oral History, Women: A Cultural Review*, the *International Journal of Heritage Studies*, and the *European Journal of Women's Studies*. Her book *Feminism, Digital Culture and the Politics of Transmission: Theory, Practice and Cultural Heritage* was published in 2015.

Re-enacting the past: vivifying heritage 'again'

Mads Daugbjerg, Rivka Syd Eisner and Britta Timm Knudsen

Aarhus University; University of Zurich and Aarhus University

What do the Mexican tourism concept *Caminata Nocturna* (running since 2004), the British *Battle of Orgreave* event staged by Jeremy Deller in 2001, Joshua Oppenheimer's prize-winning 2012 documentary *The Act of Killing* and the international grassroots *Society for Creative Anachronism* have in common? In all of them – although for different reasons – people engage in *re-enactment*: they utilise, dramatise and revitalise selected events, episodes or even atmospheres of the past, whether those pasts concern illegal crossings of the US–Mexican border, the violent clashes of the 1984–1985 UK miners' strike, the massacres of supposed communists in Indonesia during the 1960s or the arts and skills of pre-seventeenth-century Europe.[1]

This special issue deals with processes of re-enacting as they relate to heritage. Re-enactment as activity and concept implies a number of challenges to conventional understandings of 'heritage' and many of the taken-for-granted qualities and assumptions usually associated with the term, such as fixity, conservation, 'listing', ownership or authenticity, to name but a few. The contributions in this volume work, we hope, to unsettle many such 'givens', forcing us to critically interrogate the scope of conventional heritage thinking; to ask whether heritage can be thought and analysed, instead, along lines of impermanence, performance, flux, innovation and creativity – and if so, how such lines of scrutiny might afford new possibilities and potential identifications within heritage work, while at the same time acknowledging a set of new or recast problems and issues not easily dealt with when 'heritage' is approached through the lens of re-enactment.

Re-enactment is hardly an understudied phenomenon these days, and the present volume must be seen as a contribution to a growing field of research that spans several disciplines, including history, anthropology, performance studies and film studies (for some important, recent contributions, see Agnew and Lamb 2009; McCalman and Pickering 2010; Jackson and Kidd 2011; Magelssen and Justice-Malloy 2011; Schneider 2011; Kalshoven 2012; ten Brink and Oppenheimer 2012).[2] What we have sought to provide in the present context is an open, curious and, importantly, cross-disciplinary set of studies and explorations of re-enactment as practice, problem and/or potential, and relate these to the field and insights of heritage studies.

Why and how, one may ask, should re-enacting and re-enactment be seen as a particularly pertinent field of study within heritage studies just now? Following from our identification of the 'challenging' nature of re-enactment, above, we would identify four clusters of reasons for this:

(1) Re-enacting could be said to produce *ontologically intensive knowledge*, to adopt Lash's (2010, 8) term, in which the observer is placed in the world with the things or beings that she studies. According to Lash, globalisation

processes engender simultaneous 'extensive' and 'intensive' tendencies. As an example of an extensive yet also intensive, global network, the *Society for Creative Anachronism* spans more than 30,000 members all across the world.

(2) Re-enacting is profoundly *experiential*, attesting to the fact that 'meaning is not interpretative; it is doing, it is impact' (Lash and Lury 2007, 12; and see Knudsen and Waade 2010), pointing to the fact that 'culture' – or, more precisely, the products and by-products of the cultural industries – have become so ubiquitous as to dominate economies and the experiences of everyday life. Post-Fordist economies turn increasingly experiential (Pine and Gilmore 1999; Boswijk, Thijssen, and Peelen 2007), and everyday life is vitally intensified through events and peaks. 'Culture' today must be conceptualised as *matter for immersion*, not mere signs for interpretation.

(3) Re-enacting *transcends conventional Western mind-matter dualisms*, biology-culture dichotomies and self-other divides in producing new agencies (Barad 2007) and inter-corporealities with inherent possibilities of establishing dialogues (Harrison, 2012), kinetic empathy (Thrift 2008), sympathetic imagination (Weissman 2004) or haptic communication; in all of which it becomes crucial how a body feels and how energies, sensations, forces and intensities move between bodies and entities (Blackman 2012, 13).

(4) Re-enacting means *performing and producing in the present*, stressing immediacy, liveness and participation (Auslander 1999; Gumbrecht 2004; Jenkins 2006; Marriott 2007; Tomlinson 2007; Kelty et al., 2015). Such logics of immediacy, partly created and powerfully supported by various forms of digital media, travel and spread across the social fabric at astonishing rates. They provide increasing user-generated possibilities for virtual and global interconnection, supplementing more conventional systems of history making and heritage work (but also often provoking or destabilising those apparatuses; see Pietrobruno, this volume).

The time of re-enactment

Following the flow of a 'script', as most re-enactments do to some degree, means that the re-enacted past upholds a complex temporality: it is not entirely present or completely constructed in the here and now, but neither does it, obviously, allow access to an unmediated past. To borrow an eloquent double negation from Schneider (2011, 43), we may say that the re-enacted past is *not not* the past (Schneider 2011, 43).[3] Or, following film scholar Bill Nichols, we may say that re-enactments 'effect a fold in time', a 'temporal vivification in which past and present coexist in the impossible space of a fantasmatic' (2008, 88; see also ten Brink 2012). His term 'vivification' is astute, in our view, since it captures the effect of re-enactment as something distinct from conventional representation. 'Vivification is neither evidence nor explanation. It is, though, a form of interpretation, an inflexion that resurrects the past to reanimate it with the force of a desire' (Nichols 2008, 88).

Performing history in the form of re-enactment is thus paradoxical because it is both 'bound by the past', obliged on the sceneries and scripts it seeks to recreate, and also necessarily forcing participants to experience that past from the position and reflexive hindsight of the present. Moreover, re-enactments are also often used to perform 'work' in the present and/or for the future, capable of generating and assembling new collectives, sympathies or movements in the present and sometimes providing participants with a powerful experience of individual or collective agency, of 'having a say' in the shaping or even revision of history (Thompson 2004; de Groot 2009; Daugbjerg, this volume).

This dimension of felt agency is closely tied to the embodied and experiential forms of knowledge that re-enactment thrives on. Contrary to conventional representations, re-enactments commonly feature bodily and immersive performances of material and digital 'archives' (Taylor 2003) that have the capacity to substantially transform participants' or witnesses' relations to the events or memories in question. While critics have argued that re-enacting is often – or, according to some, generically – characterised by a hollow, superficial, commercialised, politically traditionalist or otherwise dangerously compelling relation to history (e.g. Agnew 2004; Cook 2004; Walsh 1992), we argue against such an ingrained scepticism, stressing instead how re-enactment in some senses arguably 'digs deeper' than standard modes of history and heritage representation, exactly because it includes the sensual, the corporeal and the kinesthetic (Cromby 2007; Schneider 2011; Waterton and Watson 2013). This is in line with classical phenomenological points on the cognitive profoundness of embodied being and of 'dwelling' (Dijk, Smith, and Weiler 2012), and also informed by work in non-representational theory (e.g. Thrift 2008; Anderson and Harrison 2010; and see Grewcock, this volume).

In our view, to put it briefly, the haptic and experiential character of re-enactment holds promise and potential for work within the heritage field. This does not mean that we encourage uncritical embracement of any and all attempts at re-enactment. We do believe, however, that re-enactment does not, as some critics tend to argue, of and by itself 'distort' or 'falsify' history or heritage, and we hold that an academically reflexive dialogue and critique – in some cases, even, co-participation – may, in fact, be productive in shaping fresh awareness, heightened reflexivity and counter-narratives, and increased access for new audiences around heritage. Joram ten Brink, in his thoughtful discussion of Collingwood's continued relevance for filmic uses of re-enactment, insists that re-enactment is, at its core, 'a process of critical thinking' (2012, 178). He is also acutely aware, however, that many popular re-enactment activities today, such as battle re-enactments, tend to 'perpetuate ideologies rather than question them' (184; see also West 2014). Echoing this, Phillips states that '[r]e-enactment, it is true, has often served as a vehicle for the politics of traditionalism, but (…) it is a mistake to assume fixed correlations between form, affect, and ideology' (2013, 12).

In agreement with such calls for critical but open-minded research engagements that set out to explore, discuss and influence the contemporary state, power and impact of re-enactment in different heritage contexts – while always insisting on the specificity of each particular context – we invite the reader to delve into the wide-ranging case studies and interdisciplinary discussions of the following pages.

The state of re-enacting: the essays and case studies

The contributions in this special issue engage a range of media, from digital recordings and platforms to the blurred boundaries between dance, parade, ritual and protest, to imaginative acts of refashioning the material objects and whole livelihoods of very present pasts. Culturally and geographically, the authors explore the legacies of colonial and post-colonial criss-crossing between Asia and Europe, the evolving memories and current (re)enactments of protest in the United Kingdom and Ireland, alternative Mevlevi Sema Ceremony practices and their online interventions, the struggle to reclaim American Civil War narratives and the desire to relive Iron Age Nordic pasts. Each essay differently unearths the politics of these complicated heritage re-enactments and raises questions about 'authenticity' and 'originals', the nature and multisensory textures of experience, embodiment and material culture, and the impulses driving our era's increasing thirst for re-living heritage.

Deborah Withers begins the volume with her study of the online Women's Liberation Music Archive. She explores the archive as a continuing record of performative practices rather than as authentic, finished products. Withers illuminates how the archive's in-process, activist recordings underscore and propel the unfinished political work of protest and help keep it alive and effective within the present. Working with a different sort of living, evolving heritage practice, Michael Falser retells the fraught history of Cambodia's Royal Khmer Ballet. Falser investigates the confluence of what he calls 'French colonial reinvention, postcolonial/ nationalist essentialisation, and global commodification' that have shaped Khmer classical dance and our (mis)understanding of its 'architectural stage' of Angkor Wat. His study makes clear the problematics of UNESCO-branding practices and the necessity of careful historical analyses. History is also at stake in Mads Daugbjerg's essay as he shifts focus to the personal perspectives and private lifeworlds of American Civil War re-enactors. Daugbjerg charts the vitality of objects within practitioners' experience of touching – as well as their aspirations to claim and change – the past and present. Looking at heritage re-enactment in terms of what he calls a 'holistic' and yet, also 'unfinished' practice of 'patchworking', Daugbjerg shows how these present-day confederate soldiers critique conventional museum-based practices of learning about and experiencing the past.

In her investigation of the Mevlevi Sema Ceremonies of Turkey through the medium of online YouTube videos, Sheenagh Pietrobruno takes heritage re-enactment research into new technical and performative cyber territories. Through extensive knowledge of the ceremonial practice and its practitioners, as well as the algorithmic workings of YouTube, Pietrobruno forwards her claim that user-generated content becomes a critical archive of the changing nature of Mevlevi Sema re-enactments. This unofficial archive helps counter the 'freezing' tendency of official UNESCO videos as well as question the conservative and nationalist politics bound up in the ritual's status as heritage. Continuing the theme of change within embodied practice, Duncan Grewcock offers a performative essay that simultaneously discusses and demonstrates his call for more performance-centred forms of 'doing' heritage studies. Drawing on non-representational theory and performance-research approaches, Grewcock interweaves description and analysis of the Lord Mayor's Show ritual with the Occupy London Stock Exchange protest movement as they encounter each other in the public streets. The resulting document is itself an evocative record and re-enactment of the heritage about which it speaks.

In *The time-travellers' tools of the trade: some trends at Lejre,* Cornelius Holtorf returns to questions of authenticity, experience and material culture with his participatory study of an open-air archaeological museum in Denmark. Following a larger trend, the Lejre museum is undergoing transformation from research site to what Holtorf terms an 'archaeological theme park' where families vacation together and partake in heritage tourism, or 'time travel', as both an experiential learning and leisure activity. A vital, underlying question running throughout this essay is, to what extent historical accuracy matters in this and other living history and heritage tourism sites: what is gained and what is lost if accuracy is not a priority? In the final essay, Rivka Syd Eisner discusses Vietnamese-French choreographer Ea Sola's *Drought and Rain* dance trilogy as a site and practice of performatively layered and unfinished, cross-border cultural heritage. Seeking to bring heritage studies into greater dialogue with performance studies perspectives, Eisner engages *Drought and Rain* in order to propose four performance-centred dynamics of heritage re-enactment that may be of value for forging new pathways into heritage studies scholarship.

Notes

1. For a study of the performative power of the *Caminata Nocturna* tours, see Magelssen (2011). For a discussion of Jeremy Deller's *Battle of Orgreave* re-enactment, see Correia (2006). The Indonesian context to Joshua Oppenheimer's *The Act of Killing* is detailed in Anderson (2012). For an inquiry into the role of material culture in the *Society for Creative Anachronism*, see Sparkis (1992).
2. Earlier landmark studies that continue to inform the field include Snow (1993); Samuel (1994); Crang (1996); Handler and Gable (1997); Handler and Saxton (1988); Kirshenblatt-Gimblett (1998). In the philosophy of history, Collingwood's (1946) seminal theories on re-enactment as (intellectual, historiographical) method form an important, if often indirect, backdrop to much current work.
3. Here, Schneider draws on Schechner's (1985) foundational dictum in performance studies of what he called 'restored behaviour' and the 'not not me', indeed making her own phrase a form of recast re-enactment in itself.

References

Agnew, V. 2004. "Introduction: What is Reenactment?" *Criticism* 46 (3): 327–339.
Agnew, V., and J. Lamb, eds. 2009. *Settler and Creole Reenactment*. Basingstoke: Palgrave Macmillan.
Anderson, B. 2012. "Impunity." In *Killer Images. Documentary Film, Memory and the Performance of Violence*, edited by J. T. Brink and J. Oppenheimer, 268–286. New York: Wallflower Press.
Anderson, B., and P. Harrison, eds. 2010. *Taking-Place. Non-Representational Theories and Geography*. Farnham: Ashgate.
Auslander, P. 1999. *Liveness. Performance in a Mediatized Culture*. London: Routledge.
Barad, K. 2007. *Meeting the Universe Halfway. Quantum Physics and the Entanglement of Matter and Meaning*. Durham: Duke University Press.
Blackman, L. 2012. *Immaterial Bodies. Affect, Embodiment, Mediation*. London: Sage.
Boswijk, A., T. Thijssen, and E. Peelen. 2007. *The Experience Economy. A New Perspective*. Amsterdam: Pearson, Prentice Hall.
ten Brink, J. 2012. "Re-Enactment, the History of Violence and Documentary Film." In *Killer Images. Documentary Film, Memory and the Performance of Violence*, edited by J. ten Brink and J. Oppenheimer, 176–189. New York: Wallflower Press.
ten Brink, J., and J. Oppenheimer, eds. 2012. *Killer Images. Documentary Film, Memory and the Performance of Violence*. New York: Wallflower Press.
Collingwood, R. G. 1946. *The Idea of History*. Oxford: Oxford University Press.
Cook, A. 2004. "The Use and Abuse of Historical Reenactment: Thoughts on Recent Trends in Public History." *Criticism* 46 (3): 487–496.
Correia, A. 2006. "Interpreting Jeremy Deller's the Battle of Orgreave." *Visual Culture in Britain* 7 (2): 93–112.

Crang, M. 1996. "Magic Kingdom or a Quixotic Quest for Authenticity?" *Annals of Tourism Research* 23 (2): 415–431.

Cromby, J. 2007. "Towards a Psychology of Feeling." *International Journal of Critical Psychology* 21: 94–118.

Dijk van, P. A., Smith, L. D. G, and Weiler, B. 2012. "To Re-Enact of Not to Re-Enact? Investigating the Impacts of First- and Third-Person Interpretation at a Heritage Tourism Site." *Visitor Studies* 15 (1): 48–61.

de Groot, J. 2009. "Historical Re-Enactment." In *Consuming History. Historians and Heritage in Contemporary Popular Culture*, 105–123. London: Routledge.

Gumbrecht, H. U. 2004. *Production of Presence. What Meaning Cannot Convey*. Stanford: Stanford University Press.

Handler, R., and E. Gable. 1997. *The New History in an Old Museum. Creating the past at Colonial Williamsburg*. Durham: Duke University Press.

Handler, R., and W. Saxton. 1988. "Dyssimulation: Reflexivity, Narrative, and the Quest for Authenticity in 'Living History'." *Cultural Anthropology* 3 (3): 242–260.

Harrison, R. 2012. *Heritage: Critical Approaches*. London: Routledge.

Jackson, A., and J. Kidd, eds. 2011. *Performing Heritage. Research, Practice and Innovation in Museum Theatre and Live Interpretation*. Manchester: Manchester University Press.

Jenkins, H. 2006. *Convergence Culture: Where Old and New Media Collide*. New York: New York University Press.

Kalshoven, P. T. 2012. *Crafting the Indian. Knowledge, Desire and Play in Indianist Reenactment*. Oxford: Berghahn.

Kelty, C., A. Panofsky, M. Currie, R. Crooks, S. Erickson, P. Garcia, M. Wartenbe, S. Wood 2015: "Seven dimensions of contemporary participation disentangled". *Journal of the Association for Information Science and Technology* 66(3): 474–488.

Kirshenblatt-Gimblett, B. 1998. *Destination Culture. Tourism, Museums and Heritage*. Berkeley: University of California Press.

Knudsen, B. T., and A. M. Waade, eds. 2010. *Re-Investing Authenticity. Tourism, Place and Emotions*. Bristol: Channel View.

Lash, S. 2010. *Intensive Culture: Social Theory, Religion and Contemporary Capitalism*. London: Sage.

Lash, S., and C. Lury. 2007. *Global Culture Industry: The Mediation of Things*. Cambridge: Polity Press.

Magelssen, S. 2011. "Tourist Performance in the Twenty-First Century." In *Enacting History*, edited by S. Magelssen and R. Justice-Malloy, 174–202. Tuscaloosa: The University of Alabama Press.

Magelssen, S., and R. Justice-Malloy, eds. 2011. *Enacting History*. Tuscaloosa: The University of Alabama Press.

Marriott, S. 2007. *Live Television. Time, Space and the Broadcast Event*. Los Angeles, CA: Sage.

McCalman, I., and P. A. Pickering, eds. 2010. *Historical Reenactment. From Realism to the Affective Turn*. Basingstoke: Palgrave Macmillan.

Nichols, B. 2008. "Documentary Reenactment and the Fantasmatic Subject." *Critical Inquiry* 35 (1): 72–89.

Phillips, M. S. 2013. "Introduction. Rethinking Historical Distance: From Doctrine to Heuristic." In *On Historical Distance*, edited by M. S. Phillips, B. Caine, and J. A. Thomas, 1–19. Houndmills, Basingstoke: Palgrave Macmillan.

Pine II, J. B., and J. H. Gilmore. 1999. *The Experience Economy. Work is Theatre and Every Business a Stage*. Boston, MA: Harvard Business School Press.

Samuel, R. 1994. "Living History." In *Theatres of Memory. Past and Present in Contemporary Culture*, 169–202. London: Verso.

Schechner, R. 1985. *Between Theatre and Anthropology*. Philadelphia: University of Pennsylvania Press.

Schneider, R. 2011. *Performing Remains. Art and War in times of Theatrical Reenactment*. New York: Routledge.

Snow, S. E. 1993. *Performing the Pilgrims. A Study of Ethnohistorical Role-Playing at Plimoth Plantation*. Jackson: University of Mississippi Press.

Sparkis, S. 1992. "Objects and the Dream: Material Culture in the Society for Creative Anachronism." *Play & Culture* 5 (1): 59–75.

Taylor, D. 2003. *The Archive and the Repertoire. Performing Cultural Memory in the Americas*. Durham: Duke University Press.

Thompson, J. 2004. *War Games. Inside the World of 20th-Century War Reenactors*. Washington, DC: Smithsonian Books.

Thrift, N. 2008. *Non-Representational Theory*. London: Routledge.

Tomlinson, J. 2007. *The Culture of Speed. the Coming of Immediacy*. London: Sage.

Walsh, K. 1992. *The Representation of the past: Museums and Heritage in the Post-Modern World*. London: Routledge.

Waterton, E., and S. Watson. 2013. "Framing Theory: Towards a Critical Imagination in Heritage Studies." *International Journal of Heritage Studies* 19 (6): 546–561.

Weissman, G. 2004. *Fantasies of Witnessing. Postwar Efforts to Experience the Holocaust*. Ithaca, NY: Cornell University Press.

West, B. 2014. "Historical Re-Enacting and Affective Authority: Performing the American Civil War." *Annals of Leisure Research* 17 (2): 161–179.

Mads Daugbjerg
Aarhus University

Rivka Syd Eisner
University of Zurich

Britta Timm Knudsen
Aarhus University

Re-enacting process: temporality, historicity and the Women's Liberation Music Archive

Deborah Withers

Independent Researcher

This article uses the Women's Liberation Music Archive (WLMA) as a case study to explore re-enactment as the performative 'doing' of history. As an archive composed of music-making processes rather than commercial 'products', the article argues this is an invitation to consider the time of history as one of action and enlivenment. The article frames the dissemination of material in the WLMA as a delayed event that is made possible by the digital technologies, in particular free web tools, such as blogs. It explores the implications of the resurfacing of marginal cultural histories within the present moment, and how this can transform conceptions of historicity and time. Finally, the article asserts the value of digital archives within the context of music histories, thus challenging the notion that effective historical encounters can only occur through engagement with original objects.

The Women's Liberation Music Archive (WLMA) is an online blog archive that documents the histories of music making in the UK Women's Liberation Movement (WLM) 1970–1989. Launched in May 2011, it contains digitalised music, film and photographs, oral history excerpts, written personal narratives, songbooks, fliers and other ephemera from a wide range of bands and solo artists connected to feminist political communities during the 1970s and 1980s. For many of the acts documented on the blog, it is the only evidence they ever existed, even if that was only for one spontaneous performance at an agit-prop cabaret event in Hackney, London in 1981. The blog uses the possibilities afforded by free 2.0 web tools to address the marginalisation of these women's contribution to alternative music history. These are histories that even in the early twenty-first century still cast only a cursory glance to oppositional music made by women, including within so-called radical accounts (see Lynksey 2011).

This article explores how the WLMA digitally *re-enacts* the histories of feminist music making. By using the term 're-enactment', I deliberately deploy it in a different way to theorisations of historical re-enactment that tie it to the *practices* of historical re-enactment societies, or the re-enactment of historical events and situations on television, radio and film. Vanessa Agnew, who has written about practices of re-enactment in popular culture, does however suggest that the term can be utilised in a wider way. A consideration of re-enactment, she argues, 'enables us to map trends within historical thought, examine the implications for our understanding of the past and interrogate history's social and political uses' (Agnew 2007, 301). I engage with the flexibility of recent theorisations of re-enactment that suggest when the past is brought 'to life', it can create openings for relating to history in affective, empathetic and corporeal ways. Jerome de Groot echoes this by highlighting the potential of re-enactment to 'undermine the controlling and disciplining claims of an all-encompassing, authoritative historical mainstream' (de Groot 2011, 588).

This article is especially inspired by the work of Rebecca Schneider in *Performing Remains* (2011), which explores re-enactment as the encounter between performance theory and historiography. Schneider's engagement productively highlights the particular temporal dimension and experience communicated by re-enactment practices: that of 'liveness' and the performative 'doing' of history. However, crucially in Schneider's characterisation of historical re-enactment, 'liveness' is not just 'a matter of temporal immediacy, happening only in an uncomplicated now, a "transitory" present, an im-mediate moment [… it can be] punctuated by, syncopated with, indeed charged by, other moments, other times' (Schneider 2011, 92). The materials in the WLMA, I argue, are a particularly rich source to think through a re-enacted historical 'liveness' and the attendant playing with time because the remains left by these communities are 'incomplete', 'fragmentary' or 'unfinished' and thus communicate the *processes* of feminist music making. They are examples of histories that are 'utterly impossible to conserve in 'representations' that can be taken along in the hand luggage with which we traverse time' (Runia 2006, 305). Finished representations embody and enact a particular temporal logic – we arrive to the event or object *after* it takes place or has been made. The process-based materials of the WLMA, however, communicate a wholly different temporal dimension. Encountering these materials is comparable to arriving at event in the middle of its duration, or to the construction of a building as it is being made, while simultaneously suspending the expectation that the event will end, or the house will ever be built. This kind of temporal retraining is integral to understanding what the re-enacted histories of the WLMA *do*. As they are read through the lens of performance theory's proximity to liveness, and how digital media facilitates high levels of networked relationships, linear time is muddled, as past, present and future touch and rebound in unexpected ways.

Digital media platforms are the crucial and transformative vehicle for the re-enactment of Women's Liberation music histories in the contemporary moment, and the theoretical significance of this will also be explored in the article. In the case of the WLMA, the free online digital platform creates the possibility for the large-scale circulation of non-commercial music that was simply not possible during the time it was created: feminist music making was embedded in a certain time and place, and within particular communities. In terms of mainstream popular culture, it may as well have not existed—such was its invisibility. Women's liberation music making subsequently disappeared, only to re-emerge as a digitally mediated 'untimely history', as will be discussed later. The re-circulation of historical materials or 're-presence of the past' (Sobchack 2011, 323) via digital networks has also been theorised as changing temporal experiences and relations in a similar way to Schneider's use of re-enactment. Digitally 'networked re-enactments' create what

Katie King calls '*pastpresents*, run together all in one word, in which pasts and presents very literally mutually construct each other' (King 2012, 12). In this article, then, I bring together the different ways performance theory, historiography and media studies have implicitly or explicitly theorised re-enactment, so that the term can be used to understand different experiences of historicity and time using the WLMA as my case study.

This article is split into three areas that explore the re-enactment of feminist music making in the contemporary moment. The first section provides context about women's participation in music making within wider culture, highlighting that participation still remains uneven among the genders, from grassroots to professional levels. This is followed by explanations about why the music of the WLM has remained largely invisible until its dissemination on the WLMA. The next section frames the re-enactment of feminist music making as a delayed event, exploring the temporal implications of their untimely emergence in the present through the vehicle of digital technologies. The final section explores the question of digital re-enactments and the value of digital archiving, and whether digitally re-circulated artefacts can engender affective and corporeal historical experiences. To begin the article, I will elaborate the cultural situations that have shaped the emergence of the WLMA.

Women and music: a fragmented legacy

In 2013, women are still massively under-represented in the music industry, from grassroots to professional levels. In 2010, the UK-based Performing Rights Society (PRS) noted that men who registered as songwriters and music creators with the organisation outnumbered women from 6 to 1 (PRS 2010). While in 2009, 77% of people working in promotion and management work in the music industry were men (Guardian 2009). The marked gender discrepancy within the UK is clear. Although there are a number of reasons for this, the lack of access to the histories of women who have made music in the past, and the lack of visible role models in the public sphere as a consequence, is arguably one of them.

The aim of the WLMA, and its partner exhibition project *Music & Liberation*,[1] is to organise and communicate the varied histories of women's music making in the UK WLM. Saving some acts like Spoilsports and The Fabulous Dirt Sisters from obscurity, and bolstering the knowledge of established music makers such as Maggie Nicols, Frankie Armstrong and Carol Grimes, the archive aspires to create an enduring legacy that sticks permanently into the grooves of culture. The blog aims to create a sense of tradition to allow for a 'temporal depth rooted in [the] continuities' of feminist music making, affording those histories a 'disposition to value' (Cubitt 2007, 181) that has previously been denied to them because of their ephemerality, unknown and non-commercial nature. Of course, it does not necessarily follow that greater access to women's musical histories will equate with more balanced opportunities for women musicians in the future. However, allowing these histories to *circulate* on the Internet and other public spaces creates possibilities for people to collide with them. This can happen deliberately or through more opportunistic means, such as following the trails of hyperlinks from other websites, or clicking through to the site after search engine terms such as 'list of bad haircuts,' 'female playing congas' or 'blue cow music record' list the WLMA as part of the search results.[2]

The cultural interventions made by feminist music makers have largely been invisible prior to their dissemination on the blog in 2011. Much of the evidence of feminist music making from the 1970s and 1980s has been locked away at the back of cupboards, stuffed into old shoeboxes, largely forgotten and sometimes deemed unimportant by the music makers themselves.[3] Or, if the music has been collected in archives, such as the Women's Revolution Per Minute archive that was stored at Birmingham public library for over 10 years, the recordings languished in an archival basement, without the facilities to listen to the music. The WRPM collection moved in 2012 to the Women's Art Library at Goldsmiths, London, which should now improve access to the material, with regular opening hours and listening equipment available.[4]

Despite the lack of discernible legacy of WLM music in mainstream and alternative music histories, the personal collections of people involved in WLM music making generated large amounts of material. Recordings were stored on now obsolete formats such as ½ and ¼ inch Ampex tape, U Matic and Betamax videotape, or on more common analogue formats such as audiotape and vinyl. The launch of the WLMA has been a catalyst for the small-scale digitisation of some of this material, but this has often not been to archive quality standards because it has been reliant on domestic digitisation technologies that tend to output highly compressed mp3 files, rather than uncompressed WAVs or AIFFS. The Heritage Lottery Funded *Music & Liberation* project did provide resources for high quality, professional transfers, and this has further facilitated the digitisation of rare material.

Explaining invisibility

There are a number of specific reasons for the enduring invisibility of the histories of feminist music makers that are worth mentioning here. Firstly, there was a deliberate political strategy of some bands to purposely eschew the popular, capitalist 'malestream', which meant groups positioned themselves outside the dominant popular culture (including against punk), and were more concerned with creating and controlling their own means of cultural production. As the Women's Liberation Music Projects Group, who was instrumental in organising debates related to feminism and music in London in the late 1970s, stated in their introduction to the songbook *Sisters in Song*:

> We are firmly against feminist music being taken up by the music industry and commercialised in any way. We are involved in taking control over our own music, which means not only playing and singing, but also gaining knowledge about instruments, equipment, sound engineering and recording – usually a male domain, and having control over the distribution of our music, etc (WLMP n.d., 4)

Such an attitude meant that women had to find ways to be independent, but this also meant that feminist bands had limited public exposure. The commercial popular music industry was a particular target for feminist criticism because it melded capitalism and sexism in oppressive ways, as the Northern Women's Liberation Rock Band challenged in their manifesto: 'these songs help to keep women in their accustomed role of wives and mothers, dependent on men, because they hide the real conflicts in women's lives and relationships with men and so prevent them from understanding their oppression' (1974). Opportunities for participating in music making were limited too in the 1970s: at worst women were excluded outright, at best they could occupy limited, stereotypical roles, such as a genteel backing singer.

Another factor affecting the audience reception of women's liberation music was that much of the music was written for circulation within feminist communities. Lyrics celebrated taboo subjects such as lesbianism, and often referred to the dynamics of being in the movement itself. To a large degree, the subject matter of the songs reflected the 'world' of the WLM, and drew on and created specific codes that would have been relevant only to women who were also participating. The appeal to 'outsiders', and the potential to engage wider audiences, was therefore arguably limited. There were exceptions, of course, with bands such as The Guest Stars having a good degree of popular success throughout the 1980s.[5]

Another important reason for the lack of a well-known legacy for WLM music making was financial: finding funds to support activities such as practising, acquiring equipment and organising gigs was difficult, and this compromised the sustainability of women's ventures. Lack of money also impacted on many music makers' capacity to realise practical aspects of music making, like recording music in studios. Making a record of 'studio quality' music and releasing it on an album or 7" single is one way to make a concrete legacy of musical activity, whether done professionally or in a more amateur setting. Having such recordings can facilitate 'canonisation', a crucial technology of recognition in popular music history, and of course, wider culture (Von Appen and Doehring 2006). Yet many feminist music makers did not manage to do this with all of their work, although there are exceptions. Ova, for example, set up their own recording studio in 1986 and managed to record four full-length albums during their career. In the late 1970s, music studios were very expensive to use. Although Portastudios (portable recording equipment) came into usage in the late 1970s and early 1980s, home recording was in no way as accessible, high quality or common as it is today. Recording studios could also be intimidating places for women who had little or no experience of working in such a context that was, for the most part, the exclusive domain of men. To put it simply, a lot of music made by women in the 1970s and 1980s went unrecorded. There are far more recordings of demo tapes, practices and live performances than studio recordings available. It is this basic lack of music and legible musical 'products', that render it difficult to recognise the legacy of Women's Liberation music making within the terms of recognition afforded by mainstream popular music histories.

The circulation of Women's liberation music

The circulation of the music made within the Women's Liberation was therefore minimal by commercial music standards. Some bands existed for a few shows, never recorded music and only played in their local area. Others lasted for years, toured extensively but only recorded one record. Jam Today is a pertinent example of this. In a career that spanned eight years (and three different line-ups), they only recorded and released the four songs on *Stereotyping* EP (1981),[6] and they had to borrow the money to do it. Even *if* or when the music was recorded, there was then the issue of distribution. This could be an exhausting and pain staking experience, particularly if you were organising and funding the activity yourself, as Figure 1 indicates.

Given the limited resources of women's liberation music makers, organising recording music *and* distributing it was exceptionally hard work. Women's Revolution Per Minute (who are mentioned in Figure 1) was the only distribution company that sold 'women's music' in the UK. They sold cassettes, records and later CDs through a catalogue, at events, in women's bookshops such as Sisterwrite in London, and at radical bookshops across the UK. The re-distribution of artefacts on the WLMA re-enacts all aspects of music making, and does not just focus on 'finished' musical products, or the success stories. Sales lists, as included in Figure 1, sit along-side album covers, budget books next to photographs of live performances. The archive thus communicates process, doing and action. It re-enacts this sense of 'live-ness,' and relays the cultural interventions made by feminist music makers.

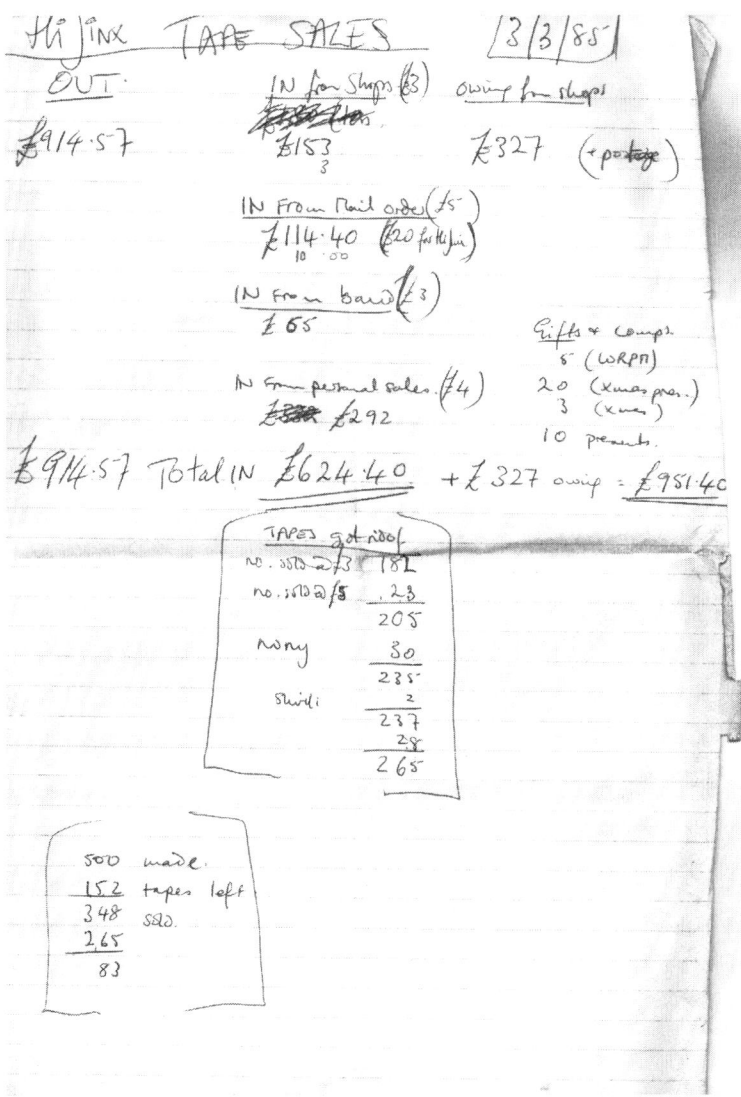

Figure 1.   Hi-Jinx Tape Sales. Image illustrates the financial pressures of women recording and distributing their own music in Women's Liberation music-making communities. Item appears courtesy of Ros Davies who funded the recording of the one Hi-Jinx album *Stepping Over and Out.*

Given the nature of legacy material described above, prior to setting up the WLMA the circulation of Women's Liberation music histories across time and generations has been minimal. To give a sense of this point, I want to share here my own opportunistic encounter with the music of the WLM. In 2007, I became interested in the histories of the WLM and regularly visited the Feminist Archive South (FAS) in Bristol. The archive was then based in the back room of a public library. Posters hung on the walls and the periodicals protruded invitingly for visitors. The material was as accessible as it could be; it was largely an 'open archive.' In 2007, I was very involved in feminist music making myself (albeit in a different context), and was generally interested in uncovering the 'cultural' legacies of the WLM. The FAS has a fairly good collection of tapes and vinyl but had no facilities on which to play the items. Very few of the bands featured in the archives had further information about them on the Internet. It was frustrating, but also tantalising, to see and touch what felt like cultural secrets in a space that was relatively accessible for the public. Significantly, should I be seeking a similar experience today it would not be possible. In 2009, the FAS moved to premises at Bristol University so that trained archivists, rather than volunteers, can look after the archives. While this may be a key step toward institutionalising these histories, it also makes it far more difficult for people to have chance encounters with marginal cultural histories in public spaces.

To create the possibility for public encounters is precisely what motivated the creation of the WLMA and its exhibition project, *Music & Liberation*. In January 2013, 18 months after being launched, the site has had over 45,000 unique visitors. Considering the limited audiences for such music during the time it was being performed, this is a staggering number. The online archive has the potential to reach audiences across the world and with great speed, as Anna Reading summarises: 'digital media technologies and digitization enable the capture and storage, management and reassembly of data records in ways that in relation to earlier mediated memories are less costly, globally connected, and reproducible across different media' (Reading 2011, 242). Although people have viewed the blog across the world, the highest numbers of visitors to the site come from the UK, USA, Canada and Australia.

Women's Liberation music histories as a 'delayed event'

For many of the bands in the WLMA then, being documented on the site was the first time the material was subject to large-scale media circulation. Before the archive was launched these histories were the province of temporally and spatially located communities of interest, reliant on oral transmission, personal and collective memories and the distribution of analogue recordings for their coherence and communication. In the digital age however, this has radically changed as they have become accessible to far wider and diverse publics. The WLMA acts as an example of what Victoria Browne, following Christine Battersby's reading of Nietzsche, calls an 'untimely history':

> the untimely event is not simply used up as it occurs. It does not fall back into the past: spent and wasted, but nor is it swept up and appropriated [...] Nietzsche's untimely events and forgotten ideas are not subsumed within historical time. Nor do they disappear from it. They remain on the fringes of cultural memory and pop up again at unforeseen moments, to break apart and disrupt the sedimented time frames and

syntheses that cannot entirely suppress or contain them. This upsets the linear ideal of history as a simple succession or step-by-step accumulation of events. (2012, 11)

Such a description seems fully appropriate to describe what happened to the music making histories of the WLM. The potential of such histories was not 'used up' at their time of happening because they simply did not reach that many people to have a substantial impact. Moreover, the specific, anti-capitalist and woman-focused nature of music making meant that they were also too 'difficult' to be appropriated, unlike other radical musical movements of the time. Punk's oppositional stance, for example, became commodified, at least at an aesthetic level, almost as soon as it arrived on 'the scene'. Women's Liberation music making, however, has remained on the fringes of cultural memory and still has the capacity to surprise: 'who knew feminist rock was full of sax? Not me' wrote music critic Alexis Petridis in *The Guardian* in an article about the WLMA (2012). Arguably it is only with the technological conditions of the early twenty-first century, in particular digitisation; that provide a fertile context where these histories can emerge from the margins. Importantly, they do so in a different, digitised form that has implications to be explored later in this article.

The last part of Browne's quote is also indicative of what the very materials of this untimely history *do*: they break apart established historical time precisely because they re-enact the *processes* of Women's Liberation music making. They jolt time into the moment of action as we can listen to women practising together, tarrying in time, going through the motions (in the motion) and trying (but often) failing to get the song right. We do not have access to the 'final' performance because there is no such recording in existence. We can hear the chatter of 'I missed that bit' in the corner of the recordings, followed by frustrated laughter as the women attempt again.[7] These archives indicate and re-enact *learning*. Recordings of practices and demo tapes by any band can capture that similar sense of 'working things out'. Such alternative recordings allow a glimpse into how familiar recordings could have been otherwise, and challenge the sense of closure that the final mix represents. But, it is important to note that recordings of anti-commercial feminist bands' practices are very different to a commercial band like, say, the Beatles, whose recordings are overwhelmingly part of the machinery of representation that moulds temporal and cultural expectations in popular (music) culture. The difference now is that in the digital age, commercial and non-commercial, 'finished' and 'unfinished' music can circulate simultaneously. It does so with similar speed and intensity that pre-internet was only the purview of the commercial music commodity. There is no need to package the histories of the WLMA so they can be sold, they are simply distributed and re-enacted in the process.

Such techno-cultural movement creates an avenue into a time of action and doing that opens the present moment up to the possible simultaneity of past, present and future. The re-enactment of materials in the WLMA, with their emphasis on process, functions as a performative undoing of linear temporal logics. It offers a different sense of time that is continuous and historically capacious because it is grounded in 'doing' and 'liveness'. It creates an experience of 'historicality that spans the division of past, present, and future, not only revealing the past as in some way always present but also revealing the present and future as in some way already past' (Sobchack 2011, 324). This historicality is a space where normative demarcations of time recombine and flow together, liberating static conceptions of linear history that render the dissonances of 'the past' into neat caricature, naturalise an unsatisfactory present and smother visions that the future could be any different from established 'tradition'. Such time travelling antics occur when the fragmentary remains of women's liberation music making are circulated to mass audiences via versatile and freely accessible digital platforms.

Digital re-enactments: what is lost and what is gained?

The re-enactment of the women's liberation music making is then absolutely entangled with its digital dissemination. But, can digital archives open up relations to history in affective or corporeal ways, as Schneider suggests are part of the allure of re-enactment, or do they pale into insignificance when compared to original documents or recordings? Is the WLMA merely a collection of imitations and copies, and what role do embodied and affective responses play in forging relationships with historical material? For Emily Robinson 'archival research is in large part an affective experience. And it is absolutely dependent on an encounter with an original document or artefact' (Robinson 2010, 510). She goes on to state:

> The rather ambivalent response to digital records is a clear indicator of the extent to which the archival endeavour is predicated on an encounter with physical artifacts. Without doubt, digitisation has transformed the historical discipline and made it possible to pursue topics that might otherwise have seemed insurmountable [...] This does not, however, mean that the historical discipline is ready to substitute the convenience of digital archives for the *sensory experience of the real thing* (Robinson 2010, 509, italics mine).

The key part of this quote is Robinson's affirmation of the *sensorial* sovereignty of 'real thing'. However, the 'real thing' arguably becomes less important when what is historically significant are recordings stored in the object, rather than the object itself in its non-operative state. Particularly if the recordings are of live performances or practices, rough copies that were never destined to be 'the real thing' but became that way through an accident of history: a lack of money and organisation, the pressures of everyday life or the break up of a relationship.

Phillipe Le Guern has commented on the inferior value of digital recordings such as MP3s and WAVs over vinyl, suggesting that no one cares about digital copies in comparison to the awe produced by a material encounter with a record (2011). Yet, what is the value of the 'curious inadequacies of the copy', and what do 'inadequacies get [...] right'? (Schneider 2011, 6) For when there are no records or artwork, and each tape looks the same as each other (bar idiosyncratic label sticking and hastily scrawled handwriting), the digital copy really comes into its own as an affective historical experience (Figure 2).

There is nothing more pleasing, in a sensory way, than hearing a digitised version of the one live show a band collected in the WLMA did before they split up. Upon listening, there is an added excitement and sense of preservation, and that something as ephemeral as a performance has left a trace that can be re-captured, tidied up and shared with thousands of other people because of digital technology.

To privilege the 'real thing' rather than these re-enacted copies is also to miss the point of how music and sound can affect people. As Brandon Labelle suggests,

Figure 2. Abandon Your Tutu tapes. Rare recordings of live performances of London-based, avant-garde feminist band that never recorded a 'proper' album.

> Sound is intrinsically and unignorably relational: it emanates, propagates, communicates, vibrates, and agitates; it leaves a body and enters others; it binds and unhinges, harmonizes and traumatizes; it sends the body moving, the mind dreaming, the air oscillating. It seemingly eludes definition, while having profound effect. (Labelle 2006, xi)

The re-enacted music contained in the WLMA requires no original because of the primacy of the *embodied* musical encounter it presents. Here, digital material provides an invitation to reconsider traditional historiographical methods that privilege the authenticity of original objects. If archival research is no longer dependent on an encounter with an original object but is part of the everyday media-scape most people in the world inhabit, it indicates that these modes of re-enactment and what they can 'do' have the potential to reach people and transform the *conditions* of historicity. This distinct sense of historicity is, ironically, unleashed by digital formats, smothering the social with simultaneous encounters that circulate 'presence' that meld past, present and future in a continuous and capacious now. This sense of time is characterised by an

> endless rhythm of things appearing and disappearing [...] The continuing-across of things [...] To grasp time, as apart from the being in or out of time of any particular thing, or even of all things, you must look to the middle, to the continuing, where appearance and disappearance cross, returning the instance to itself. Time has no loose ends, only existential interweave'. (Massumi 2006, 204)

However, I want to stress here that digital formats are not omnipotent. I do not want support fantasies of 'superhuman digital programmability' (Chun 2011, 185) that assume that digital presence will always exist in 'perfect', preserved form. Digital formats degrade and require similar forms of intervention and management as other forms of data. Wendy Hui Kyong Chun suggests we must try to 'grasp a present that is always degenerating [and] the ways in which ephemerality is made to endure' (Chun 2011, 200). Yet, it is precisely the circulation of digitised ephemeral artefacts that characterise the content of WLMA. The WLMA re-enacts material culture practices that never had a stable referent or origin within culture. The conditions of the culture were always ephemeral and transitory.

Paradoxically, in the age of the enduring ephemeral such low-budget, marginal histories come to claim a space that had previously eluded them. As a consequence, the 'long-term survival of data [which] tends to depend on some combination of dissemination and concentration' (Cubitt 2007, 183) is realised through digital resources in a moment of ephemeral compatibility. Indeed, it is the specific conditions of the digital age that have made the materials in the WLMA *legible* and, consequently, *legitimate*. People have become adept at reading operational, ephemeral forms of media such as the 'imperfect' youtube video, video footage from mobile phones and news reporting told through fragmentary 'tweets'. This means the partial qualities of the WLMA seem to be 'in time' with the digital present as these histories merge consequentially into the everyday landscape of infinite archive and pervasive media.

If it is true then that we are living in a cultural moment that privileges the circulation of transient and marginal cultural histories at the same velocity as monumental, established histories, we are arguably 'much closer within the globital memory field' (Reading 2011, 249) to an egalitarian historicity. In taking the risk of stating what may seem like a naïve declaration, I feel it is worth doing because of the possibilities that free web tools such as blogs and wikis offer marginalised cultural groups wishing to share their histories. As they do so they move from an invisible periphery to a diversely populated memory centre. Web 2.0 allows for hidden, untimely histories to become quickly visible to global audiences, as Ana Laura Lopez de la Torre from the Remembering Olive Collective, a community history and blog-based project focused on the life of British Black Panther Olive Morris, states:

> As information was coming into [us we could] publish it straight away so it is very immediate and that really appealed to us. [...] There is some information there [...] that is not published on the internet at all. There is nothing, for example on the British Black Panthers, and if you type 'British Black Panthers' we come on top so I think it has been really instrumental in contributing to filling a gap about information online about this. (de la Torre 2009)

Of course, such online presence needs to be concentrated in other areas, such as exhibitions and physical archives, in order to provide multiple and varied sites where these histories can be re-enacted. Yet, the potential cultural reach of the Internet in such a context is unquestionable.

Web archiving projects, as conducted at the British Library (of which the WLMA and Do Your Remember Olive Morris? is part of), are also important for documenting the process of archival activity on the Internet. The intermittent snap-shots capture sites as information is accumulated, and taken away. They provide important backup for information, preserve vulnerable histories and mitigate their disintegration. As Cubitt asserts, memory 'data' survives within culture through a combination of dissemination *and* concentration, and the blogs offer un-funded and oppositional cultural histories a vital porthole into the world. And importantly, through their re-enactment they not only circulate 'presence' but also rework the flow of time itself, ensuring that the past protrudes into the present in a way that denies its past-ness and declares its enlivenment.

Conclusion: the value of re-enactment to historiography

This article has explored re-enactment as the performative 'doing' of history, a recirculation of the time of action and process facilitated by free digital platforms. I have thought through the digital re-enactment of the marginal, untimely history of the WLMA in terms of 'liveness', not only in terms of immediacy, but as being 'punctuated by, syncopated with, indeed charged by, other moments, other times' (Schneider 2011, 92). Re-enactment is premised in the time travelling, affective his-torical encounter that can bring history *alive* in a continuous present where past, present and future interweave. Such an action forces those that encounter historical materials to become intimate with the rough edges of process, to refuse narrative accounts and in their place attend to the 'presences' that circulate within culture. Within the context of the WLMA, the re-enactment of histories allows the materials to speak for themselves because they clearly betray the processes of their produc-tion. And, fortuitously, it is through their digital re-enactment that those processes become intelligible within a current cultural context amenable to their articulation.

While the effects of such profound transformations cannot necessarily be quanti-fied, qualitative shifts in time, historicity and cultural value are undoubtedly discern-ible. These shifts have created affective and corporeal openings to what was once known as 'the past', but can arguably no longer be called so, as the undeniable force of lived events rubs into and beyond a 'now' that is changing its temporal complexion in the process. Because of these changes new historiographical termi-nologies are needed to cope with the challenges a capacious and continuous time offers. As Jussi Parikka writes: 'similarly as the photographic and new image cultures in the early part of the twentieth century forced not only a rethinking of perception but also of collection, memory and organisation [...] now software cultures demand a rethinking of similar extent' (2012, 90).

One such historiographical terminology is re-enactment. It is a useful tool because it does not deny the performative force of 'doing' history. It wears its process openly, allowing for affective, textual, spatial, digital and corporeal engage-ment to be part of its 'onto-epistemology' (Barad 2007, 34). What is lost in re-enactment's 'objectivity' is gained in greater potential for intimacy and proximity to historical action. Thinking through re-enactment with the WLMA has been a productive exercise because the archive materials resist representation and are instead grounded in the time of action and process. Through combining these two areas, my aim has been to show the potential of re-enactment as the performative 'doing' of history, as well as asserting the value and difference of cultures that resist commercialism can make to historiographical methodology. Through their re-enactment in digital culture, it creates opportunities for these enduringly ephemeral histories to become legible and widely available in a profoundly trans-formed present.

Notes

1. *Music & Liberation*, which was funded by the Heritage Lottery Fund in 2012, is an exhibition that draws on the material collected in the Women's Liberation Music Archive. It aims to create an 'open archive', where people can watch and listen to archive material, as well as look at objects and ephemera collected as part of the project.
2. These are some of the search terms people have used which has led them to the archive.
3. During interviews conducted as part of *Music & Liberation* one interviewee questioned the importance of the histories, and expressed doubt if anyone wanted to know about them or not.
4. See http://www.gold.ac.uk/library/collections/wrpmcollection/.
5. The Guest Stars were however part of the evolution of feminist music making in the 1980s, and wouldn't have necessarily seen themselves as part of the WLM in the same way that a band like Jam Today would have.
6. See http://youtu.be/vsyIh6ISLzE for the film 'Jam Today 3 at the Moonlight Club and More'.
7. The recording of the Jam Today 2 practice 'Where Do We Go From Here?' is a good example of this. Available online: http://womensliberationmusicarchive.wordpress.com/j/

References

Agnew, V. 2007. "History's Affective Turn: Historical Reenactment and Its Work in the Present." *Rethinking History* 11 (3): 299–312.
Barad, K. 2007. *Meeting the Universe Halfway: Quantum Physics and the Entanglement of Matter and Meaning*. Durham, NC: Duke University Press.
Browne, V. 2012. Backlash, Repetition, Untimeliness: The Temporal Dynamics of Feminist Politics. *Hypatia*. doi: 10.1111/hypa.12006.
Chun, W. H. K. 2011. "The Enduring Ephemeral, or, The Future is a Memory." In *Media Archaeology: Approaches, Applications and Implications*, edited by E. Huhtamo and J. Parikka, 184–207. Berkeley: University of California Press.
Cubitt, G. 2007. *History and Memory*. Manchester, NH: Manchester University Press.
de Groot, J. 2011. "Affect and Empathy: Re-Enactment and Performance as/in History." *Rethinking History* 15 (4): 587–599.
de La Torre, A. L. L. 2009. Personal Interview with Deborah Withers, 21 September 2009.
Guardian. 2009. 'Behind the Music: Where are the Female A&Rs?' (accessed March 7, 2012) http://www.guardian.co.uk/music/musicblog/2009/jul/23/behind-music-female-a-rs.
King, K. 2012. *Networked Reenactments: Stories Transdisciplinary Knowledges Tell*. Durham, NC: Duke University Press.
Labelle, B. 2006. *Background Noise: A History of Sound Art*. London: Continuum.
Le Guern, P. 2011. Keynote Address at the *Sites of Popular Music Heritage* conference, Liverpool University, 8–9 September, 2011.

Lynksey, D. 2011. *33 Revolutions per Minute: A History of Protest Songs*. London: Faber.

Massumi, B. 2006. "Painting: The Voice of the Grain." In *The Matrixial Borderspace*, edited by B. Ettinger, 201–215. Minnesota: University of Minnesota Press.

Northern Women's Liberation Rock Band. 1974. Nothern Women's Liberation Rock Band Manifesto. (accessed January 24, 2013) http://womensliberationmusicarchive.wordpress.com/n/.

Parikka, J. 2012. "Archives in Media Theory: Material Media Archaeology and Digital Humanities." In *Understanding Digital Humanities*, edited by D. M. Berry, 85–105. Palgrave: Basingstoke.

Petridis, A. 2012 "Who knew feminist rock was full of sax? Not me." in *The Guardian*, 11 March 2012. (accessed March 16, 2012) http://www.guardian.co.uk/culture/2012/mar/11/critics-notebook-alexis-petridis.

PRS. 2010. "Where are the women in music?" (accessed March 7, 2012) http://www.prsformusic.com/aboutus/press/latestpressreleases/Pages/Wherearethewomeninmusic.aspx.

Reading, A. 2011. "Memory and Digital Media: Six Dynamics of the Globital Memory Field." In *On Media Memory: Collective Memory in a New Media Age*, edited by M. Neiger, O. Meyers, E. Zandberg, 241–252. Basingstoke: Palgrave.

Robinson, E. 2010. "Touching the Void: Affective History and the Impossible." *Rethinking History* 14 (4): 503–520.

Runia, E. 2006. "Spots of Time." *History and Theory* 45 (3): 305–316.

Schneider, R. 2011. *Performing Remains: Art and War in Times of Theatrical Re-Enactment*. London: Routledge.

Sobchack, V. 2011. "Afterword: Media Archaeology and Re-presencing the past." In *Media Archaeology: Approaches, Applications and Implications*, edited by E. Huhtamo, and J. Parikka, 323-335. Berkeley: University of California Press.

von Appen, R., and A. Doehring. 2006. "Nevermind the Beatles, Here's Exile 61 and Nico: "the Top 100 Records of All Time": A Canon of Pop and Rock Albums from a Sociological and an Aesthetic Perspective." *Popular Music* 25 (1): 21–39.

Women's Liberation Music Project Group. n.d. 'Introduction' to *Sisters in Song*. (accessed March 7, 2012) http://womensliberationmusicarchive.files.wordpress.com/2010/10/introduction-to-the-songbook.pdf.

From a colonial reinvention to postcolonial heritage and a global commodity: performing and re-enacting Angkor Wat and the Royal Khmer Ballet

Michael S. Falser

University of Heidelberg

It is a commonplace that cultural heritage is not only a highly contested concept of modern times, full of nationalistic undertones, cultural stereotypes and essentialist topoi such as past grandeur and enduring cultural purity. Cultural heritage has also become *the* easiest and most profitable prey for today's global tourism industry. These observations apply with particularly dramatic consequences to young emerging, postcolonial nation states with a rich repertoire of built (tangible) and performed (intangible) culture – especially if elements of this repertoire are branded 'UNESCO World Heritage' without considering their contested formation histories. Few other iconic heritage sites are more instructive in showcasing these observations than the temple site of Angkor, by charting the transcultural trajectories of Cambodia's heritage construction through the processes of French colonial reinvention, postcolonial/nationalist essentialisation, and global commodification. This paper focuses on the 'Royal Khmer Ballet' as cultural performance and heritage re-enactment in combination with the twelfth-century temple of Angkor Wat as architectural stage. References to similar 'heritagisation' processes in the (post)colonial Dutch East Indies (now Indonesia) will help to anchor this transcultural enquiry.

The spectacle starts [...] music [...] One of the back doors opens; one small, adorable and almost chimerical creature rushes into the middle of the hall: an Apsara of the temple of Angkor! Impossible to make a more perfect illusion of it; she has the same features because she is of the same pure race, she has the same enigmatic smile [...] the small Apsara from the old ages, slipped away from the holy bas-reliefs [of Angkor Wat, MF] [...] these poses are the ancient tradition of this country, as the stone figures which inhabit the ruins [...] May France, the protector of this country, understand that this royal ballet of the kings of Phnom Penh is a sacred legacy, an archaic marvel which should never be destroyed![1]

Pierre Loti: Un pèlerin d'Angkor (1912, 204–213)

This article was originally published with errors. This version has been corrected. Please see Erratum (http://dx.doi.org/10.1080/13527258.2013.815495)

1. Introduction: history, heritage, performance and re-enactment

'History is not about [a passive] past as such, but rather about our [active] ways of creating meaning from the scattered, and profoundly meaningless debris we find around us' (Kellner 1997, 136–137). If *heritage* can be defined as 'history processed through mythology, ideology, nationalism, local pride, romantic ideas or just plain marketing, into a commodity' (Schouten 1995, 21), and 'the use of the past for contemporary purposes' (Tivers 2002, 188), then both history and heritage are *made* by concrete agency. Our inquiry asks about this agency behind contested heritage constructions in general, and focuses on *cultural performances* in particular. 'To study performance is not to focus on completed forms, but to become aware of performance as itself a contested space, where meanings and desires are generated, occluded, and of course multiply interpreted' (Diamond 1989, 69). We include 'not only supposedly 'pure' performances or idealised versions of traditional genres but also tourist shows, hybrids, and genres in the midst of [these] profound disturbances and/or transformations' (Schechner and Appel 1990, 2), which particularly characterise the modern history of country we are examining: Cambodia. Furthermore, we will analyse a specific type called *heritage performance* which is characterised by a site-specific 'unity of kinaesthetic imagination and the affirmation of cultural memory' (Carlson 2000, 247) and which materialises and spatializes in so-called *historical re-enactments*. With the goal of exactly restoring ancient history or 'socially relevant events' or both with the latest multi-media (Arns 2007), historical re-enactment aims to make it possible to experience 'living history' directly. They employ supposedly 'authentic' actors with historical apparatus, and often take place, as in our case, on original cultural heritage sites (Agnew 2004, 2007; Cook 2004). By blurring the boundaries between fact and fiction, heritage performances in the form of historical re-enactments contribute today to an ever-growing *global heritage tourist industry*. Since the 1980s, they have become parasitic and even instrumental in the *global heritage politics* under UN's Educational, Scientific and Cultural Organisation (UNESCO)'s leadership. This combination helps to 'fossilise and commodify heritage' (Brosius and Polit 2011, 6). This trend is, as we shall see in our combined case study on Cambodia's temple of Angkor Wat (as a tangible heritage) and 'Royal Khmer Ballet' (as an intangible heritage), especially menacing to young emerging nation-states with a rich built and performed heritage, which is today both 'salvaged' by the global heritage community, locally exploited by profit-oriented national(ist) elites, and instrumentalised to overwrite memories of recent postcolonial traumata.

Chronologically, we will traverse three decisive moments of culturo-political transformation in Cambodia's modern history: French colonialism (1863–1953/4), Cambodia's independence as a period of extensive cultural nationalism (1954–1970) and Cambodia's globalised rebirth process after 1990 as Asia's youngest nation state. Cambodia's heritage landmarks, the temple of Angkor Wat and the Royal Khmer Ballet, as transcultural hybrids, with their colonially reinvented, postcolonially appropriated and globally commodified elements, will be contextualised along six parameters: the source material used to reconstitute cultural performances and re-enactments; the media used to develop them; the events of representation and their audiences; the specific sites and spatial components; the temporalities employed; and, most importantly, the concrete agency behind these scenarios, ranging from individual cultural brokers, national decision-makers, and elites and institutions, to the global heritage community and cultural heritage industry.

2. The French colonial reinvention of the danseuses cambodgiennes

2.1. From Louis Delaporte 1880 to the National Colonial Exhibition of 1906 in Marseille

Louis Delaporte – French captain, draughtsman and participant of the French Mekong Expedition of 1866–1868 – presented the twelfth-century sandstone temple of Angkor Wat in his 1880 book entitled *Voyage au Cambodge: L'architecture Khmer*. Two aspects of his drawings were remarkable: firstly, although the call for the reclamation and restoration of the decayed ninth-to-thirteenth-century temples of the Angkor region (until 1907 on Siamese territory!) was an essential part of the French colonial rhetoric in Indochina at this time, Delaporte depicted Angkor Wat in a picture-perfect condition (Delaporte 1880, 206–207) (Figure 1). Secondly, his drawing did not correspond to the French narrative of Angkor as the abandoned site of a vanished civilisation; on the contrary, he placed a row of four dancing and bare-breasted women with stylised skirts, necklaces and crown-like headgear on the temple's central causeway as a perfect stage. He named them 'tévadas' or 'celestial nymphs', as they were 'sculptured on the walls of Angkor-Vaht' to represent the 'living female beauties themselves' (Delaporte 1880, 344–346). Delaporte's ideal reconstitution of the temple as a stage setting and background for a re-imagined historical dance performance remained a powerful pictorial combination for the decades to come. During his second mission to Indochina (1873–1874), Delaporte collected original sculptures and made moulds of selected bas-reliefs of the Angkorian temples and shipped them back to France. His collection was finally opened in the mid-1880s as the *musée Indo-chinois* in the Parisian Trocadero palace, just opposite Viollet-le-Duc's *musée de Sculpture comparée* containing plaster casts of mainly Gothic French architectural sculpture. At this point, the

Figure 1. *Angkor-Vaht (Vue restituée)*, as depicted in Louis Delaporte's 1880 publication *Voyage au Cambodge* (Delaporte 1880, 206–207).

celestial maidens of Angkor Wat had been 'translated' through the medium of plaster casts to France, but were, for the moment, only depicted on these thin replicated facade elements, which were, in the following decades, reassembled to create fantastic temple pavilions in Universal and Colonial Exhibitions in Paris and Marseille (Falser 2011).

The 1889 Universal Exhibition in Paris staged the first free-standing Angkor pavilion in its French colonial section, but Khmer dance performances were not yet carried out. In these early European exhibitions, 'imaginative representations of the exotic 'East' gave little heed to cultural specificities' (Cohen 2010, 4), as long as a random combination of architectural stereotypes and 'traditional' dance elements could form a compelling amalgam for the Occidental voyeuristic gaze. Thus, it was right next to the *palais d'Angkor* that the *kampong Javanais* (a 'traditional' Javanese village) was installed to stage cultural performances from colonial Southeast Asia. A remake from the 1883 Colonial Exhibition at Amsterdam, the scenario was executed as a private enterprise by Dutch planters from Java to promote their products. Additionally, the sacred *danseuses Javanaises*, in reality 'prostitute dancers from the princely courts of Java' (Chazal 2002, 114), presented a hybrid cultural performance imitating 'traditional' court dance elements together with a gamelan orchestra provided by the plantation owners. Visiting along with other prominent guests, such as the sculptor Auguste Rodin and the composer Claude Debussy, the painter Paul Gauguin not only satisfied his Oriental sexual fantasies with a member of the show, but also reportedly confused Javanese art with the Khmer art of the neighbouring pavilion (Chazal 2002, 131; Cohen 2010, 17; compare Bloembergen 2006, 106–163). Ironically, the French press itself celebrated the Javanese dancers' 'splendid costumes as almost identical reproductions from the bas-reliefs of the Khmer ruins' (Lombard 1992, 122). How the architectural and performative elements from an imagined colonial Far East became exchangeable and even combinable in European spectacles was shown by the indoor installation of the *Tour-du-Monde* during the 1900 Universal Exhibition in Paris, where the painted architectural panorama of Angkor Wat was enhanced (re-enacted) with living Javanese dance performers (Décordet-Ahiha 2004, 39) (Figure 2).

With 'authentic' actors from the colonies in front of their reconstituted village huts or temples, these performative displays (a) facilitated the European voyeuristic gaze on the exotic 'Other' with its pre-modern and static tradition, or better timeless 'ethnographic present' (Fabian 2002, 80), and (b) exhibited the primitive, underdeveloped status of the colonies to self-justify the exhibiting imperial nation's supposedly altruistic project of 'cultural uplifting' around the planet (Blanchard 2011). In the case of Angkor, the 1906 National Colonial Exhibition at Marseille marked a decisive turning point. Two years previously, the Francophile Sisowath had followed the former Cambodian King Norodom on the throne in Phnom Penh and was strongly backed by the French colonial authorities. In 1906, he was invited to France with the highest diplomatic honours, but with no real political power. Encouraging the French population's curiosity about exotic French colonial Indochina, the king was also made the official head of an 'authentic' royal ballet troupe for the Marseille Exhibition. In reality, this ballet group was the creation of the French representative in Phom Penh, George Bois, and composed of mostly private dancers and only a few 'real' court dancers (Cravath 2007, 125, referring to Bois 1913). The 'Royal Ballet troupe' enjoyed great success and was invited to

LE TOUR DU MONDE — LA PAGODE D'ANGKOR ET LES DANSEUSES JAVANAISES

Pays de rêve, que les poètes et les musiciens ont chanté... Les ruines fabuleuses d'Angkor, aux profondeurs inconnues, et qui cachent sous leurs pierres écroulées d'inestimables trésors. Et devant ces vestiges de l'empire Khmer, des danseuses javanaises, très modernes, les sœurs peut-être — ou les filles — de celles qui eurent tant de succès en 1889.

Figure 2.   Inside the *Tour-du-Monde* panorama of the 1900 Universal Exhibition in Paris. The French explication reads (in English translation): 'Le Tour du Monde – La pagode d'Angkor et les danseuses Javanaises. Land of dreams that the poets and musicians sang about... The fabulous ruins of Angkor, of unknown profoundness, hide under their collapsed stones inestimable treasures. And in front of these vestiges of the Khmer empire, the Javanese female dancers, very modern, the sisters perhaps or the daughters of these which already had such a success in 1889.' (Baschet 1900: plate 166; photographer Neurdein frères et Maurice Baschet).

Paris to perform during Sisowath's visit to the French president. Its reputation as an 'icon of [the Khmer] traditions, of their eternal religious rites and of the immutability of the Cambodian culture' (Vilain 2006, 29) was only established at this very moment with Rodin executing about 150 drawings and paintings of the graceful gestures of the Khmer ballet. As cited by Bois in 1913, Rodin, in 1906, formulated what would become – from the time of French colonial politics to UNESCO's intangible heritage listings today (see below) – an essentialist cultural stereotype of the Khmer Ballet, like the Orientalists Loti and Groslier in 1913 (see quotations):

> There are stones which are so ancient that one cannot describe them with the terms of historic epochs. And looking at these stones, one thinks about thousands of years [...] These Cambodian female dancers gave us all that real antiquity can contain: their own antiquity which equals ours. In three days we experienced three thousand years. It is impossible to see human nature in a higher state of perfection. (Auguste Rodin about the *danseuses Cambodgiennes* in 1906, cited in Bois 1913, 275).

26

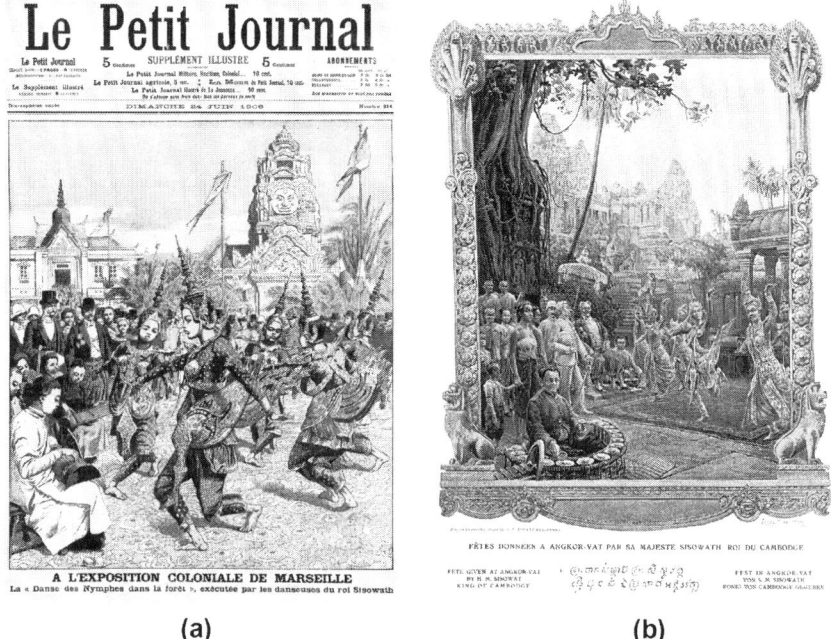

Figure 3. Left (a): cover page of *Le Petit Journal* of 24 June 1906, entitled *À l'Exposition Coloniale de Marseille. La 'Danse des Nymphes dans la forêt', exécutée par les danseuses du roi Sisowath*. Right (b): illustration of Dieulefils' 1909 trilingual publication *Indo-China picturesque and monumental. Ruins of Angkor* with a water colour by Lorant-Heilbronn entitled *Fete given at Angkor-Vat by H.M. Sisowath King of Cambodge* (Dieulefils 1909: plate 2).

This version of the 'Royal Khmer dance' already contained many of the characteristics of a 'cultural performance': it was performed for a specific occasion with a structured programme and it used actors to satisfy the gaze of a defined audience (Diamond 2005, 390; Fischer-Lichte 2003, 11–37). Press releases like the one in the *Petit Journal de Marseille* from 24 June 1906 (Figure 3(a)) described the Khmer ballet performances in Paris and Marseille as 'animated bas-reliefs of the temples of Angkor' (cited in Vilain 2006, 25, compare Beau 1906, 177), accompanied by illuminated fountains and electrical colour projections. At this time, the transcultural travel of this topos of Angkor's built and performed antiquity was in full swing. The Marseille performances combined the scenario with the royal ballet dancers in 'traditional costumes' performing original gestures to authentic music, with the Khmer King as the ballet's patron and guarantor of an unbroken tradition stretching back to Khmer antiquity, Angkor Wat temple architecture as a stage and background; the public and representatives of the ruling French authorities were very quickly re-translated back to the original spot (Figure 3(b)).

2.2. George Groslier and the rebirth of the Khmer dance from the bas-reliefs of Angkor Wat

> They are in agony, the Khmer dancers! [...] They're dying! The charming traditions and poetry of yesteryear are dying! Our steamships and automobiles generate a smoke in which *champa* flowers wither. Soon, mysterious actresses, we will no longer see you gather the ancient poems and lost beauties floating thick in the air of festival nights. [...] What will artists and poets do tomorrow in this chosen land? They will be told that, only yesterday, there still remained one hundred twenty Vestals in whom the entire past and all its rituals were preserved; that these Vestals were sometimes seen emerging from their mystery and dancing slowly in splendid costumes with graceful harmony, under streaming lights [...] but that now [all this] is gone! (George Groslier: *Danseuses cambodgiennes anciennes et modernes* (1913, 120, translated in Davis 2010, 107)

In 1907, the temples of Angkor became part of the French protectorate of Cambodia and the primary cultural concern of the French *mission civilisatrice* in Indochina. The earlier romanticised imaginings of Angkor were now replaced with scientific research *in situ*. More importantly, the new political 'owners' of Angkor wished to reconnect the whole contemporary canon of Cambodian culture to ancient Angkor. This procedure, intended to recreate the present within a *pure* Angkorian past tradition without foreign influences, was a delicate task. In reality, Angkor had been captured by the Siamese in the fifteenth century, and royal court dance – like some of the Cambodian kings themselves – only survived until the nineteenth century at the Siamese court in Bangkok, the cultural influences of which were still considerable around 1900. Now, the entire system of art education in Cambodia was systematically grouped around the French intention of rescuing the traditional Cambodian art scene from – a typically colonial topos – 'degeneration'. The central figure was George Groslier (1887–1945), the first French citizen born in Cambodia, a Parisian *École des Beaux-Arts* graduate, and gifted artist and writer. Between the establishment of the *École royale des arts décoratifs* in 1907 and its reformulation as *École des arts cambodgiens* in Phnom Penh (with Groslier as its first director), he had also studied the decorative reliefs of Angkor. Observing a contemporary crisis of religious beliefs, traditional morals, and performing arts (citation above), his 1913 book *Danseuses cambodgiennes anciennes et modernes* was the first modern in-depth study about the royal court dancers. In his sketches, Groslier let the ballet dancers emerge – or be reborn in their purest reincarnation – from the celestial maidens on the bas-reliefs of Angkor Wat (Figure 4). However, from an iconographical standpoint, the latter had never been conceived as earthly dancers per se, but as celestial guardian figures for the entertainment of a dead king after apotheosis, serving to mediate between him and the heavenly skies. Concluding his study, Groslier re-imagined a 'spectacle grandiose' of an ancient procession at Angkor Wat – altogether a virtual re-enactment of the past including back translated elements of contemporary dance performance. This hybrid reconstruction would serve as a perfect script for the *son-et-lumière* shows performed at the Exhibitions in France, the spectacles at Angkor Wat during Cambodia's independence, and, finally, for the mythic re-enactments for a cultural heritage industry on site after 1990:

Figure 4. A series of sketches on the revived bas-reliefs of Angkor Wat by George Groslier in his 1913 publication *Danseuses Cambodgiennes anciennes et modernes* (Groslier 1913: 135, 128, 161, 133).

> Now the extraordinary ritual lies clearly before me! [...] mysterious harmonies, dripping down the stones like the drops of some sonorous rain, fade before a procession that has suddenly appeared. Sixteen *devadasi* advance. The crowd is prostrate, like green rice bending in the wind. [...] What a spectacle! The huge, pale sky of Cambodia, the dying sun, the nine towers, the sacred academy, the King, the prostrate crowd. [...] Royal elephants, each enclosed in its golden carapace. Then, atop the sculpted mountain, before the shadow of the sanctuary where all powers dwell suspended, the sixteen symbolic *devadasi*, resplendent like stars in the night! Yes, I see it quite well, the extraordinary ritual. [...] Absolute Beauty stands complete before me. [...] Of this absolute Beauty she is the sole pure expression [...] Alone, she returns from the past to offer us her flower, while all else about her crumbles. (Groslier 1913, 172–173, in Davis 2010, 154–159)

Groslier even translated the arm gestures of the actual dance *back* into the ancient stone surface of the Angkor temples (compare UNESCO's video on the listed 'Royal Ballet of Cambodia' later in this paper):

> Today's [...] giant poses resemble those of the characters set in the sandstone of Angkor. There is a direct line of descent, and absolute relationship between the parts and the whole. In fact, the line of descent is so direct that if *lokhon* [dance] in the modern aesthetic were suddenly to turn to stone, we could precisely superimpose their gestures carved in the past. (Groslier 1913, in Davis 2010, 153)

Groslier established a small photo studio in the *musée Albert Sarraut* (today the National Museum) in Phnom Penh to study the dance gestures through fragmented photographic series. Years later, Sappho Marchal, the daughter of the General Angkor Conservator Henri Marchal, published a detailed study on the costumes and hairstyles of the '1700 devatas' of the Angkor Wat temple (Marchal 1927, 2). Both Groslier's and Marchal's publications would serve as a perfect catalogue and pattern book to re-Khmerise and purify the Royal Ballet à la *angkorienne* (Figure 5). However, when King Sisowath died in 1927, private dance troupes were already performing in front of the Angkorian temples for the fast growing tourist industry.

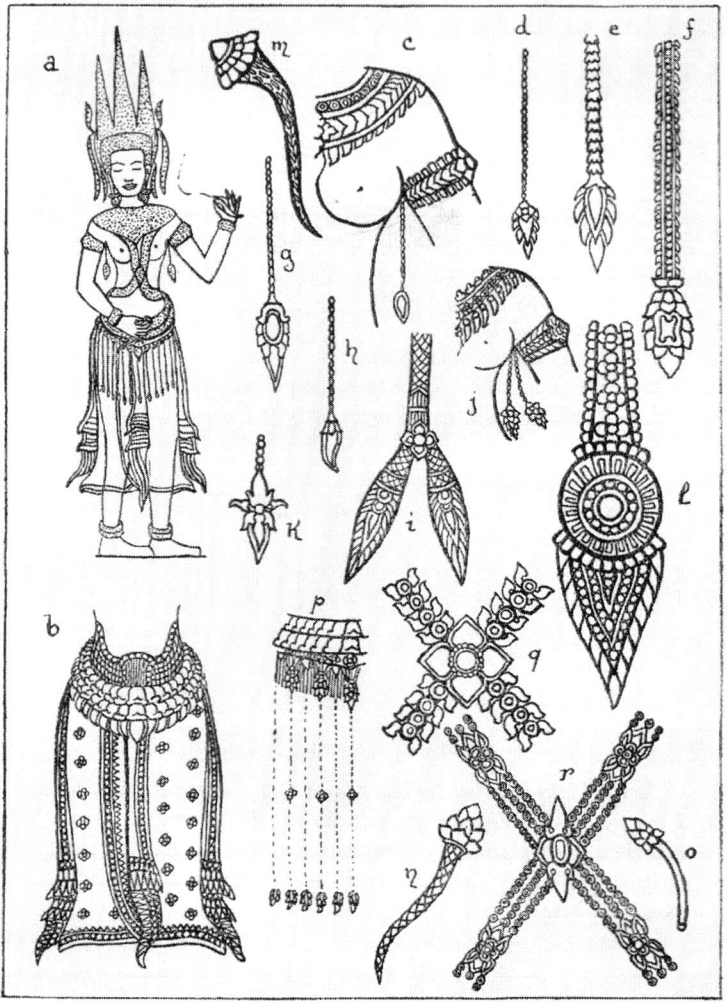

Figure 5. A study on the costumes of the Cambodian dancers in Sappho Marchal's 1927 publication *Costumes et parures khmèrs d'après les Devatâ d'Angkor-Vat* (Marchal 1927: plate XL).

2.3. Reconstitutions of Angkor Wat and the Royal Ballet in Marseille 1922, Paris 1931 and on the 'real' spot

In 1908, the position of a Conservator General was established to supervise the installation of the so-called *Archaeological Park of Angkor* (Falser 2013) under the colonial tutelage of the newly founded *École française d'Extrême-Orient*. Along with Groslier's studies of Cambodia's applied and performing arts, the architectural and stylistic knowledge of the Angkor temples was increasing exponentially, and the ephemeral Angkor Wat pavilions for the Colonial Exhibitions in Marseille 1922 and Paris 1931 resembled more and more their 'original' source (Falser 2011). Now stereotyped as 'direct descendants of the Apsaras on the bas-reliefs of Angkor Wat' (Artaud 1923, 207), the dancers' magic night performances now took place in front

L'apothéose lumineuse du temple d'Angkor le soir.
Suivant les heures, le temple se trouve coloré par des projecteurs en jaune d'or, rouge, vert ou bleu.

Figure 6. *L'apothéose lumineuse du temple d'Angkor le soir*, as depicted in the special issue of *L'Illustration* in 1931 on the *Exposition Coloniale Internationale de Paris 1931* (L'Illustration 22 August 1931, special issue: Exposition Coloniale Internationale de Paris 1931, n.p.).

of the giant Angkor Wat replica and they were, after their performance at the Paris Opera, praised again for their 'authenticity, purity and timelessness' (de Miomandre 1923, 213). Nine years later, the Parisian Colonial Exhibition of 1931 topped all earlier undertakings of exotic representations in scale, variety, and performance. The 'illuminated apotheosis of Angkor [Wat]' (de Beauplan 1931) reached the 1:1-scale of its Cambodian source and the theatrical effect of its central causeway was enlarged into a cruciform square for cultural performances (Figure 6).

In the meantime, the French authorities in Phnom Penh had tried in vain to keep complete control over the 'real' Royal Ballet in order to save it from 'decadence' and 'agony' (Groslier 1918). The great success of dance performances in Marseille in 1906 and 1922 had proved their political significance, tensions concerning their proper use broke out and an official invitation for the 1931 Paris Exhibition was turned down by the new Cambodian king, Monivong. The French then chose Say Sangvann, the wife of a member of the royal family who had already organised performances for the *Résident Superieur* in Phnom Penh, for a dance troupe. As a substitute of the real dance group, the one in Paris in 1931 was a private enterprise equipped with costumes and masks from Groslier's art school and subsidised by the French authorities (Cambodian Information Agency 1963, 19, Edwards 2007, 171–173). With this essential shift, the border between 'authentic' cultural performance and commercialised folklore was irreversibly crossed, even though the show was still sold as 'original' Khmer and 'of the greatest purity even from the viewpoint of Siamese *connoisseurs*' (Thiounn 1930, 31, 58). As a staged heritage commodity, the Cambodian ballet in front of the Angkor Wat pavilion was now inter-changeable with the Balinese troupe in front of the Dutch Indies pavilion or the 'fetish dancers' from French Africa in front of faked adobe architecture (Cadilhac 1931).

These configurations in the French *métropole* had, from our transcultural viewpoint, considerable consequences for the real site back in Cambodia: the aesthetics of folkloric dance spectacles in torch-lit or electric floodlight atmosphere in front of mysterious temple skylines in France were re-imported back to the real site (Cravath 2007, 143). Say Sangvann's private troupe had gained 'the monopoly to perform the dance for tourists at Angkor Vat' (Sasagawa 2005, 429) and her dancers now posed in gestures and costumes even more perfect than the depictions on the ancient bas-reliefs behind them.

3. A new identity rooted in antiquity: re-enacting Angkor and the invention of the Apsara dance during Cambodian independence

The fight for the monopoly over the 'authentic' Khmer ballet continued into the early 1940s. Princess Kossamak, the mother of the young Norodom Sihanouk, who had become king in 1941, played a crucial role. She took advantage of (a) the detailed studies on the Khmer ballet by Groslier and Marchal, who had re-established its direct and 'purified' link to the imagined origins of the bas-reliefs of Angkor Wat; and (b) the rising international popularity of Cambodia's glorious built and performed past in the mass spectacles in France. Feeding the movement of an 'anti-colonial cultural nationalism', she initiated a major reconfiguration of the royal dance performance, ironically based on French colonial ideas. She changed the choreography to form a group-precision dance, added entertaining effects and shortened the previous day-long private royal dance ritual into a two-hour programme. Outwardly, the result was meant to underline the new cultural self-confidence of the Khmer nation on the occasion of international state visits, and inwardly to symbolically demonstrate the authority of the new king who was rooted in a continued Angkorian antiquity back to his direct ancient royal ancestors (Cravath 2007, 153–167). With this shift, the status of the Khmer dance changed again, now from its folkloristic effect at French exhibitions to a deeper political meaning back in Cambodia. With its (ostensibly) apolitical appearance beyond a specific time, space and direction, the royal dance with its ritual components was in fact the perfect performative medium with which to minimalise tensions or bridge the liminal spaces that opened up in Cambodia's violent 'transition from a colonial to a postcolonial state figuration' (after Bachmann-Medick 2009, 113–130, compare Turner 1982, 28–94). After Cambodia's independence in 1953, Kossamak succeeded in 're-Khmerising' and politicising the royal dance with a new central element: she invented the so-called *Apsara Dance* or *roban Apsara* which perfectly served the new Khmer national ideology. In the best fulfilment of Groslier's 1913 study, the whole choreography itself staged five *apsaras* which materialised out of the bas-reliefs of Angkor Wat, only to perform a dance of salutation before disappearing again into the stone surface (Heywood 2008, 76). In order to densify the ideological dimension of a supposedly pure continuity from the ancestors of Angkor up to the current ruling political power, Kossamak made the Apsara dance the showpiece for Buppha Devi, the prima ballerina of the Royal Ballet and daughter of King Sihanouk (Figure 7). During Cambodian independence, the 'Apsara dance' with Buppha Devi of the newly named *Royal Corps de Ballet* became the entertaining centre piece of all diplomatic visits to Cambodia, and during Sihanouk's own interna-

Figure 7. Left (a): a photograph in *Cambodge Aujourd'hui* 1962 of Bopha Devi as Apsara dancer in front of the bas-reliefs of Angkor Wat, entitled 'Women in Angkorian history - Past and present: a 12th century bas-relief and Princess Bopha Devi' (Cambodge Aujourd'hui, July-August 1962, 46). Right (b): a dance performance of the revived Royal Khmer Ballet with a painted architectural background as depicted in Thiounn's 1956 reprinted publication *Danses cambodgiennes* of 1930 (Thiounn 1930, reprint in 1956, n.p.).

tional state visits abroad. In the medium of cultural performance, cultural nationalism was poured into Sihanouk's strategy of 'cultural diplomacy', most importantly with his visit to France in 1964, where the dance was performed (one more time after 1922) in the Paris Opera (Cambodian Information Agency 1963). Now, the peaceful 'Khmerness' full of unbroken tradition and cultural purity could be staged all around the world using a movable stage set quoting Angkorian architecture. In this context, Khmer and Javanese dance performances met each other once again after their career during Dutch and French colonialism in Southeast Asia: Indonesia's first president Sukarno fused Javanese and Balinese dance elements into one coherent performance as a cultural instrument of the 'peaceful' internationalisation of his country during the first decades of Cold War politics (Cohen 2010, 214–219). He himself visited Cambodia in 1962 and reportedly fell in love with Sihanouk's daughter during her dance with the Royal Khmer Ballet.

The French invention of an ephemeral Angkor pavilion also came back to modern Cambodia when the second *Games of the New Emerging Forces* were organised in Phnom Penh's new Olympic Stadium in 1966 and portable 'Bayon towers' formed a part of the opening ceremony. As an additional component to the political parcours by Phnom Penh's new and highly symbolic city planning (including the Angkor-styled Independence Memorial), important diplomatic state visits to non-aligned Cambodia were now combined with dance performances at the real site of Angkor Wat with fireworks above the illuminated temple – just like those above the temple's replica in Paris about 30 years earlier.

When General Charles de Gaulle, President of the French Fifth Republic, was brought to Angkor Wat for a *son-et-lumière* show, the Khmer Ballet was turned from a cultural performance into historical re-enactment. A unique blend of 'collapsing temporalities' and the recreation of a 'historical continuity, exploited for ideological ends' (Agnew 2007, 309) took place on 1 September 1966: the king of a postcolonial nation let the pre-colonial, 'authentic past' of his direct ancestors at

Figure 8. A double page on the visit of Charles de Gaulle to Cambodia in 1966 with a *son-et-lumière* show at Angkor Wat, as depicted in Norodom Sihanouk's publication *Photo-Souvenirs du Cambodge* in volume 7 (*Le prestige au plan international du Cambodge*) (Sangkum Reastr Niyum 1969, 167–168).

the original, 'credible setting' (an important feature of re-enactments, Gapps 2009, 403) be theatrically re-enacted in front of the head of the former colonial power (Figure 8). In a 'reconstitution historique grandiose' (Sangkum 1969, 167, compare Groslier 1913), 900 laymen and 600 monks in historical and religious costumes participated in the re-enactment of a historic royal coronation ceremony and procession of an Angkorian king in which the actual children of the real King Sihanouk, Prince Naradipo and Princess Botum Popha, staged the historic royal couple in order to 'narrow the mimetic gap' (Agnew 2004, 332) between fact and fiction; the gigantic illumination of Angkor Wat had been designed by Sihanouk's gifted state architect Vann Molyvann.[2] Even though, in 1969, he would explicitly correct his own father's invention of the 'dancing maidens emerging from the bas-reliefs of Angkor Wat'[3], the acting General Angkor Conservator, Bernard-Philippe Groslier (the son of George Groslier!), wrote the text *The voices of one night in Angkor* for this retro-travel into Angkor's re-staged past (Groslier 1966). As the 'most beautiful and perfect temple of Asia' and the 'summit of the first thousand years of glory', Groslier aligned Angkor Wat with the Egyptian pyramids, Rome, and Byzantium. He announced the dancers as a 'thousand stone figures which dreamlike came to life that early night as shadows out of our time, [as] celestial dancers that descended to earth' and, finally, the king himself as divine reincarnation. Bringing his audience back to present times, Groslier described the 'procession that vanished in the dark like a sign of the dying time' and was followed by Buddhist 'holy monks'. His text concluded – highly relevant for the political aspect of re-enactments in the form of 'pageantry' – with a direct and 'affirmative address' to the French president and the

Cambodian king (Lamb 2008, 243): he spoke of the actual affinities of both nations to each other as regards the temple of Angkor Wat as an 'object of joint, caring interest'. Here, King Sihanouk used this staging of the Khmer emergence myth to subliminally communicate a new political self-confidence to his former colonial master (Sangkum 1969; Sihanouk 1981, 319–320).

Ironically, this event was repeated two years later for a political guest at the other end of the ideological spectrum. When Josip Broz Tito, President of the Socialist Federal Republic of Yugoslavia, visited his non-aligned brother country, a reduced de Gaulle version was performed on 19 January 1968. Grolier's text from 1966 was modified to have socialist undertones. Now, the Romans did not conquer the Gauls, but 'Trajan and Hadrian brought the *pax romana* to the Dacians', and both the Cambodian and the Yugoslav nations were now 'united in a common history of battles' against imperial politics (Sihanouk 1968, 16, 20). However, this was just a minor detail in a much larger political programme in the name of reborn Khmer antiquity. King Sihanouk was a brilliant politician in staging himself as the 'quasi re-incarnation' of the glorious King Jayavarman VII (Garry 1964), and he re-enacted himself in processions à la *angkorienne* and circulated his enormous production of song, poem, and film productions, including *Apsara* (1965) or *The little Prince* (1967), where his own son played himself in reference to the ancient king Jayavarman.

4. The globalised rebirth of Cambodia and the commodification of Angkor and the Apsara dance

In 1970, Cambodia descended into civil war when Sihanouk's former minister of defence, Lon Nol, came to power. Although backed by the United States, he was himself overthrown by the Maoist terror regime of the Khmer Rouge, which ruled between 1975 and 1979 and committed a horrifying auto-genocide in order to re-install a pre-industrial, rural state, meant to be (we remember George Groslier) 'puri-fied' of Western influences. The Khmer Rouge refashioned a female dance group with the typical revolutionary dresses, and Angkor was still present in the propaganda material (Gosh 1998, 1–53; Shapiro-Phim 2002). On the Western side of the Thai-Cambodian border, the refugee camp *Khao I Dang* became the second largest city in Thailand, housing some 130,000 Cambodians. In 1980, the first Khmer dance perfor-mances were carried out there by dancers who later emigrated to the USA to form a new traditional dance troupe. Here, Khmer and Javanese dance troupes, the first formed by refugees and exiles and the second sponsored by the Indonesian Suharto government, might have met for a third time in their modern history.

The Cambodian scene changed dramatically with the end of the Cold War around 1989, and when final national peace was within reach after the Paris Agree-ment of 1991. The *United Nations Transitional Authority in Cambodia* (UNTAC) supervised free elections in 1993 to re-install a constitutional monarchy. What had been de-contextualised, fragmented, reassembled and altogether re-invented during French colonial times, and then essentialised during cultural nationalism and diplo-macy in Cambodia's Sihanouk-led era of independence, was now, with a total of twenty years without any creative development, incorporated into the new identity construction of the reborn Cambodian nation state: the representational modes of the Angkorian temple site and the *Apsara Dance* were back on the spot. They were, quasi overnight, 're-colonised' by a globalised heritage machinery, now including newly-found national agencies of heritage protection led by returning Khmer elites, and by government-encouraged mass tourism.

Following the partly justifiable, however neo-colonial narrative of the 'imminent danger of the total loss of Cambodia's tangible and intangible culture' – but this time with an unforeseen speed and the direct impact of international expertise, financial support and ad hoc-infrastructure (some call it 'NGOisation') – the UNESCO stepped onto the stage. From 1989, with a series of international work-shops and conferences, agreements and declarations, and with the regional (old and new) political key players, France and Japan, together with many other countries, from the USA to Germany, Italy to China and Indonesia, UNESCO helped to place the *Angkor Archaeological Park* in 1992 on the *World Heritage List (of Danger)*. With a draught management plan for the protected zone which correlated roughly with the borders of the French colonial *Parc archéologique d'Angkor* of 1925/1930, 'adequate protective legislation, a national protection agency, permanent boundaries and buffer zones and a international coordination' were, at this point, still a desider-atum (UNESCO 1992); these were only established with the national protection agency *APSARA* years later (Ang et al. 1996). Under the slogan 'Save Angkor', the newly founded *Bulletin* of UNESCO's Phnom Penh representation reported on 'national and international steps to protect the ancient city of the Khmer kings, an authentic symbol for the Cambodian people, from the corrosive fingers of time, the incursions of nature and the destruction by man' (UNESCO Cambodia 1992, 2).

A decade later, after the Angkor temples, the *Royal Ballet of Cambodia* (unlike the Angkor temples, Cambodia's performing arts had indeed suffered near-extinc-tion during and after the Khmer Rouge), too, had become another target of the global (neo-colonial) 'salvage paradigm, reflecting the desire to rescue something 'authentic' [and pure] out of destructive historical changes' (Clifford 1989, 73). UNESCO's 2002 publication *Rehabilitation of Cambodian performing arts* spoke about the 'revival of previously lost forms of performing arts' and judged the *Roban dance* (invented by Kossamak) to be deeply rooted in antiquity, since 'Angkor's temple walls [were] literally saturated with dancing images, notably the heavenly nymphs of Apsaras' (UNESCO 2002, 2, 3). An *Inventory of intangible cultural heritage of Cambodia* based its research on Cambodia's performing arts on the new global heritage norms and standards (Ministry of Culture and Fine Arts 2004). After UNESCO's 'Safeguarding project' from 2005 to 2008, the *Royal Ballet of Cambodia* was inscribed in 2008 on UNESCO's *List of the Intangible Cultural Heritage of Humanity* based on its *Convention for the Safeguarding of Intangible Cultural Heritage* of 2003 (UNESCO Convention 2003). To this day, UNESCO's homepage for the *Intangible Heritage List* reconnects the *Royal Ballet of Cambodia* 'with the Khmer court for over one thousand years'. UNESCO's online video on this inscribed property is – like George Groslier's sketches (Figure 4) – a neo-colo-nial invention of tradition in the best Hobsbawmian sense: as a kind of virtual re-enactment for the global internet user, a 'real' apsara rises from a filmed bas-relief of Angkor Wat, and starts to dance in front of the screen of the spectator while a male voice-over explains the unbroken and unchanged link from antiquity to the present (UNESCO 2008) (Figure 9).

Despite sincere intentions of sustainable protection, Cambodia's tangible heritage (the temples of Angkor) suffers from touristic over-exploitation (Hauser-Schäublin 2011; Winter 2007). Its intangible heritage (the performing arts, including the Royal Khmer Ballet) is frozen in time by folkorisation. The combination of faked apsaras

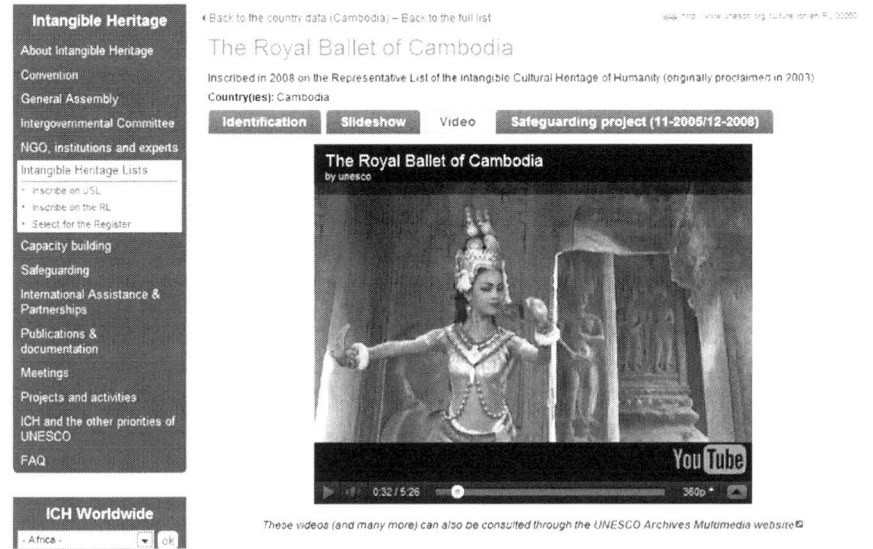

Figure 9. Screen shot of UNESCO's homepage of the *List of the Intangible Cultural Heritage of Humanity*, featuring *The Royal Ballet of Cambodia* (UNESCO 2008).

re-enacting in front of Angkor Wat has become a fossilised and static, but lucrative stereotype of Khmer culture, whereas the 'real' ballet's conditions of training and instruction were and are consequently constricted (Burridge and Frumberg 2010; Diamond 2005; Shapiro-Phim and Thompson 2001; Turnbull 2006). Strongly supported by the ex-colonial (French and Japanese) and global protection community, the ruling Khmer elites in their cultural ministries under president Sun Sen (an old Khmer Rouge member), and the national protection agency of Angkor *APSARA*, the heritage package of Angkor as a historic temple site, a place of cultural performances and re-enactment of Angkor's past, and of cultural mass tourism as the most profitable national income, has become a great source of income for the Cambodian post-conflict nation (Winter 2007). Random examples underline these global, national and local alliances: *Les nuits d'Angkor Vat* (also the title of the Sihanouk-de Gaulle re-enactment in 1966) staged as 'illumination events' *in situ* in December 2002, were organised by the French Cultural Centre with the support of Cambodia's Ministry of Culture and Fine Arts, and presented Khmer and French dance performances (Figure 10(a)). The *Angkor Wat Show* 'took place' in 2008/ 2009. According to its webpage, the re-enacted French discoverer of Angkor, Henri Mouhot, was 'on his dreamlike journey through Khmer legends' and followed by an apsara from the bas-reliefs of Angkor Wat. The show was organised by *Siem Reap's Bayon CM Organised Co Ltd,* a joint venture with *Bayon TV* and 'put together with the cooperation of the Ministry of Tourism and the Ministry of Culture and Fine Arts […] All historic and cultural details of the show, the script and choreography were developed and supervised by Proeung Chhieng, vice rector and dean of the Faculty of Choreographic Arts, at Phnom Penh's Royal University of Fine Arts' (Angkor Wat Show 2008) (Figure 10(b)). The ASEAN Congress of 2009 chose the same iconography for their publication (Figure 10(c)) and the

(a)   (b)   (c)

Figure 10 (a–c).   Collected flyers on Angkor Wat shows and publications between 2002 and 2009 (Personal Archive Michael Falser).

Cambodian Pavilion at the Shanghai Universal Exhibition 2010 presented 'dancing Apsaras' in front of Angkorian temples – just as Louis Delaporte had imagined it almost 150 years earlier and UNESCO propagates it on its homepage today.

5.   Three conclusions, or: the last meeting of the Javanese and Khmer dancers

Firstly, our case study has demonstrated that cultural heritage is not a god-given fact or natural property of modern nation states and on World Heritage lists, but a contested construction, full of constantly reloaded ideological conflicts and shifting cultural interests in changing political regimes. Understanding cultural heritage in its manifold manifestations thus implies the dissection of the concrete, ever-changing – individual, institutional, collective – agency behind it. Something called the 'Royal Khmer Ballet' is not a static cultural entity directly from Angkorian antiquity, but a dynamic modern hybrid of different interpretations, re-inventions, and reactivations, and therefore a constant de- and re-evaluation of ancient pasts for contemporary purposes. Cultural heritage *itself* is an ongoing 'performance of meaning making' (Smith and Akagawa 2009, 4): the Khmer dancers in Delaporte's drawing of 1880 were not the ones at the Marseille Colonial Exhibition of 1906; the Khmer ballet surviving at the Bangkok or Phnom Penh royal courts until the nineteenth century was not the one reinvented in George Groslier's purifying sketches from Angkor Wat's bas-reliefs in 1913; and Sihanouk's post-colonial diplomatic *Royal Corps de Ballet* dancing in the *son-et-lumière* show at Angkor Wat or the Paris Opera in the 1960s was not what is performed today in Phnom Penh's Royal Palace, featured for bus-loads of international tourists in Siem Reap's luxury hotels near Angkor, or, finally, propagated on UNESCO's exclusive World Heritage List homepage. However, all these bits and pieces participate in this specific complex heritage construction called 'Royal Khmer Ballet'.

Secondly, as our case study was able to show, an adequate reading of today's complex – *synchronically* locally, regionally, nationally *and* globally entangled – cultural heritage constructions necessitates a new methodological approach. The so-called 'Area Studies', such as Asian or Southeast Asian, or in our case Khmer Studies, have themselves contributed largely to the hermetic and essentialist conceptualisation of cultural products within supposedly well-defined political and geographical borders, national centres and cultural peripheries. On the contrary, we have tried to sketch the *transcultural trajectories* which the so-called 'Khmer Ballet' has travelled with changing cultural brokers (e.g. George Groslier or Norodom Sihanouk), regimes (French colonialism, Cambodia's independence and globalisation), and institutions (e.g. Groslier's colonial art school, UNESCO), and in different cultural and political spaces between Europe and Asia, in our case between France and Cambodia, or Paris-Marseille and Angkor-Phnom Penh. The *transcultural concept of cultural heritage* works against nationalist narratives and stereotypes, and deconstructs – within the emerging discipline of Global Art History – essentialist terms such as 'the pure, original, traditional, and authentic' in heritage constructions (Falser and Juneja 2013).

Thirdly, our case study has pinpointed the enormous risks and dangers in UNESCO's new cultural branding strategy called 'intangible heritage', which still borrows much from its original concept of 1989, to 'safeguard traditional culture and *folklore*'. *After* 1989, when the Cold War blocks collapsed, new emerging nation states such as Cambodia re-established their new identity construction by re-imagining ancient cultural glory and imperial power, by reviving post-colonial nationalism, but also by overwriting recent collective traumata of violent decolonisation (Chau-Pech Ollier and Winter 2006, 1–19). With its elitist listing strategy, UNESCO had, instead of 'supporting the continuity of knowledge and skill' and 'the conditions' per se for a creative further development of the Khmer Ballet, only given the 'national government a tool to proclaim the richness of their cultural heritage' and give, as our case has shown, 'the endangered or outmoded a second life as an exhibition of itself' (Kirshenblatt-Gimblett 2004, 56, 61). At this moment, the Javanese and Khmer dancers meet for a fourth and maybe last time: just as the 'staged authenticity' (MacCannell 1973) of a Khmer Ballet à la *Angkorienne* frozen in time helps to block the necessary artistic-performative expression of the recent post-colonial trauma of the Khmer Rouge genocide, the folkloric 'Javanese dance troupes' as government-sponsored 'cultural missions' around the globe help to 'erase' the memory of post-colonial massacres in Indonesia (1965–1966). Or, as an international 'Javanese dance performer' of the 1990s put it, and as a Khmer Ballet dance might equally say:

> I was reminded and forced to admit that my body functioned as an eraser, and at the same time provided a reconfiguration of a 'nationalized body' to enter the global discursive space. This (re)formation of (new) identity, although presented through the presence of the marked body on the global stage, is always sown as a celebration of 'diversity'. Everyone's 'National Dress', and my dance as well seem to commemorate the presence of 'differences' while in actuality this celebration has already passed through many layers of violence in the process of its replication [...] Javanese court dance dominates cultural mission presentations [meaning] the 'Javanese replica' [...] The replica dances a cultural form categorized as 'third world', but a third world with 'high, royal arts' or sacred, ancient origins that remains valuable to the people with whom it originated (Larasati 2006, 167, quoted in Cohen 2010, 224)

Notes

1. This and all following English translations from French sources are by the author of this paper.
2. The author would like to thank Vann Molyvann and his wife Trudy for this information provided during an interview in Phnom Penh, in March 2010.
3. 'The monuments themselves give only us only a little precious information on the dance. Not that the female figures are rare on the Angkorian temples, but it does not make sense to see in them only dancers. As protective deities, praying and following the almighty and mysterious god who lives in the cella, they are here to surround him, to serve him and to adore him, forever perpetuated in stone. *At Angkor Wat, the god-serving enchantresses are multiplied* ad infinitum, *however they do everything but dance* [italics MF]. On the bas-reliefs we can only find at most two or three dancing poses' (Groslier 1969, 91).

References

Agnew, V. 2004. "What is Re-enactment?" *Criticism* 46 (3): 327–339.

Agnew, V. 2007. "History's Affective Turn: Historical Re-enactment and its Work in the Present." *Rethinking History* 11 (3): 299–312.

Ang, C., E. Prenowitz, and A. Thompson, eds. 1996. *Angkor. A Manual for the Past, Present and Future*. Phnom Penh: APSARA, UNESCO.

Angkor Wat Show. 2008. "The Legend of Angkor Wat – When History Comes to Life." Accessed June 15 2010. http://www.angkorwatshow.com/.

Arns, I. 2007. "Strategies of Re-enactment in Contemporary (Media) Art and Performance." In *History Will Repeat Itself*, edited by I. Arns and G. Horn, 37–63. Frankfurt/Main: Revolver.

Artaud, A. 1923. *Exposition National Coloniale de Marseille, Rapport Général*. Marseille: Imprimerie du Semaphore.

Bachmann-Medick, D. 2009. *Cultural Turns. Neuorientierungen in den Kulturwissenschaften*. 3rd ed. Reinbeck bei Hamburg: Rowohlt. (Performative turn: 104–143).

Baschet, R., ed. 1900. *Le Panorama, 1900. Exposition Universelle*. Paris: Baschet (photographer Neurdein frères et Maurice Baschet).

Beau, M. 1906. *L'Indo-Chine à l'Exposition Coloniale de Marseille* [Indochina at the Colonial Exhibition of Marseille]. Marseille: Imprimerie Marseillaise.

Blanchard, P., G. Boëtsch, and N. J. Snoep, eds. 2011. *Exhibitions. L'Invention du Sauvage* [Exhibitions. The Invention of the Savage]. Paris: Actes Sud.

Bloembergen, M. 2006. *Colonial Spectacles. The Netherlands and the Dutch East Indies at the World Exhibitions, 1880–1931*. Singapore: NUS Press.

Bois, G. 1913. *Les danseuses cambodgiennes en France* [The Cambodian Dancers]. Hanoi, Haiphong: Imprimerie d'Extrême-Orient.

Brosius, C., and K. Polit, eds. 2011. *Ritual, Heritage and Identity. The Politics of Culture and Performance in a Globalised World*. London: Routledge.

Burridge, S., and F. Frumberg, eds. 2010. *Beyond the Apsara. Celebrating Dance in Cambodia*. London: Routledge.

Cadilhac, P.-E. 1931. "L'heure du ballet [The Hour of the Ballet]." *L'Illustration*, no.4616, 89th year, 22 August 1931, n.p.

Cambodian Information Agency. 1963. *Royal Cambodian Ballet*. Phnom Penh: Government Press.

Carlson, M. 2000. "Performing the Past: Living History and Cultural Memory." *Paragrana* 9 (2): 237–248.

Chau-Pech Ollier, L., and T. Winter, eds. 2006. *Expressions of Cambodia. The Politics of Tradition, Identity, and Change*. London: Routledge.

Chazal, J.-P. 2002. "'Grand Succès pour les Exotiques'. Retour sur les spectacles javanais de l'Exposition Universelle de Paris en 1889 [Great Success for the Exotic. Revisiting the Javanese Spectacles of the Paris World Fair of 1889]." *Archipel* 63: 109–152.

Clifford, J. 1989. "The Others: Beyond the 'Salvage' Paradigm." *Third Text* 6: 73–77.

Cohen, M. 2010. *Performing Otherness. Java and Bali on International Stages, 1905–1952*. Basingstoke: Palgrave MacMillan.

Cook, A. 2004. "The Use and Abuse of Historical Re-enactment." *Criticism* 46 (3): 487–496.

Cravath, P. 2007. *Earth in Flower. The Divine Mystery of the Cambodian Dance Drama*. Holmes Beach: DatASIA.

De Beauplan, R. "La nuit merveilleuse [The Marvellous Night]." *L'Illustration*, no.4616, 89th year, 22 August 1931, n.p.

de Miomandre, F. 1923. "Rêveries sur les Danseuses Cambdgiennes [Fantasies About the Cambodian Dancers]." *La danse* 38: 213–214.

Décordet-Ahiha, A. 2004. *Les danses exotiques en France* [The Exotic Dances in France]. Pantin: Centre national de la danse.

Delaporte, L. 1880. *Voyage au Cambodge. L'architecture Khmer* [Travel to Cambodia. Khmer Architecture]. Paris: Delgrave.

Diamond, E. 1989. "Performance and Cultural Politics." In *The Routledge Reader in Politics and Performance*, edited by L. Goodman and D. de Gay, 57–63. London: Routledge.

Diamond, C. 2005. "Emptying the Sea by the Bucketful. A Difficult Phase in Cambodian Theatre or the Creation of a Culture of Independence." In *Ethnicity and Identity. Global Performance*, edited by R. Chaturvedi and B. Singleton, 389–396. New Delhi: Rawat.

Dieulefils, P. 1909. *Indo-China. Picturesque and Monumental. Ruins of Angkor (Cambodge)*. Hanoi: Dieulefils.

Edwards, P. 2007. *Cambodge. The Cultivation of a Nation, 1860–1945*. Honolulu: HUP.

Fabian, J. 2002. *Time and the Other. How Anthropolgy Makes its Object*. New York, NY: Columbia UP.

Falser, M. 2011. "Krishna and the Plaster Cast. Translating the Cambodian Temple of Angkor Wat in the French Colonial Period." *Transcultural Studies*, 2: 6–50. Accessed March 15 2013. http://archiv.ub.uni-heidelberg.de/ojs/index.php/transcultural/article/view/9083.

Falser, M. 2013. "From Colonial Map to Visitor's Parcours – Tourist Guides and the Spatio-temporal Making of the Archaeological Park of Angkor." In *'Archaeologizing' Heritage. Between Local Social Practice and Global Virtual Reality*, edited by M. Falser and M. Juneja, 79–103. Berlin: Springer.

Falser, M., and M. Juneja, eds. 2013. *Kulturerbe und Denkmalpflege transkulturell. Grenzgänge zwischen Theorie und Praxis* [Cultural Heritage and Architectural Preservation in a Transcultural Perspective. Enquiries between Theory and Practice]. Bielefeld: Transcript.

Fischer-Lichte, E., et al., eds. 2003. *Performativität und Ereignis* [Performativity and Event]. Tübingen, Basel: Francke.

Gapps, S. 2009. "Mobile Monuments: A View of Historical Re-enactment and Authenticity from Inside the Costume Cupboard of History." *Rethinking History* 13 (3): 395–409.

Garry, R. 1964. *La renaissance du Cambodge de Jayavarman VII roi d'Angkor à Norodom Sihanouk Varman* [The Renaissance of Cambodia of Jayavarman VII, King of Angkor to Norodom Sihanouk Varman]. Phnom Penh: Department de l'Information.

Gosh, A. 1998. *Dancing in Cambodia, At Large in Burma*. Delhi: Ravi Dayal.

Groslier, G. 2010. *Danseuses cambodgiennes anciennes et modernes*. Paris: Challamel, 1913. Translated: *Cambodian dancers – ancient and modern*, edited by K. Davis, 6–158. Holmes Beach: DatASIA.

Groslier, G. 1918. "L'agonie de l'art cambodgien [Agony of Cambodian Art]." *Revue Indochinoise*: 547–560.

Groslier, B. P. 1969. "La musique et la danse sous les rois d'Angkor [The Music and the Dance of the Kings of Angkor]." In *Mélanges sur l'archéologie du Cambodge (1949–1986), Bernard-Philippe Groslier* [Miscellanies on Archaeology of Cambodia (1949-1986), Bernard-Philippe Groslier], edited by J. Dumarcay, 89–93. Paris: EFEO.

Groslier, B. P. 1966. "Les voix d'une nuit d'Angkor. Texte de spectacle 'son et lumière' offert au Général de Gaulle, sur le parvis d'Angkor Vat, par le Royaume du Cambodge, le 1er septembre 1966 [The Voices of a Night at Angkor. The Text for the Sound and Light Show for General Charles de Gaulle in front of Angkor Wat]." In *Mélanges sur l'archéologie du Cambodge (1949–1986), Bernard-Philippe Groslier* [Miscellanies on Archaeology of Cambodia (1949–1986), Bernard-Philippe Groslier], edited by J. Dumarcay, 79–84. Paris: EFEO.

Hauser-Schäublin, Brigitte, ed. 2011. *World Heritage Angkor and Beyond. Circumstances and Implications of UNESCO Listings in Cambodia. Göttingen Studies in Cultural Property, vol. 2*. Göttingen: Universitätsverlag Göttingen.

Heywood, D. 2008. *Cambodian Dance. Celebration of the Gods*. Bangkok: River Book Press.

Kellner, H. 1997. "Language and Historical Representation." In *The Postmodern History Reader*, edited by K. Jenkins, 127–138. London: Routledge.

Kirshenblatt-Gimblett. 2004. "Intangible Heritage as Metacultural Production." *Museum International* 56 (1–2): 52–64.

Lamb, J. 2008. "Historical Re-enactment, Extremity, and Passion." *The Eighteenth Century* 49 (3): 239–250.

Larasati, R. D. 2006. "Dancing on the Mass Grave: Cultural Reconstruction Post Indonesia Massacres." PhD diss., UC, Riveside. (unpublished).

Lombard, D. 1992. "Le Kampong javanais à l'Exposition Universelle de Paris en1889 [The Javenese Kampong at the Paris World Fair of 1889]." *Archipel* 43: 115–130.

Loti, P. 1912. *Pelerin d'Angkor* [A Pilgrim of Angkor]. Paris: Grevin.

MacCannell, D. 1973. "Staged Authenticity: Arrangements of Social Space in Tourist Settings." *American Journal of Sociology* 79 (3): 589–603.

Marchal, S. 1927. *Costumes et parures khmèrs d'après les Devatâ d'Angkor-Vat* [Khmer Costumes and Attires After the Devatas of Angkor Wat]. Paris: G. van Oest.

Ministry of Culture and Fine Arts, UNESCO Phnom Penh, eds. 2004. *Inventory of Intangible Cultural Heritage of Cambodia*. Phnom Penh: JSRC Printing House.

Sangkum Reastr Niyum. 1969. *Photo-Souvenirs du Cambodge. Sangkum Reastr Niyum 1955–1969 (Vol. 7: Le prestige au plan international du Cambodge)* [Photo-Souvenirs of Cambodia. Sangkum Reastr Niyum 1955–1969 (The International Prestige of Cambodia)]. Phnom Penh: Sangkum Reastr Niyum (to the visit of Charles de Gaulle, see 128–9, 136–7, 156–7, 160–7, 174–8).

Sasagawa, H. 2005. "Post/Colonial Discourse on the Cambodian Court Dance." *Tonan Ajia Kenkyu (Southeast Asian Studies)* 42 (4): 418–441.

Schechner, R., and W. Appel, eds. 1990. *By Means of Performance. Intercultural Studies of Theatre and Ritual*. Cambridge: CUP.

Schouten, F. 1995. "Heritage as Historical Reality." In *Heritage, Tourism and Society*, edited by D. T. Herbert, 21–31. London: Mansell.

Shapiro-Phim, T. 2002. "Dance, Music, and the Nature of Terror in Democratic Kampuchea." In *The Anthropology of Genocide*, edited by A. L. Hinton, 179–193. Berkeley: UCP Press.

Shapiro-Phim, T., and A. Thompson. 2001. *Dance in Cambodia*. Kuala Lumpur: OUP.

Sihanouk, N. 1968. *The Glory of Angkor – Son et Lumière. After the idea of Samdec Norodom Sihanouk, Chef d'Etat. In honor of His Excellency Mr. Josip Boroz Tito, President of the Socialist Federal Republic of Yogoslavia* [in Serbo-Croatian, National Archives, Phnom Penh, Cambodia].

Sihanouk, N. 1981. *Souvenirs doux et amers* [Sweet and Bitter Memories]. Paris: Hachette.

Smith, L., and N. Akagawa, eds. 2009. *Intangible Heritage*. London: Routledge.

Thiounn, S. C. 1930. *Danses cambodgiennes* [Cambodian Dancers]. Hanoi: Imprimerie d'Extrême-Orient.

Tivers, J. 2002. "Performing Heritage: The Use of Live 'Actors' in Heritage Presentations." *Leisure Studies* 21 (3–4): 187–200.

Turnbull, R. 2006. "A Burned-out Theatre: The State of Cambodia's Performing Arts." In *Expressions of Cambodia. The Politics of Tradition, Identity, and Change*, edited by L. Chau-Pech Ollier and T. Winter, 133–149. London: Routledge.

Turner, V. 1982. *From Ritual to Theatre. The Human Seriousness of Play*. New York, NY: Performing Arts Journal Publications.

UNESCO. 1992. *Angkor, UNESCO World Heritage* Accessed on March 15 2013. http://whc.unesco.org/en/list/668/.

UNESCO. 2002. *Rehabilitation of Cambodian Performing Arts*. Phnom Penh: UNESCO Publications.

UNESCO. 2003. "Convention of the safeguarding of intangible cultural heritage." Accessed March 15, 2013. http://www.unesco.org/culture/ich/index.php?lg=en&pg=00022#art2.

UNESCO. 2008. "UNESCO List of the Intangible Cultural Heritage of Humanity: The Royal Ballet of Cambodia." Accessed March 15, 2013. http://www.unesco.org/culture/ich/index.php?lg=en&pg=00011&RL=00060.

UNESCO Cambodia. 1992–4. *Save Angkor*. News Bulletin 1–4. Phnom Penh: UNESCO.

Vilain, J. 2006. *Rodin et les danseuses cambodgiennes. Sa dernière passion* [Rodin and the Cambodian Dancers. His last Passion]. Paris: Editions du musée Rodin.

Winter, T. 2007. *Post-conflict Heritage, Postcolonial Tourism. Culture, Politics and Development at Angkor*. London: Routledge.

Patchworking the past: materiality, touch and the assembling of 'experience' in American Civil War re-enactment

Mads Daugbjerg

Aarhus University

This article investigates the power of things and materials in the context of historical re-enactment. Based on ethnographic fieldwork among costumed re-enactors reinvigorating the American Civil War, it explores participants' close connections to specific objects and ensembles of objects and the crucial role awarded to 'experience' and 'touch' in this genre of relating to the past. It is argued that three interrelated propositions derived from my analysis allow a better understanding of this popular heritage practice: (1) Re-enactment can be understood as a human-material 'patchworking' process, (2) Re-enactment comprises a 'holistic' enterprise and (3) A key motivation in re-enactment derives from its 'unfinishedness'. By attending to these dimensions through a detailed analysis that takes the role of objects and their experiential potential seriously as going beyond 'representation', I argue that the re-enacted Civil War serves as an often implicit and non-verbal – but, precisely, *enacted* – critique of conventional approaches to learning about and exhibiting history and heritage, such as those epitomised by the conventional museum.

When I was handed the greyish jacket, I sensed right away that it constituted far more than a mere piece of worn cloth. I was in Chestertown on the Eastern Shore of Maryland, USA, to take part in the local Memorial Day parade and witness the annual re-enactment of the Chestertown tea party.[1] Even though the town's Tea Party Festival, an event marketed as 'celebrating colonial resistance to British rule',[2] was mainly centred on the 1770s and the period of the American Revolution, I was here as a Civil War private from the 1860s. The company of re-enactors I had joined had strong ties to this particular place, and we were set to march in the afternoon parade, unconcerned about potential anachronism. In fact, my biggest concern on that late May day in 2010 was the soaring heat building up, threatening to destabilise a native Scandinavian like myself who had recently acquired an expensive and well-crafted, but also thick and woollen, reproduction of a Confederate army coat. This is when I was handed that other jacket. It was much thinner than my fancy woollen one, but more importantly, it carried so much more power. We may perhaps with Benjamin (1969) speak of 'aura', but this was not an original historical piece from the actual Civil War. It did however possess a history and an authority that I could tap into, closely tied to its owner, a local hero and old-time re-enactor, now in his 60s, who had 'been there and done that' when the re-enactment hobby was finding its feet in the 1960s and 1970s. On that day in Chestertown, 'Warren', as we may call the old-timer,[3] had been inspecting my amateurish attempts at getting dressed for the parade, and was evidently not happy with my appearance, or, more precisely, with my 'impression' – the re-enactment term for the total look and feel of the part you bring to the show. Grudgingly, he went to his pickup, took out his well-worn Confederate jean jacket, and said 'put this on instead'. From the faces of my company comrades I could tell immediately that this was not simply an order not to be disputed; more than that, it constituted a generous offer from a local legend who did not have the energy (or indeed the need) to be in the frontline himself anymore, but whose powerful apparel I was now invited to don, give life to and carry on for a little while. As I marched the hot roads of Chestertown that day, I was thus not only re-enacting the 1860s but also in a sense celebrating and reconsolidating the potency of Warren's early ventures in the hobby. The dirty jacket, holding so much accumulated experience and grit, was much cooler – in both senses of that term.

This article investigates the power of things and materials in the genre of historical re-enactment. Based on ethnographic fieldwork among costumed hobbyists reinvigorating the American Civil War, it explores participants' close connections to specific objects or ensembles of objects, and the crucial role these play in establishing moments of historical 'experience'. In doing so, I draw inspiration from studies in materiality and heritage that pay special heed to processes of 'assembling' and the establishing of 'connections' between human actors, artefacts and places (Bennett 2007; Macdonald 2009; Byrne et al. 2011; Bille 2012; Harrison 2012). As I took part in the restagings of the nation's bloodiest ever conflict (bloodiest, that is, when measured by the number of lost *American* lives), I was struck again and again by my battle brothers' close connections to their 'stuff' (Miller 2010), and especially to their personal uniform, weapons and gear, known in re-enactment terminology as their 'kit'. These material connections, and the senses in which you as a re-enactor can touch, take on and literally 'inhabit' and give life to the materials – as I did with Warren's jacket – lie at the heart of the experience of re-enactment.

Working through a selection of my ethnographic material from the US Civil War scene, I describe and analyse three central, but partly overlooked, dimensions of re-enactment that may improve our understanding of the genre's powerful popular appeal: Firstly, in line with my comments above, I elaborate on the 'connectivity' between persons and things (Harrison 2012), or, as I term it, the human-material 'patchworking' lying at the heart of these performances. Secondly, I argue that the aspirations of re-enactors are fundamentally 'holistic' in that they pursue moments of bodily and temporal resonance that go beyond rational learning about history and embrace broader 'sensescapes' (Classen and Howes 2006). And thirdly, I suggest that a key part of the fascination of Civil War re-enactment is its quality as 'unfinished business', an engagement with the past that allows for human and material agency and thus not just for reviving but also for *revising* selected pasts (Schneider 2011, 7–13). As such, the re-enacted Civil War also serves, I propose, as an often implicit (but, precisely, *enacted*) critique of conventional approaches to learning about and exhibiting history and heritage. Before delving into these three analytical clusters, I provide, below, a brief contextualisation of my study and of the key concepts with which I grapple.

Contextualising historical re-enactment, materiality and experience

The American Civil War, it has been claimed, 'has supplanted the Revolution as the war that made the nation' and 'has become, over the years, an event to rank with the myths and legends of a very distant age' (Grant 1998, 164–165). Indeed, mytho-logical parallels were invoked almost as soon as the smoked cleared, for instance at the iconic field of Gettysburg, where, in the immediate aftermath, '[n]ewspapers described the battle within the providential sweep of history, labelling it an Ameri-can Waterloo, Thermopylae, or Armageddon' (Weeks 2003, 13). The Civil War's importance for American identity and memory can hardly be overstated, continu-ously being reasserted on many levels and scales, not least in the never-ending cycle of anniversaries such as the 150-year commemorations that are currently sweeping over the USA (in 2011–2015). Any attempt, past or present, to revamp fragments of this 'struggle over the nation's soul' (Fornieri 1994, 45) inevitably finds itself enmeshed in a web of major American socio-political issues, including the relation-ship between continued warfare, mass death and patriotism, the discussion over the extent of federal 'government', or the persistent question of racism and segregation (Bodnar 1996; Savage 1997; Fahs and Waugh 2004; Faust 2008). As Blight (2001, 2002) has convincingly demonstrated, the reconstruction of 'white' America has taken place on a backdrop of continued, and in some periods even increasing, racial segregation (see also Linenthal 1991, 90–91; O'Leary 1996).

Civil War re-enactors, dabbling also in 'reconstruction', albeit on a much more tactile and hands-on level, often seem to sidestep, exclude or even consciously deny such larger political issues in their celebration of the common soldier and his Civil War 'experience' (which I address below). While a number of important studies have examined historical re-enactment and 'living history' interpretation,[4] indeed informing and inspiring my own work in the field, relatively little attention has hith-erto been paid to the *material* dimension so key in these contexts, and to the role that objects and tangibles play in shaping a desire for 'more than representation' (see Lorimer 2005; Thrift 2007; Grewcock 2014 this volume). Indeed, a lot of aca-demic effort has been invested precisely in discussing how re-enactment can or (especially) cannot be said to provide for adequate representation of past events, often from a critical standpoint (e.g. Walsh 1992; Bennett 1995; Agnew 2004, 2007; Cook 2004). While such debates are important in their own right, in this article I am primarily indebted to scholars who insist, instead, on scrutinising the performative and affective aspects and potentials of re-enactment, and of a detailed (often ethno-graphically inspired) unpacking of these dynamics (especially Crang 1996; Magelssen 2007; Schneider 2011; Kalshoven 2012). In a larger theoretical landscape, my focus on the intimate relationship between people and things and on the ways in which concrete human-material constellations empower and engender particular acts and activities is fueled by an interest in Actor–Network Theory and in the idea of analysing social gatherings as 'assemblages' emanating from this body of theory (e.g. Law 2004; Latour 2005; Harrison et al., 2013), as well as from the work of Deleuze and Guattari (2004; and see Harrison 2012, 33–35). 'Taking an assemblage perspective on heritage', as Macdonald has observed, 'directs our attention less to finished 'heritage products' than to processes and entanglements involved in their coming into being and continuation' (2009, 118). In my case, such entanglements are supremely material and also connected to a tactile desire to *touch* the past and in turn, to be touched (Hetherington 2003; Schneider 2011, 35).

The yearning for touch and 'experience' – as opposed to something we may, crudely, term 'representation' – is fundamental in historical re-enactment (Handler and Saxton 1988; de Groot 2009). As I immersed myself in the local concerns of 'my' company of Confederate re-enactors,[5] I found that my probes into grander political and moral dimensions, such as those connected with the role of slavery, were most often deflected with responses circling around the celebration of the typical, average or common man, uninformed in politics and merely 'fighting for what he believed was right'. This corresponds well with Thompson's findings, in her in-depth study of World War I and II re-enactment, of the widespread 'fascination with this mythic common man' propelling re-enactors to 'represent, honour, and come closer to understanding the common war experience' (2004, 88). Time and again, my informants came back to the crucial dimension of experience that they considered lacking from other ways of approaching the Civil War past. For example, Jonathan, one of the leaders of my company, told me that 'I got into it because I wanted what the books couldn't give me'. He elaborated:

> I started studying the American Civil War when I was in middle school, and I just automatically got hooked, and read everything I could get my hands on. Ken Burns came out with his Civil War [television] documentary at the same time I was getting into it. And as I am reading it, and seeing it, I am always wondering, "what was it like, what was it like", you know, walking a mile in somebody's shoes? And when I found out they did reenactment, I was like: I gotta try that, I gotta do that. And then I found the first local reenactment unit in my area (…) and I joined them. And it was really amazing, to really walk a mile in their shoes, and to get that experience.

Jonathan's perceived clash between bookish knowledge and lived experience is typical of my informants' attitudes. Although he, like many others in the re-enactment society, possessed a vast and detailed knowledge of the Civil War, obtained from an almost obsessive devouring of war literature, battle descriptions and drill manuals, such theoretical knowledge was understood to be inadequate for capturing and communicating a "real" sense of 'what it was like'. Along with the stereotype of the conventional (glass-case, fenced-off, no-touch) museum, other major institutions and emblems of learning such as 'the book' and 'the school system' were commonly invoked by re-enactors as providing inadequate, flawed or sometimes downright false history.[6] In their worldview, they all lack the crucial resonating power of personal experience.

In seeking to grasp what we should, in this context, take an 'experience' to mean, an useful starting point is the distinction between the two German terms Erfahrung and Erlebnis. While *Erfahrung* denotes the cumulative and 'temporally elongated notion of experience based on a learning process' (Jay 2005, 11), *Erlebnis* refers to the 'inner' or 'lived' experience of the individual and 'generally connotes a more immediate, pre-reflective, and personal variant of experience' than Erfahrung (ibid.). This last variant, connected to momentary, sensorial impact and rush, is central for my purposes. Robert Desjarlais, in his tracing of the term's history from Romanticism over hermeneutics and phenomenology and into modern anthropology, argues that experience is crucially connected to a holistic aspiration, 'an appeal to wholeness' (Desjarlais 1996, 74; see also Ankersmit 2005, 117–119). Further, he argues, 'a set of phrasings of depth, interiority, and authenticity, sensibilities of holism and transcendence, and practices of reading and writing, have, in the modern era, crafted a mode of being that many in the West call experience' (Desjarlais 1996, 75).

It is far from revolutionary to assert that experience is crucial for re-enactors. Indeed, in a classic paper, Handler and Saxton describe what they term an 'authenticity of experience' as a key ambition for the 'living historians' of their study (Handler and Saxton 1988, 245). This includes a wish to communicate or teach history as accurately as possible to *others*, but it is also – to many re-enactors more than anything – about the sensing of an authentic past *themselves*, and, in doing so, simultaneously obtaining a sense of a 'real self'. 'An authentic experience, to be achieved in the practice of living history, is one in which individuals feel themselves to be in touch both with a "real" world and with their "real" selves', Handler and Saxton state (ibid., 243). In another seminal piece, Crang argues, likewise, that 'the quest for the real in reenactments is considerably more of a self-knowing performance than is often suggested – and it is this that makes living history such an exemplary dramatisation of modernity' (1996, 417).[7] Building on insights such as these, my own aim in the present study can be described as a commitment to understanding the practical work entailed in this – understanding how such an experiential sense of authenticity *comes about* – part of which, as we shall see, involves paying close attention to the things as things as opposed to mere representations (cf. Henare et al. 2007; Miller 2010).

Re-enactment as processes of 'patchworking'

To re-enactors, the pursuit of the ultimate Civil War experience includes an unending fascination with materials and material qualities, and especially with those that come together in one's personal 'kit': uniforms, clothing, weapons and equipment. Coming across as authentic depends to a large degree on the quality of your kit, constituting the material basis of your 'impression' – a complex cover term used to denote both the particular part a given group is expected to fulfil in a specific re-enactment (e.g. 'in this battle, our impression will be the 15th Alabama') and the degree to which one's portrayal is credible or accurate (e.g. 'a fantastic impression'). Impression in this understanding thus concerns a great deal of *expression*, and it also comprises and binds together a number of less outright material factors such as stature and pose, facial work, and fidelity and skill. In turn, the quality of your personal impression relies heavily on your company and its collective orchestrations. A convincing impression thus distinguishes the serious re-enactor – called 'campaigners', 'progressives' or 'hard cores' – from the 'mainstreamer', the 'weekend warrior' or the 'farb'.[8] And while not in itself sufficient, a quality kit is a prerequisite for a quality impression. Thus, even though we may, with Handler and Saxton, speak of an 'authenticity of experience' comprising largely intangible sensations, atmospheres and emotions, such qualities cannot be separated from a number of tangibles and their powers – indeed, they revolve around them. The stuff is crucial in facilitating the experiential authenticities. A great deal of concrete labour, assembly work, or what I refer to as 'patchwork', is invested in producing, maintaining and improving your kit, involving processes of selection and priority juggling and also, very often, actual sewing work or other repair and maintenance duties. Jonathan described his movement within the hobby from 'mainstreaming' towards 'campaigning' as follows:

When I first started, it was more of a mainstream unit, and we didn't carry everything on our backs. And our uniforms were all machine sewn, and synthetically dyed, and they never fell apart, and we never lost a button, and we slept in tents, on cots, with coolers. But, you know, for the past seven, eight years, maybe even longer, I've been doing the campaign side of reenacting, where, you know, our uniforms are mostly handstitched, and they *do* fall apart, and you *have* to stitch them up, and you *do* lose buttons, and you carry everything on your back.

Patchworking, in this sense, summarises the processes of stitching together and combining bits and pieces, on the tactile level of the object but in combination with 'bits and pieces' of accumulated and shared knowledge. In discussing 'assemblage' as a process of 'tentative and hesitant unfolding', Law (2004, 41–42) adopts Derrida's suggestion that we should understand assemblage as 'the complex structure of a weaving, an interlacing which permits the different threads and different lines of meaning – or of force – to go off again in different directions, just as it is always ready to tie itself up with others' (Derrida 1982, quoted in Law 2004, 42).[9] Importantly, the objects facilitate 'patchworking' in a more-than-representational sense (Lorimer 2005). That is to say, for my informants, a quality kit and a convincing impression were not merely symbolic marks of distinction (Bourdieu 1984) – although they were clearly also that – but involved a sense of craft and authenticity going well beyond surface symbolism (see also Kalshoven 2012, 181–221). Your materials, posture and knowledge all had to come together to shape a convincing and deep impression that could not be reduced to a semiotic signifier of 'capital' but must be filled with experience, given life, inhabited.

In a discussion of the relationship between knowledge and experience in museums, or between what she terms 'science' and 'magic', Macdonald has pointed out that experiential approaches seem to be gaining ground across the heritage sector, and that 'the balance of emphasis in the "new museums" may be tilted towards other matters such as providing enjoyment, entertainment or spectacle' (2005, 216; see also Hall 2006; Daugbjerg 2011). Re-enactment must be seen as part of such a broader heritage landscape in which the knowledge/experience relationship is being reshuffled. Macdonald also notes the increasing 'direct appeal to, and mobilisation of, the enchanted properties of objects' in the newer experiential museums (ibid.). This resonates well with my findings from the Civil War re-enactment scene in which objects, sites and moments are certainly often ascribed enchanted or hallowed properties and agencies. Indeed, the so-called 'magic moment' has a special place in re-enactment mythology. These rare points or 'spots of time' (Runia 2006a) constitute especially dense and often short glimpses in which a particularly strong sense of 'being there' is felt and shared.[10] Cushman has described an urge in re-enactors 'to lose track of time, to fool themselves, to experience a mystical moment when the seemingly impermeable boundary between the present and the past suddenly dissolves' (Cushman 1999, quoted in Amster 2007, 21).

There is, of course, no room for such a 'mystical' dissolving or connection in a conventional Western conception of history and being, revolving around what Lash has called 'the rationality of Cartesian space and Newtonian time' (1999, 1). Thus, such insistences on the part of my informants – say, of 'walking a mile in their shoes', to re-quote Jonathan – imply a challenge to rational thought, and to the black-and-white common-sense distinction between being there and not actually being there. They attempt to capture the experiential enjoyment derived from occupying the grey zone in-between now and then. Schneider suggests similarly that re-enactment can be said to contest 'tightly stitched Enlightenment claims to the forward-driven linearity of temporality' (2011, 29). In her suggestive phrasing,

> a reenactment *both* is *and* is not the acts of the Civil War. It is *not not* the Civil War. And, perhaps, through the cracks in the 'not not,' something cross-temporal, something affective, and something affirmative circulates. Something is touched. (ibid., 43, italics in original)

What the books could not give someone like Jonathan was exactly an experience of touching, or of 'being' in the shoes of a historical Civil War soldier. The shoes, and the rest of Jon's kit, were crucial. When viewed from the safe territory of Western rational thought, 'their shoes' must of course be interpreted rather liberally, since the actual shoes walked in by Jon were relatively recently produced copies based on 1860s designs. Still, they remain at the core of the experience. They do not, however, *in themselves* hold the magic moments or powerful experiences – they do not possess 'agency' per se – but must be animated, worn, given life. Like the Chestertown jacket allowing me to join in on and momentarily touch the materialised memories of Warren, and add my own minimal amount of wear and tear to its accumulated value, the power of my company comrades' equipment and accoutrements was strongly dependent on their continuous use, on on-going human engagement, and on the specific entanglements with other tangibles.

Re-enactment as a 'holistic' enterprise

The physicality of sites and materials thus works in concert with their human invigorators in bringing about such multi-layered moments and experiences. These processes are also, as I noted with Desjarlais, characterised by a 'holistic' ambition and arguably contain an implicit critique of the conventional museum's focus on detached parts and causal chains of chronology and explanation. In re-enactment, material and bodily elements work together with already existing knowledge and imaginations to co-produce entire atmospheric assemblages speaking to many senses at once. Thus, for example, at the 2010 Gettysburg annual re-enactment, Mark, a young and enthusiastic member of my company, attempted to get across to me the difference between two modes of learning he considered oppositional. He did so by referring to what he termed the 'whole scene' accessible to us where we stood, in the sizzling summer heat of the Gettysburg event's Confederate camp:

> When you're in a classroom, and you're in this hard little desk, and you're watching a teacher sit up there at the chalkboard and drone on and on and on, you can't help but lose interest. When you're out on the battlefield, in your jeans cloth, and you're sweating, and you have black powder in your teeth, and you can smell the smoke in your nose, and you see the banners flapping, and the glint of the metal, and... the whole scene is ... [gestures with both arms as if to physically embrace the surrounding landscape] playing out before your eyes, you feel that you're part of it, and you start to feel you can *understand* what it must have ... been like for them.

Kirshenblatt-Gimblett reminds us that 'wholes' are of course 'not given but constituted, and often they are hotly contested' (1991, 389). Nevertheless, in the case of re-enactment, these co-productions are also meant to be *re*-productions. However, no matter how ambitious and grand the spectacles may be – and some of the restaged Civil War battles involve thousands of participants – they are also commonly understood by participants to be Quixotic (Crang 1996) and invariably incomplete in comparison to the historical nodes of references to which they point. Mark was rather clear on this sense of lack, unattainability and of how his own experience (of, say, the Battle of Gettysburg) was so much thinner than the real deal of the 1860s. He told me that to him, re-enactment was about 'respecting men far better than me'. When I asked him why he had chosen to side with the Confederacy, he elaborated:

> The South was agrarian. It was almost chivalric. Almost… a very knightly society. I can respect that cavalier attitude, and I emulate it in my daily life. And the North, of course, [was] industry, and merchants, and bankers. And I see it as being a conflict between the farmer and the banker, literally. And, well, the rest of history was written by the fact that the bankers and the merchants won. (MD: And you would side with the farmers?) Every time. Anybody that wants to … preserve the countryside as a pristine area – I mean, it's beautiful – trees and creeks and stones, those are beautiful. I think cities are ugly. And stinky, and just… not pleasant places to be.

The wholes assembled, even at the biggest or most painstakingly elaborate re-enactments, were thus also full of absence, of nostalgic yearnings for a past that might never have been (but that might also, or perhaps, according to people like Mark, *should* have been),[11] of that which cannot be retrieved (see Stewart 1993). The spectacles of re-enactment therefore also, in indirect but profound ways, revolve around those elements of the past that are forever gone, for good or bad. As noted by Till, 'when we return to a place, remember an experience in place, and perform a rendition of the past through a place, we may feel haunted by that which appears not to be there in material space but is, in fact, a powerful presence' (2005, 13). To Mark as to many other re-enactors, the hobby – often described as much more than a hobby – concerned a desire to stitch together, through concrete material and bodily practice, historical wholes they knew could never be complete but whose unfinishedness constituted not just a dissatisfaction but also a key fascination (further elaborated below). There was 'almost a teleological ideal of progress towards authenticity which knowingly will never be attained' (de Groot 2009, 108).

In his work on the power of touch, Hetherington (2003) has suggested the relevance for museum and heritage studies of the notion of *praesentia*, a concept he adopts from Brown's (1981) study of the significance and the power of mediaeval saintly relics in Christianity. Praesentia is 'concerned with how the absent divine and the holy dead can be made manifest through the presence of a seemingly insignificant fragment of ordinary material made extraordinary by association' (Hetherington 2003, 1940). Further, praesentia 'is concerned with the experience of mingling: distance and proximity; presence and absence; secular and divine; human and nonhuman; subject and object; time and space; vision and touch' (ibid.). Such an 'experience of mingling' comes close to capturing the dimension of human-material connectivity that I have described as a primary drive for my informants. Not unlike the power of Christian relics, the materials and artefacts involved in historical re-enactment arguably work as vehicles for establishing a link or a presence of the past in the present. As I have stressed already, these links and presences are not established or activated by the materials in themselves, but only in the human appropriation, use and habitation of them. The shoes have to be worn, their connections to feet, legs and mind mobilised and felt, in order for the experiences of temporal resonance to occur. The meaningful wholes are produced, woven together, made effective and affective, through such sustained efforts of bringing together humans and materials into moments of touch and 'mingling'.

Re-enactment as 'unfinished business'

Along with its patchworked nature and its holistic ambitions, a key attraction in re-enactment springs from its dimension of unfinishedness. To qualify my use of this term, we may look first to Horwitz's bestselling account of Civil War re-enactment, *Confederates in the Attic* (1999), subtitled 'Dispatches from the Unfinished Civil War', and the ways in which the unfinishedness I aspire to describe differs from his account. This book, in which Pulitzer Prize-winning journalist Horwitz chronicles his joining up with a group of hardcore re-enactors on a 10-state tour to explore the living legacy of the Confederacy, is generally disliked in the re-enactment community because of its witty but also exoticising and occasionally derogatory descriptions of the hobby. Still, it deftly pinpoints a number of intricacies and paradoxes of the present-day Civil War memory widespread in the US South. In this, we find strong remnants of the 'Lost Cause' mythology, the nostalgic literary and cultural movement in which 'many white southerners found intellectual and psychological comfort in the (…) depiction of a cavalier South, valiantly losing a war over states' rights, republicanism, and Christianity to the industrial might of Yankeedom' (Carmichael 2011, 9).[12] The 'unfinishedness' that Horwitz documents thus primarily refers to a political and symbolic level; to discourses and narratives through which the Civil War legacies continue to assert influence in US society. The recurring debate over 'states' rights' vs. federal 'government' central to today's Tea Party movement is but one example.

While related to such arguments in intimate ways (as we shall see below), my own exploration of the unfinished is different. It relates first and foremost to a dimension of experienced, embodied, *felt* historical agency intimately tied to the physical-material realities of re-enactment. The appeal of the unfinished that I encountered during my fieldwork worked on the level of concrete interaction where one – through collaborative effort, and by 'thinking through' objects (Henare et al. 2007) – could cultivate a powerful experience of shared agency and thus of 'having a go' or 'a say' in the production and dissemination of history and remembrance. This resonates well with Thompson's finding that re-enactors seek a degree of 'ownership' over history, (2004, 181; see also de Groot 2009, 109). This tendency is connected to an understanding of the past described by Schneider as 'never complete, never completely finished, but incomplete: cast into the future as a matter for ritual negotiation and as yet undecided interpretive acts of *reworking*' (2011, 33, italics in original; see also Cooper and Law 1995).

Importantly, these open-ended (and therefore, to re-enactors, attractive) amalgams of experience, magic or 'touch' are not merely individual bubbles of meaningful connection, but are supremely situational and social in nature. They require collective effort and a will to agreement. As an example of such a context of concerted memory practice, I will end this article with a discussion of an event which immediately caught my interest when I saw it advertised in the local re-enactment media: a so-called 'Gathering of Civil War Eagles' taking place in the Old Court House Civil War Museum in Winchester, Virginia, in June 2010. Borrowing its title from *A Gathering of Eagles*, a 1963 (cold) war movie starring Rock Hudson as a tough B-52 Air Force Colonel, this weekend was set to bring together commanders from both sides of the Civil War for a curious symposium: 'Suppose the War Between the States was over', as the event website announced (utilising the label for the conflict preferred by many Southerners), and suppose further that 'the principal Commanders and both Presidents survived and all were gathered together for a round of discussions regarding the contest.'[13] Said to include 'the nation's most prominent impressionists' of famous Civil War figures, who would be at hand to 'engage in debates throughout the weekend and offer themselves to you for those questions you've always wanted to ask', this sounded like a golden opportunity to witness a dialogic form of re-enactment of an event that had never actually happened.[14] Since we were obviously dabbling in the counterfactual, 're-enactment' may not be the right word. Still, the séances that followed and the cast of important, named characters included a profound amount of restaging, if always in a quasi-historical framework.

In seeking to understand the power of materiality in this case, I mean to include in the 'material' realm not only the many small-scale tangibles at hand, such as the period costumes of actors and the physical stage 'props' they utilised. More than that – and pointing back to my argument on holism – what *mattered* here was the atmospheric framing and the 'whole scene' surrounding and sustaining the event. This whole comprised the immediate physical site of the performances, the museum's historical courtroom, organised with a centre 'stage' area surrounded by wooden benches for the audience. But any consideration of the event as a whole must also incorporate a larger contextual dimension in which the museum is seen as an institutional entity layered with specific meanings, values and powers. We may describe this as its *atmosphere* if, with Böhme, we accept that 'atmospheres' must be conceived 'not as free floating but on the contrary as something that proceeds from and is created by things, persons or their constellations' (Böhme 1993, 122).

To give an example, as I arrived at the museum it was immediately clear to me that I had crossed the line to the South. Even though Winchester was a mere one-and-a-half hours' drive from my fieldwork base in Gettysburg, Pennsylvania – where I had grown used to the ubiquitous celebration of Abraham Lincoln as the Civil War's undisputed hero and saviour of the Union – I sensed the shifting sympathies right away. It is impossible to pin this atmospheric shift down to one isolated factor; we may say with Böhme that it emerged, rather, as 'something that proceeds from and is created by things, persons or their constellations', including historically ingrained, intangible qualities clinging to the place and the human and non-human actors assembled there. Outside the museum, I was greeted by a friendly event organiser wearing period Confederate costume and introducing himself as 'General Corse', one of General Robert E. Lee's trusted men. He proceeded, right away, to explain to me why the Civil War was not primarily about slavery, as school history books insisted, but more fundamentally about 'states' rights', the extent of 'government', and above all about economics. A man with a mission, 'Corse' was clearly out to re-enact, but also in a sense to re*vise* history, speaking up against what he considered a flawed set of myths, largely the product of a North-Eastern, urban and politically liberal elite.[15] He was not alone in this; indeed, a flavour of revisionism permeated the courthouse sessions over the following days, manifesting itself in words, gestures and ritualistic performance. Here, the Lost Cause was temporarily un-lost, as the potentials of the unfinished Civil War took material and performative shape.

The North was, in fact, present in Winchester. Indeed, President Abraham Lincoln himself was there, in the shape of an immaculately clad and impressively goatee-bearded lookalike ('impersonator' or 'impressionist' are the preferred terms) who did chip in with 'his' views on the war in the debates and sessions that followed. But the moral high ground belonged safely to the South, and especially to General Robert E. Lee. Lee was evidently the folk hero here, cheered along by a sympathetic audience benched in the intimate historical courtroom, and 'Lee' the impersonator also acted, tellingly, as main host and facilitator of the event as a whole, guiding us through the three-day programme.[16] Even though the North was thus given voice, and 'Lincoln', 'Grant' and many other key Union figures spoke in the dialogues that followed, the South prevailed again and again, with spectators rooting for and supporting the Confederate cause virtually unchallenged. In all of this 'Lincoln', so revered in Gettysburg a few hours north, was clearly under pressure. Perhaps, this was what made him stumble during his signature moment, the re-enacting of the Gettysburg address – the famous three-minute speech from November 1863, delivered in the midst of the Civil War, and handed down in (mainstream) American history as a stage-setting moment for the Reconstruction of the Union – as Lincoln the impersonator, in the middle of speaking, suddenly went blank. The long moment of embarrassment, as 'Lincoln' literally did not know what to say – indeed had somehow forgotten his most renowned argument – summed up the unsuccessful Northern presence at the gathering, before a lady in the audience finally helped poor Abe back on track and he completed his address.

It is important to note that even though the air in Winchester was indeed thick with Southern sentiment, it was never characterised by aggression but rather full of emotion and nostalgia. To the majority of its participators, the event was evidently 'touching' in the sentimental sense, connecting them to Southern memories, landscapes and 'chivalric' moments, as Mark the re-enactor put it (quoted earlier). The emotional high point of the gathering was a one-hour evening musical performance by a self-made songwriter and playwright from Georgia, Stan Clardy.[17] Dressed in period clothing and utilising 'historical' props such as Confederate flags, weapons and other military paraphernalia, Stan performed his play Soldiers in *Gray* to an audience already perfectly attuned to its melancholic messages. The play, supposedly an 'educational, musical journey of a soldier's life and feelings during the war' which 'will encourage you to preserve and honour our southern heritage',[18] consisted of a series of acts about a fictional Confederate soldier's journeys to and from the fields of the Civil War and his return to his beloved Georgia home, which had been ravaged in his absence. In a remarkable sentimental climax, Clardy invited participants in the room to join him on stage and kneel in honour of the South. Astounded by this virtually biblical devotion to the cause, I watched as a long chain of kneeling Confederate patriots formed around the performer, and witnessed the tear-swollen eyes of bystanders and participants that, in concert and perfect resonance, raised the spirits in the room to something close to a sense of *communitas*, as described in Turner's classic studies of ritual (1969).

In the wake of this extraordinary outburst of Southern sentiment, Clardy and his wife turned to the merchandise side of things. I promptly acquired two music CDs as well as a copy of a novel authored by the performer himself, entitled *TimeLight: a journey into the past* (Clardy 2003). I will end my discussion of the Winchester event with a few words on this intriguing if obscure publication, which blends historical fact and science fiction in a melodramatic interpretation of the Civil War seen from an entrenched Southern perspective. Not unlike the Winchester social gathering itself, the book can be viewed as a fictional but purportedly historically based 're-enactment' of sorts that endeavours to creatively restage and reinterpret the American Civil War; to raise the 'what ifs' not allowed by conventional historical accounts and standard scientific rationalities. The novel, in a genre we may call historical sci-fi, is said (on its back cover) to be 'inspired by the mysteries surrounding the *Hunley*', a Confederate submarine that operated in defence of the city of Charleston, South Carolina, during the Civil War, sank in 1863, and for long was surrounded by myth and legend. Its wreck was located in 1995, raised from the bottom of the sea in 2000, and is now on exhibition in Charleston. On this factual background Clardy weaves a mysterious fiction of time-travelling, dripping with critique of current American policies. 'In a future where heritage is outlawed and history is corrupted', as the author informs potential readers on his website,

> three men take a desperate and dangerous chance. They will travel into the past in an attempt to save the future and the last remnants of their Southern birthright. They journey to Charleston, South Carolina, to aid the builders and crew of the H.L. Hunley, a Confederate submarine which may hold the key to victory for the Southern cause. Along the way they make an unexpected discovery as they uncover the truths of a history that has been hidden from them and their society.[19]

TimeLight, in its weird mix of futurism and time-travel, heritage romanticism and historical revisionism, constitutes a remarkable example of how the 1860s are reinvoked in ever more surprising ways. The book can be seen as a condensed expression of the assembling, the binding together, of humans, things, places and moments to a purported Confederate 'whole'. The temporal gymnastics involved are particularly complicated, with a heroic cast of neo-Confederates set in a dystopian, Orwellesque future and then returning to the ('repressed', 'hidden') past of their homeland in order to 'save the future', thereby also saving the South. Relating to the arguments on materiality I have sought to stake out, the novel precisely celebrates the powerful presence of the object, the refound *Hunley*, the 'reality of history lying before me', as the author argues in his afterword, 'not a fable, a myth or a legend anymore' (Clardy 2003, 253). Thus, along with his coming face-to-face with the re-emerged submarine during his research trips leading up to the writing of the novel, Clardy claims, 'came the realisation that no longer could lies be told about the *Hunley* or its brave crews' (ibid.). In this profoundly partial perspective (Haraway 1988), the raising of the submarine at the turn of the new millennium is celebrated as a supremely concrete symbol – a hard, steely fact – of the resurfacing of suppressed Southern memories that have allegedly been stowed away for too long by the victorious liars of the North.[20]

Conclusion: past-making as patchworking

As Basso has noted, 'place-making is a way of constructing history itself, of inventing it, of fashioning novel versions of 'what happened here' (1996, 6). He adds:

> Building and sharing place-worlds, in other words, is not only a means of reviving former times but also of *revising* them, a means of exploring not merely how things might

have been but also how, just possibly, they might have been different from what others have supposed. (ibid., italics in original)

Although in this paper I have been focusing less specifically on place-making than on past-making, Basso's observations nicely sum up the broader processes of 'patch-working' that have concerned me here. The Winchester gathering seemed very much to revolve around a reconfiguration of 'what others have supposed' about the conflict usually known (but not here) as the American Civil War. Likewise, battle re-enactors' personal and collective engagements with reconstructed objects and places are literally novel versions of 'what happened here' that, even as they restage events and honour participants, also reshape and refuel their significance. I have explored such processes of connectivity, the entangled ways in which specific things, places and times come to surface and acquire power in concerted, collective action. I have argued that this patchworking, holistic at base, and working along principles of *praesentia*, lies at the core of re-enactment practices. In the often senti-mental spectacles that *take place* – and notions of place and belonging are of course key facets of this – re-enactors can thus be seen implicitly to challenge accepted sci-entific boundaries and 'question temporal singularity' by striving, in Schneider's for-mulation, to 'loosen the *habit* of linear time' (2011, 19, italics in original).

These temporal blurrings are also profoundly material, and their materiality matters; it is not merely that today's version of the 1860s indicates an affective turn where the past is set to 'work in the present' (Agnew 2007; see also Trouillot 1995) in a political or discursive sense. While this is of course always the case, what I have sought to highlight here are some of the central ways in which such 'work' inevitably includes a powerful material dimension and requires ceaseless human investment. I have argued, indeed, that the very ceaselessness and its necessarily 'unfinished' and uncertain nature constitute a core fascination in historical re-enactment – a fascination that sets it fundamen-tally apart from the distance-based approach towards understanding 'history' as it has been institutionalised in the conventional museum with its glass-cased, sealed and 'finished' truths. In the terminology of Cooper and Law (1995), re-enactors long for 'proximal' knowledge (as opposed to 'distal' or vision-centred knowledge). A key trait of this mode of knowing is, precisely, its unfinished character:

> Proximal thinking deals in the continuous and the "unfinished"; it is what is forever approached but never attained, it is what is approximated but never fully realised. The proximal is always partial and precarious, forever fated to repeat itself in an effort to reach (but never attain) completion. (Cooper and Law 1995, 239; see also Hetherington 2003, 1935)

As we saw earlier, unattainability is a recurring aspect of re-enactors' quest for fulf-ilment. The wholes so desperately sought for, so relentlessly approximated, are, pre-cisely, 'forever approached but never actually attained'. Their precarious character is intimately connected to the very materiality itself or, better, to the concrete 'proxi-mal' subject-object connectivities of specific re-enactments. While they may not be relics in a religious sense, the materials brought together and set to work to bring the Civil War to life again cannot be reduced to symbols or representations; their thinghood requires careful academic attention.

Notes

1. The Chestertown 'tea party' is the name of a historical incident inspired by the more famous 1773 Boston Tea Party (from which the contemporary American populist/political movement takes its name). It refers to the rebellious actions taken by local Marylanders in response to the British Tea Act, which introduced taxes on tea imported from Britain into the American colonies, raising money for the Imperial motherland. On 23 May 1774, a band of Chesapeake patriots, following the Boston example, forced their way onto a British brigantine and dumped its cargo of tea into the Chester River.

2. http://www.chestertownteaparty.org/. Accessed 7 March, 2012.

3. This is not Warren's real name. All informant names in this paper have been changed for purposes of anonymity.

4. Earlier landmark studies include Anderson (1984), Handler and Saxton (1988), Snow (1993), Bruner (1994), Samuel (1994), Crang (1996), Handler and Gable (1997), Horwitz (1998), Kirshenblatt-Gimblett (1998).

5. The ethnographic fieldwork informing this article was conducted over the spring and summer of 2010. It entailed basing myself in Gettysburg, Pennsylvania, for a five-month period, during which I investigated and took part in various branches of the local and regional Civil War industry, including joining one of the many groups that conduct historical re-enactment in the area.

6. Thompson describes how the World War I and II re-enactment scene is dominated by a similar belief that the 'real and common stories of war have been buried by inadequate educational systems, distorted by Hollywood, and silenced or lost by the veterans themselves, especially as veterans die off with their stories unheard' (2004, 91).

7. In a broader argument on tourism as a 'self-finding' practice, Neumann has suggested that while many tourist sites may be materially inauthentic, they are nevertheless places where people work toward 'selfrealization' and meaning, 'attempting to fill experiential vacancies that run through contemporary life' (Neumann 1992, quoted in Oakes 2006, 239). The literature on authenticity as a core concept of modernity is vast. Classics include Trilling (1972) and Taylor (1991); for some influential signposts within tourism and heritage studies, see MacCannell (1973), Clifford (1988), Cohen (1988), Bruner (1994), Wang (1999), Hall (2006), Knudsen and Waade (2010). For an useful overview, see Lindholm (2008).

8. The terms 'farb' and 'farby' are used in derogatory fashion to refer to re-enactors or elements considered inauthentic, lacking or out of place, typically used to frown upon those with a historically incorrect impression or attitude. Nobody seems to know exactly where the term stems from, although some say it derives from the phrase 'far be it authentic'. See Thompson (2004, 212–215), Amster (2007, 18), Hart (2007, 111).

9. This may be likened to the Lévi-Straussian notion of 'bricolage' (Lévi-Strauss 1966, 21), with the important difference that this term, for Lévi-Strauss, described a 'science of the concrete' (ibid., 1–33) operating strictly on the mental and symbolic level; where 'the concrete', in other words, was utilised in the service of thinking and *not* appreciated for its material or experiential capacities per se.

10. Such moments of felt temporal resonance are also sometimes referred to as 'period rush' or 'Civil War moments'. See Handler and Saxton (1988, 245–246), Agnew (2004, 330), Thompson (2004, 167–173), Amster (2007, 19–24), Schneider (2011, 39–42).

11. Here I am inspired by Schneider's note: 'The fight to get the times right – to *touch* the Civil War – was for many [reenactors] an effort to go back to an idealised time, and the drive to authenticity was a drive to an authenticity that *should have been*, according to reenactors' interpretations, not necessarily an authenticity that was' (2011, 55, italics in original).

12. On the cultural power of the Lost Cause, see also Savage (1997, 129–161), Blight (2001, 255–299), Goldfield (2002), Brundage (2005), Carmichael (2011). The Lost Cause, according to Blight, 'came to represent a mood, or an attitude towards the past. It took hold in specific arguments, organizations, and rituals, and for many Southerners it became a natural extension of evangelical piety, a civil religion that helped them link their sense of loss to a Christian conception of history' (2001, 258).

13. http://www.civilwargatheringofeagles.com/about.html. Accessed 13 March 2012. The conflict known in most accounts as the American Civil War goes under many different

names. Most Americans simply call it the Civil War, though a few refer to the 'War of the [Southern] Rebellion'. Among sympathisers with the Confederate cause, the 'War Between the States' is the preferred term – implying a rejection of the label 'Civil War' since the conflict, in such a perspective, was not fought between two parties belonging to the same state – although the 'War for Southern Independence' or even 'The War of Northern Aggression' are also sometimes heard. Some of my informants semi-jokingly referred to the conflict as the 'Second War of Independence' (following in the wake of the American War of Independence fought against Great Britain 1775–1783).

14. http://www.civilwargatheringofeagles.com/about.html. Accessed 13 March, 2012.
15. On the argument over the role of slavery vs. states' rights as primary causes for secession and thus for the Civil War, see Finkelman (2011), Loewen (2011).
16. In his analysis of the early memorialisation of the Civil War, Savage (1997, 131) proposes that 'the fundamental effect of [retrospectively] installing Lee as the South's premier representative [rather than Jefferson Davis, the president of the Confederate States] was that it depoliticized the Confederacy after the fact. With Lee as the major historical actor, the story of the Lost Cause became a glorious military record rather than a political struggle to secure a slaveholding nation'.
17. In this particular case, and as an exception, I use the real name of the artist, since his business, performances and products are publically available and promoted, primarily through the internet. See http://www.stanclardy.com/. Accessed 25 March 2012.
18. http://www.stanclardy.com/web_site_revised_4_2011_002.htm. Accessed 22 March 2012.
19. http://www.stanclardy.com/web_site_revised_4_2011_003.htm. Accessed 22 March 2012.
20. On 'historical reality' considered as a 'stowaway' passenger in historical writing, 'as what is absently and unintentionally present on the plane of time', see Runia (2006b, 27).

References

Agnew, Vanessa. 2004. "Introduction: What is Reenactment?" *Criticism* 46 (3): 327–339.
Agnew, Vanessa. 2007. "History's Affective Turn: Historical Reenactment and its Work in the Present." *Rethinking History* 11 (3): 299–312.
Amster, Matthew H. 2007. "A Pilgrimage to the Past: Civil War Reenactors in Gettysburg." In *Reflecting on America. Anthropological Views of U.S. Culture*, edited by Claire L. Boulanger, 15–27. Boston: Pearson/Allen and Bacon.
Anderson, Jay. 1984. *Time Machines: The World of Living History*. Nashville, TN: American Association for State and Local History.
Ankersmit, Frank R. 2005. *Sublime Historical Experience*. Stanford: Stanford University Press.
Basso, Keith H. 1996. *Wisdom Sits in Places: Landscape and Language among the Western Apache*. Albuquerque: University of New Mexico Press.
Benjamin, Walter. 1969. "The Work of Art in the Age of Mechanical Reproduction." In *Illuminations*, edited by H. Arendt. Translated Harry Zohn, 217–252. New York: Schocken Books.
Bennett, Tony. 1995. *The Birth of the Museum. History, Theory, Politics*. London: Routledge.
Bennett, Tony. 2007. "The Work of Culture." *Cultural Sociology* 1 (1): 31–47.

Bille, Mikkel. 2012. "Assembling Heritage: Investigating the UNESCO Proclamation of Bedouin Intangible Heritage in Jordan." *International Journal of Heritage Studies* 18 (2): 107–123.

Blight, David W. 2001. *Race and Reunion. The Civil War in American Memory*. Cambridge: Harvard University Press.

Blight, David W. 2002. *Beyond the Battlefield. Race, Memory, and the American Civil War*. Amherst: University of Massachusetts Press.

Bodnar, John, ed. 1996. *Bonds of Affection: Americans Define Their Patriotism*. Princeton: Princeton University Press.

Böhme, Gernot. 1993. "Atmosphere as the Fundamental Concept of a New Aesthetics." *Thesis Eleven* 36: 113–126.

Bourdieu, Pierre. 1984. *Distinction. A Social Critique of the Judgement of Taste*. London: Routledge.

Brown, Peter L. 1981. *The Cult of the Saints: Its Rise and Function in Latin Christianity*. Chicago: University of Chicago Press.

Brundage, William F. 2005. *The Southern Past: A Clash of Race and Memory*. Harvard: Harvard University Press.

Bruner, Edward M. 1994. "Abraham Lincoln as Authentic Reproduction: A Critique of Postmodernism." *American Anthropologist* 96 (2): 397–415.

Byrne, Sarah, Anne Clarke, Rodney Harrison, and Robin Torrence, eds. 2011. *Unpacking the Collection. Networks of Material and Social Agency in the Museum*. New York: Springer.

Carmichael, Peter. 2011. ""Truth is Mighty & Will Eventually Prevail." Political Correctness, Neo-Confederates, and Robert E. Lee." *Southern Cultures* 17 (3): 6–27.

Clardy, Stan. 2003. *TimeLight. A Journey into the Past*. Statesville, NC: Gray Note Productions.

Classen, Constance, and David Howes. 2006. "The Museum as Sensescape: Western sensibilities and Indigenous Artefacts." In *Sensible Objects. Colonialism, Museums and Material Culture*, edited by Elizabeth Edwards, Chris Gosden, and Ruth B. Phillips, 199–222. Oxford: Berg.

Clifford, James 1988. "On Collecting Art and Culture." In *The Predicament of Culture. Twentieth-Century Ethnography, Literature, and Art*, 215–251. Cambridge: Harvard University Press.

Cohen, Erik. 1988. "Authenticity and Commoditization in Tourism." *Annals of Tourism Research* 15: 371–386.

Cook, Alexander. 2004. "The Use and Abuse of Historical Reenactment: Thoughts on Recent trends in Public History." *Criticism* 46 (3): 487–496.

Cooper, Robert, and John Law. 1995. "Organization: distal and proximal views." In *Research in the Sociology of Organizations*, edited by Samuel Bachrach, Pasquale Gagliardi, and Bryan Mundell, 237–274. Greenwich, CT: JAI Press.

Crang, Mike. 1996. "Magic Kingdom or a Quixotic Quest for Authenticity?" *Annals of Tourism Research* 23 (2): 415–431.

Cushman, Steven. 1999. *Bloody Promenade: Reflections on a Civil War Battle*. Charlottesville: University Press of Virginia.

Daugbjerg, Mads. 2011. "Playing with Fire: Struggling with "Experience" and "Play" in War Tourism." *Museum and Society* 9 (1): 17–33.

Deleuze, Gilles, and Felix Guattari. 2004 [1988]. *A Thousand Plateaus: Capitalism and Schizophrenia*. London: Continuum.

Derrida, Jacques. 1982. "Differánce." In *Margins of Philosophy*, 1–28. Hemel Hempstead: Harvester Wheatsheaf.

Desjarlais, Robert. 1996. "Struggling Along". In *Things as They Are. New Directions in Phenomenological Anthropology,* edited by Michael Jackson, 70–93. Bloomington: Indiana University Press.

Fahs, Alice, and Joan Waugh, eds. 2004. *The Memory of the Civil War in American Culture*. Chapel Hill: University of North Carolina Press.

Faust, Drew G. 2008. *This Republic of Suffering. Death and the American Civil War*. New York: Alfred A. Knopf.

Finkelman, Paul. 2011. "Slavery, the Constitution, and the Origins of the Civil War." *OAH Magazine of History* 25 (2): 14–18.

Fornieri, Joseph R. 1994. "Abraham Lincoln and the Declaration of Independence: The Meaning of Equality." In *Abraham Lincoln: Sources and Style of Leadership*, edited by Frank J. Williams, William D. Pederson, and Vincent J. Marsala, 45–70. Westport, CO: Greenwood Press.

Goldfield, David. 2002. *Still Fighting the Civil War: The American South and Southern History*. Baton Rouge: Louisiana State University Press.

Grant, Susan-Mary. 1998. "The Charter of its Birthright: The Civil War and American Nationalism." *Nations and Nationalism* 4 (2): 163–185.

de Groot, Jerome. 2009. "Historical Re-enactment." In *Consuming History: Historians and Heritage in Contemporary Popular Culture*, 105–123. London: Routledge.

Grewcock, Duncan. 2014. "Performing Heritage (Studies) at The Lord Mayor's Show." *International Journal of Heritage Studies* 20 (7-8): 760-81.

Hall, Martin. 2006. "The Reappearance of the Authentic." In *Museum Frictions: Public Cultures/Global Transformations*, edited by Ivan Karp, Corinne A. Kratz, Lynn Szwaja, and Tomás Ybarra-Frausto, 70–101. Durham, NC: Duke University Press.

Handler, Richard, and William Saxton. 1988. "Dyssimulation: Reflexivity, Narrative, and the Quest for Authenticity in 'Living History'." *Cultural Anthropology* 3 (3): 242–260.

Handler, Richard, and Eric Gable. 1997. *The New History in an Old Museum. Creating the Past at Colonial Williamsburg*. Durham, NC: Duke University Press.

Haraway, Donna. 1988. "Situated Knowledges: The Science Question in Feminism and the Privilege of Partial Perspective." *Feminist Studies* 14 (3): 575–599.

Harrison, Rodney. 2012. *Heritage. Critical Approaches*. London: Routledge.

Harrison, Rodney, Sarah Byrne, and Anne Clarke, eds. 2013. *Reassembling the Collection. Ethnographic Museums and Indigenous Agency*. Santa Fe: SAR Press.

Hart, Lain, 2007. "Authentic recreation: living history and leisure". *Museum and Society*, 5 (2): 103–124.

Henare, Amiria, Martin Holbraad, and Sari Wastell, eds. 2007. *Thinking through Things. Theorising Artefacts Ethnographically*. London: Routledge.

Hetherington, Kevin. 2003. "Spatial Textures: Place, Touch, and Praesentia." *Environment and Planning A* 35: 1933–1944.

Horwitz, Tony. 1998. *Confederates in the Attic: Dispatches from the Unfinished Civil War*. New York, NY: Vintage Books.

Jay, Martin. 2005. *Songs of Experience. Modern American and European Variations on a Universal Theme*. Berkeley: University of California Press.

Kalshoven, Petra Tjitske. 2012. *Crafting the Indian. Knowledge, Desire and Play in Indianist Reenactment*. Oxford: Berghahn Books.

Kirshenblatt-Gimblett, Barbara. 1991. "Objects of Ethnography". In *Exhibiting Cultures. The Poetics and Politics of Museum Display*, edited by Ivan Karp and D. Steven Lavine, 386–443. Washington, DC: Smithsonian Institution Press.

Kirshenblatt-Gimblett, Barbara. 1998. *Destination Culture. Tourism, Museums, and Heritage*. Berkeley: University of California Press.

Knudsen, Britta Timm, and Anne Marit Waade, eds. 2010. *Re-investing Authenticity. Tourism, Place and Emotions*. Bristol: Channel View.

Lash, Scott. 1999. *Another Modernity, a Different Rationality*. Oxford: Blackwell.

Latour, Bruno. 2005. *Reassembling the Social. An Introduction to Actor-Network-Theory*. Oxford: Oxford University Press.

Law, John. 2004. *After Method. Mess in Social Science Research*. London: Routledge.

Lévi-Strauss, Claude. 1966. *The Savage Mind*. London: Weidenfeld and Nicolson Ltd.

Linenthal, Edward T. 1991. *Sacred Ground. Americans and Their Battlefields*. Urbana: University of Illinois Press.

Lindholm, Charles. 2008. *Culture and Authenticity*. Malden, MA: Blackwell.

Loewen, James W. 2011. "Using Confederate Documents to Teach About Secession, Slavery, and the Origins of the Civil War." *OAH Magazine of History* 25 (2): 35–44.

Lorimer, Hayden. 2005. "Cultural geography: The Busyness of being 'more-than-representational'." *Progress in Human Geography* 29 (1): 83–94.

MacCannell, Dean. 1973. "Staged Authenticity: Arrangements of Social Space in Tourist Settings." *The American Journal of Sociology* 79 (3): 589–603.

Macdonald, Sharon. 2005. "Enchantment and its Dilemmas: The Museum as a Ritual Site." In *Science, Magic and Religion. The Ritual Processes of Museum Magic*, edited by Mary Bouquet and Nuno Porto, 209–227. New York : Berghahn Books.

Macdonald, Sharon. 2009. "Reassembling Nuremberg, Reassembling Heritage." *Journal of Cultural Economy* 2 (1): 117–134.

Magellsen, Scott. 2007. *Living History Museums: Undoing History through Performance.* Lanham, MD: Scarecrow Press.

Miller, Daniel. 2010. *Stuff.* Cambridge: Polity Press.

Neumann, Mark. 1992. "The Trail through Experience: Finding Self in the Recollection of Travel." In *Investigating Subjectivitiy: Research on Lived Experience*, edited by Carolyn Ellis and Michael G. Flaherty, 176–201. London: Sage.

Oakes, Tim. 2006. "Get Real! On Being Yourself and Being a Tourist." In *Travels in Paradox. Remapping Tourism*, edited by Claudia Minca, and Tim Oakes, 229–250. Lanham, MD: Rowman and Littlefield .

O'Leary, Cecilia E. 1996. "'Blood Brotherhood': The Racialization of Patriotism, 1865–1918." In *Bonds of Affection: Americans Define Their Patriotism*, edited by John Bodnar, 53–81. Princeton: Princeton University Press.

Runia, Eelco. 2006a. "Spots of Time." *History and Theory* 45 (October 2006): 305–316.

Runia, Eelco. 2006b. "Presence". *History and Theory* 45 (February 2006): 1–29.

Samuel, Raphael. 1994. *Theatres of Memory, Vol. 1: Past and Present in Contemporary Culture.* 1. London: Verso.

Savage, Kirk. 1997. *Standing Soldiers, Kneeling Slaves: Race, War, and Monument in Nineteenth-Century America.* Princeton: Princeton University Press.

Schneider, Rebecca. 2011. *Performing Remains. Art and War in Times of Theatrical Reenactment.* London: Routledge.

Snow, Stephen, E. 1993. *Performing the Pilgrims. A Study of Ethnohistorical Role-Playing at Plimoth Plantation.* Jackson: University of Mississippi Press.

Stewart, Susan. 1993. *On Longing: Narratives of the Miniature, the Gigantic, the Souvenir, the Collection.* Durham, NC: Duke University Press.

Taylor, Charles. 1991. *The Ethics of Authenticity.* London: Harvard University Press.

Thompson, Jenny. 2004. *War Games. Inside the World of 20th-Century War Reenactors.* Washington, DC: Smithsonian Books.

Thrift, Nigel. 2007. *Non-representational Theory: Space, Politics, Affect.* London: Routledge.

Till, Karen. 2005. *The New Berlin: Memory, Politics, Place.* Minneapolis: University of Minnesota Press.

Trilling, Lionel. 1972. *Sincerity and Authenticity.* Cambridge: University of Harvard Press.

Trouillot, Michel-Rolph. 1995. *Silencing the Past: Power and the Production of History.* Boston, MA: Beacon Press.

Turner, Victor. 1969. *Ritual Process: Structure and Anti-structure.* Chicago, IL: Aldine.

Walsh, Kevin. 1992. *The Representation of the Past: Museums and heritage in the Postmodern World.* London: Routledge.

Wang, Ning. 1999. "Rethinking Authenticity in Tourism Experience." *Annals of Tourism Research* 26 (2): 349–370.

Weeks, Jim. 2003. *Gettysburg. Memory, Market, and an American Shrine.* Princeton: Princeton University Press.

Between narratives and lists: performing digital intangible heritage through global media

Sheenagh Pietrobruno

Saint Paul University/University of Ottawa

Global media represents and transmits the intangible cultural heritage of nation states officially safeguarded by UNESCO. Intangible heritage sanctioned by this international institution is disseminated on YouTube videos featured on UNESCO's online intangible heritage lists including its representative list as well as within the social space of this video-hosting service. As YouTube is in large part produced by user-generated content, it has the potential to continuously store heritage as it occurs in lived circumstances, to a certain extent capturing the shifting nature of embodied practice. Whereas the UNESCO YouTube videos posted on the online representative list freeze intangible heritage (often in accordance with nationalist aims of current governments), the proliferation of user-generated YouTube videos of the very practices officially safeguarded potentially re-enacts heritage as it changes and takes on new shapes. This possibility is based upon YouTube's status as a new archival structure that transmits information through video content that produces narratives as well as through algorithms that generate lists. The claim that narratives and lists on YouTube might counter the fossilising of representations of national intangible heritage is explored through the case study of the Mevlevi Sema Ceremony of Turkey, which was officially safeguarded by UNESCO in 2005.

Introduction

What is the relation between performance as embodied practice and live performance recorded in media? Phelan (1993, 146) argued in the 1990s that performance as a live event is distinct from its renderings in media: once performance is recorded or documented it becomes something else and can no longer be classified as performance. The perspective that the original live event has an ontological status that is privileged above its documented version has been contested by theorists (Jones 1997, 16). Auslander (2006), for instance, envisions documentation as a performance in itself that produces its own presence and authenticity. Taylor (2003, 19) adds to this dialogue by showing how both embodied lived practice, which she terms the repertoire, and its storage in tangible media or the archive are mediated. Whereas the archive, for Taylor, captures live performance in durable forms of media, the embodied performance of the repertoire can be recreated and transmitted only through repeating bodily patterns and codes, a process that incorporates a type of mediation.

Debates within performance studies concerning the relation between live expressions and their documentation in media have become relevant for heritage studies. Through its 2003 *Convention for the Safeguarding of the Intangible Cultural Heritage* (Convention), UNESCO recognises and safeguards an array of living performances, including dances, rituals, ceremonies, festive events and food preparation. A means for UNESCO to raise awareness of intangible heritage, a key aim of the Convention, is through the administration and global distribution of mediated representations of living performances officially recognised as world intangible heritage. Practices tabulated on UNESCO's website featuring intangible heritage lists are shaped into textual descriptions, photographs and videos that are also posted on YouTube (UNESCO 2012). Frank Proschan (personal communication, 4 July 2012; and email communication, 18 March 2013), the programme specialist for the Intangible Cultural Heritage Section of UNESCO in Paris, outlines the relation between the Convention, official lists and YouTube videos:

> One of the four purposes of the Convention as a whole is 'to raise awareness at the local, national and international levels of the importance of the intangible cultural heritage, and of ensuring mutual appreciation thereof' (Article 1). It is in fulfilment of that purpose that videos are made available through YouTube, whether they concern elements on the Representative List, Urgent Safeguarding List or Register of Best Safeguarding.

Despite the value that UNESCO places on YouTube videos to raise awareness of the intangible heritage on all three registers, this research focuses on the Representative List of the Intangible Cultural Heritage of Humanity (Representative List). As videos featured on each of UNESCO's official lists are disseminated on YouTube, digital videotaped representations of official heritage circulate on the same video-hosting service as unofficial user-generated videos of the very practices officially safeguarded by UNESCO. Through this process, intangible heritage shifts from living performance to global media that take shape on UNESCO's official website as well as within the social space of YouTube (Pietrobruno 2013).

Inspired by Taylor's (2003) work, this exploration suggests that the circulation of intangible heritage on YouTube might allow the repertoire to move closer to the archive. As YouTube is in large part produced by user-generated content, it has the potential to continuously store performance as it occurs in lived circumstances, to a certain extent capturing the shifting nature of embodied practice. Whereas the UNESCO YouTube videos posted on the Representative List freeze intangible heritage (often in accordance with nationalist aims of current governments), the proliferation of user-generated YouTube videos of the very practices officially safeguarded has the potential to capture heritage as it changes and takes on new shapes. This possibility is based upon YouTube's status as a new archival structure that transmits information through video content that produces narratives as well as through algorithms that generate lists. Both the narrative structure of individual videos, which is reinforced through metadata and posted texts, as well as the computing processes that distribute and connect videos through lists impact the manner in which heritage as living performance is expressed through social media.

The circulation of heritage information through online videos and lists can be viewed as a re-enactment of heritage that is defined here as the repeated performances of intangible heritage that take place within both mediated and actual contexts. Digitally-mediated representations in addition to actual performances do not invariably re-enact heritage in ways that facilitate and incarnate a constant renewal of cultural forms and practices. Live contemporary performances of intangible heritage may be orchestrated to embody past and outdated practices in an attempt to resist the change and revival that is at the core of living expressions. Hence, heritage re-enacted through its reproduction in and transmission through YouTube videos as well as its circulation on lists might suppress processes of revision that are integral to living performance or may capture the manner in which intangible heritage is recreated in actual circumstances.

The claim that YouTube could counter the fossilising of representations of national intangible heritage unfolds in stages. The first section of this study examines the concretising of intangible heritage through online global lists that incorporate the fixed heritage narratives of individual nation-states disseminated through YouTube videos. The next section employs a digital humanities perspective to theories YouTube as an archive that stores cultural memory through narratives and lists. The final part illustrates how YouTube as an archive built upon lists and narratives may store intangible heritage as it changes in contemporary circumstances, countering the potential freezing of official heritage stories often put forward by nation-states. This issue is explored through the prism of the Mevlevi Sema Ceremony of Turkey. This performing art was officially safeguarded by UNESCO in 2005 through its Masterpiece Programme and then integrated into the Representative List as an element in 2008 under the Convention. The Mevlevi Sema Ceremony (Sema) of the Mevlevi Sufi Order founded in Konya, Turkey, in 1273 is based on the writings and teachings of Mevlana Jelaluddin Rumi. Along with prayer, music, poetry and movement, this mystical ceremony is distinguished by its continuous circular Sema dance, or whirling dervish dance, as it is known in Western nations.

UNESCO, intangible heritage and YouTube

The 2003 Convention aims to safeguard intangible heritage as a living process – that is, as a cultural expression that is constantly changing and adapting to its environment and the needs of its practitioners. The result of UNESCO's International Conference held in Washington, DC, in 1999, for instance, rendered its 1989 *Recommendation on the Safeguarding of Traditional Culture and Folklore* obsolete because this instrument placed more emphasis on research and researchers than on practitioner communities and the preservation of traditions as living practice (Aikawa-Faure 2009, 21). The proposed definition of intangible heritage put forward at UNESCO's 2001 Turin meeting, which lay the groundwork for the Convention, highlighted intangible heritage's link to learned processes and living communities (UNESCO 2001). The idea that intangible heritage is always in flux and cannot be concretised into an artefact is emphasised in the definition outlined in the Convention, which states that intangible heritage is 'constantly recreated by communities and groups in response to their environment, their interaction with nature and their history' (UNESCO 2003). Despite the underlying intention of the Convention to safeguard intangible heritage as living culture, the actual implementation of this instrument has the potential to freeze intangible heritage into static representations that counter its dynamic essence. This is because the sovereignty of the nation-states is legally ensured in the Convention. The legal instrument grants states exclusive rights respecting the safeguarding of intangible heritage in their territories. Consequently, the sovereignty of nation-states potentially strips communities and groups of the authority to define, determine and administer their intangible cultural heritage (Lixinski 2011, 86). As outlined in the Convention, state parties are supposed to consult all of the communities involved in order to safeguard intangible heritage in a manner that captures the ways that it is continuously reshaped by communities within national territories. Yet the Convention cannot legally compel state parties to incorporate all of the communities involved in the recreation of nationally recognised intangible heritage (Lenzerini 2011, 111–112). The Convention is powerless to prevent state parties from sidestepping communities that renew national traditions in ways that counter the political goals of the ruling government. Hence, state representatives may consult only those communities whose heritage practices conform to the state's nationalist agendas, a strategy that has the potential to concretise living practices into fixed versions.

As outlined in the Convention, one of the roles of UNESCO's Intergovernmental Committee on the Safeguarding of Intangible Cultural Heritage (Committee), which is composed of 24 state parties, is to examine the candidature files of elements of intangible cultural heritage submitted by state parties for possible inscription on UNESCO lists. If a particular candidature file meets the necessary criteria, it is inscribed on one of UNESCO's prestigious lists. Each of the elements featured on the Representative List – the register of concern in this study – is embedded in a social, cultural and political fabric that is constantly shifting as the society as a whole into which it is woven changes and transforms through time. Turning a particular living practice into an element on the Representative List uproots it from this fluctuating and dynamic process. This list making decontextualises living practices and recontextualises them in terms of the list (Goody 1977, 104; Hafstein 2009, 93). UNESCO's lists take on a life of their own by transforming heritage into a mode of cultural production that produces something new in the contemporary context (Kirshenblatt-Gimblett 1998, 149). As Smith (2006, 112) states, 'While the list may be aimed at protection, what it does first and foremost is proclaim the cultural values and meanings that are given authority and legitimacy'. UNESCO's Representative List assembles the values of nation-states through this official register but also through its digital contents. Each element on the online Representative List is described through a short textual description, a set of photographs and a YouTube video that are adapted from the candidature files put forward by nation-states. As the submission of a ten-minute video is an optional requirement within a candidature file, a few elements on the Representative List are not depicted through a YouTube video. These media representations – texts, photos and videos – also uproot living heritage from its contexts by generally featuring versions of heritage that express the political aims and ideologies of presiding national governments. These online contents, which take shape through a variety of digital media, freeze cultural change (often in accordance with the heritage visions of national authorities).

Archiving intangible heritage through lists and narratives

Official narratives of heritage encapsulated in YouTube videos circulate beyond UNESCO's online Representative List to become part of new and shifting lists on this video-hosting service. The claim that YouTube can challenge official heritage through its lists is based on an assessment of this website as an archive. However, YouTube counters the basic archival principles of provenance, custody and preservation and therefore cannot be viewed through the prism of traditional models. The conventional archive, which is composed of a founding set of documents, is generally governed by a central authority that decides its value and public access and ensures the continuous preservation of its original documents (Bastian 2003, 13). Digital media are challenging the traditional archive and providing a new framework for how the archive works in the current era (Hartley 2012). Galloway (2010, 173) claims that the archive in the networked structure no longer marks an original moment of inception or original core collection but is always in the middle since it undergoes continuous transformation through the constant labour of the machine with itself and with its users. The centralised authority of the archive has shifted in the digital era to the multiple users who both create and access it, and hence the archive in the digital era may even pose a threat to governmental power (Chun 2011, 100). Google, which has controlled YouTube since 2006, decides the structure of the site and chooses the videos displayed on the homepage (Gracy 2007, 194). This corporation also retains the right to remove any video according to its discretion. Notwithstanding these restraints, more than half of the videos uploaded to this site are posted by individuals (Burgess and Green 2009, 43–44).

When the search term 'Mevlevi Sema Ceremony' is entered on YouTube, hundreds of videos in addition to UNESCO's official video appear in a particular order that constantly shifts in accordance with changes in user-generated content and algorithms, or code. It is because of this process that YouTube could be viewed as a new form of archive produced by institutions and individuals whose contents continuously change in response to the combined efforts of the human and the machine (Pietrobruno 2013, 5). Users' involvement on YouTube takes various shapes, including uploading and downloading videos, adding metadata (i.e. descriptions, titles and tags) to videos, linking videos to appropriate and associated clips, uploading video responses, clicking on 'like' or 'dislike' and participating in the discussion forums. This user participation, when combined with algorithms, impacts the order and composition of lists under a particular search heading. In information theory and computer science, code is generally regarded as an algorithm. An algorithm is typically defined as a series of instructions that direct a computer to perform a particular task. According to digital humanities scholar Wendy Hui Kyong Chun, code is in fact more intangible than this definition allows. Chun (2011, 3) defines code as 'the behaviour of the machines when running. It is what converts their architecture in[to] action, and it is constructed with action in mind; the programmer aims to make something happen'. Algorithmic operations on YouTube are an intangible process that remains elusive to the majority of its users and even, as Chun would argue, often to programmers themselves. Chun (2011, 18) cites, for instance, the computer programmer Joseph Weizenbaum, who states that he cannot exactly 'know the path of decision making within his own programme, let alone what intermediate or final results it will produce'. Algorithmic processing, then, cannot always be traced to its source but is instead tracked through its effects, which take shape via the contents and formation of YouTube lists as user participation and algorithms merge to archive intangible heritage in an ever-shifting process of interaction between the human and machine.

YouTube as an archive of intangible heritage combines images, sound, texts and algorithms. Videos of intangible heritage on this website often transmit information through cinematic techniques that generally tell a story or produce a narrative. The narratives contained in the videos are contextualised and shaped through metadata, including titles, tags and textual descriptions as well as posted comments. At the same time, these videos that are uploaded and downloaded by users circulate and are accessed in a space that is mathematically determined by algorithmic processes. Drawing from Ernst's (2006) materialist writing on the archive, Parikka (2012, 91) notes that the archive in the digital era has been transformed into a mathematically prescribed realm where the retrieval of information, which is a key element of the perpetuation of cultural discourses and identity, is governed by computer algorithms, as opposed to 'interpretative, iconological semantics'. The mathematically established space means that information obtained under a given search heading appears in the form of lists that counter the previous ordering of information in the traditional archive. According to Ernst (as cited in Chun 2011, 212), archives are not histories or stories but instead are composed of distinct, separate units of detached discourse that are usually connected and forged into narrative representations through archival research and human interpretation. When organised into stories, the contents of traditional archives form the basis of historical interpretation. The listing produced by algorithms, according to Ernst (2006), unsettles the previous ordering in traditional archives by bringing together documents that were once detached and set apart in unconnected units. Lists that mathematically connect units in digital archives can disrupt the traditional archival order and practice, in which distinct documents are linked through interpretive narratives realised by human agency. Computation in the digital archive therefore affects the production of cultural memory, moving it from human interpretation to the machine (Parikka 2011, 56). Hayles (2007) argues that lists of data generated by algorithms do not necessarily challenge narrative and the central role of human interpretation and agency in the analysis of culture and the transmission of knowledge. The juxtapositions forged through database links require narrative to make these information connections meaningful. The interpretation of these 'relational juxtapositions' can nonetheless provide other narratives than those construed through the connection of discontinuous units in traditional archives (Hayles 2007, 1603). This analysis of the archive combines the materialist media theory of Ernst (2006) with the perspectives of Hayles (2007), Galloway (2010) and Chun (2011) to analyse the social archiving of videos of the Mevlevi Sema Ceremony on YouTube, where both lists and narratives intertwine to document heritage.

Lists and narratives of the Mevlevi Sema Ceremony of Turkey

This theoretical assessment of the archive that organises data through both narrative and lists informs the virtual ethnography, or 'netnography' (Kozinets 2009), used to analyse the way that the Sema is stored on YouTube. A virtual ethnography was conducted in July 2012 on the YouTube videos featured under the search heading 'Mevlevi Sema Ceremony,' which built upon a previous ethnography and consequent analysis conducted in September 2011 (Pietrobruno 2013). This virtual ethnography considers the way that both narrative and lists transmit information on YouTube as a digital archive. Videos, along with their metadata and posted texts, are interpreted as heritage narratives: images are analysed through cinematic codes, and voiceovers are assessed through textual analysis. The order of videos, which is constantly shifting, is simultaneously recorded to illustrate the way that the changing lists on YouTube impact the archiving of intangible heritage (Pietrobruno 2013, 10). This methodology reflects current trends in digital humanities research, which argues that images on the Internet cannot be simply studied in isolation; rather, the logic of the system, which operates via algorithms and databases, needs to be considered when analysing media representations (McPherson 2012, 152). The reading of the heritage stories concretised in YouTube videos is enriched through an actual ethnography (i.e. observation at ceremonies, informal discussions and formal interviews) of a Mevlevi community in Istanbul called the Foundation of Universal Lovers of Mevlana Jelaluddin Rumi (EMAV), which was conducted at intervals from June 2011 to August 2012. These actual and online ethnographies are informed by historical and contemporary research on the Sema in Turkey accessed through scholarly research and popular documentation. The manner in which videos are brought together on YouTube lists is also interpreted through particular narratives forged via actual ethnography as well as historical and contemporary writings on the Mevlevi Sema Ceremony of Turkey. This approach is inspired by Hayles's (2007) insight, cited above, that lists of data produced through algorithms combined with user-generated input need to be interpreted through narrative to make their juxtapositions meaningful.

When the search term 'Mevlevi Sema Ceremony' was entered on YouTube in July 2012, UNESCO's video of the same title was the first video on a list of 275 videos. The order in which the videos appear as well as each video's link to the up-next video and list of suggested videos are determined by the combined workings of user-generated content and algorithms. In conjunction with algorithms, the metadata that users attach to their uploaded videos, including titles, descriptions and tags, determine the grouping of particular videos under a specific search request and the ordered sequence that they assume. By merely viewing, rating, commenting on or flagging videos, users also affect YouTube's listed response to a particular search request (Pietrobruno 2013, 5). This process is constantly fluctuating as user-generated content changes and Google updates its algorithms (Halavais 2009, 45). That the workings of the machine are intertwined with users' input renders Ernst's (2006) theory of the archive as purely machinic and outside of human subjectivity in the digital era less relevant to YouTube. The processes that create lists on YouTube are not removed from human involvement and interpretation but instead turn the assemblage of data into lists that become meaningful when filtered through human subjective responses. At the same time, Ernst's ideas of the archive elucidate that digital media cannot be understood only through the sphere of human perception grasped via sight and sound. The algorithmic processes through which code is converted to visual and aural information also need to be taken into account (Parikka 2011, 58). Therefore, the traces of the interplay between user-generated content and algorithms on YouTube can be ascertained through an analysis of the contents of a particular video in relation to the order of videos on a list at a particular point in time.

The list of 275 videos brought together under the search term 'Mevlevi Sema Ceremony' in July 2012 included UNESCO's official version of the Mevlevi Sema Ceremony in conjunction with myriad representations of this ceremony. This stream is not a unified set of videos that necessarily emulates the spirit of the Convention in order to safeguard intangible heritage in a manner that gives expression to the constant re-creation of intangible heritage by groups and communities. Instead this list is an assemblage of videos that provides multiple perspectives in addition to capturing the varied aims of this Turkish ceremony. The following sample of a selection of videos from this stream reflects the different contexts and embodiments of this performance. The UNESCO video entitled 'The Mevlevi Sema Ceremony', which since 2010 has appeared as the first video under the above search heading, visually depicts this performance as an exclusively male practice within the Turkish context (The Mevlevi Sema Ceremony 2009). This video features entirely male performances by a group called the Galata Mevlevi Music and Sema Ensemble of the Turkish Cultural Music Association. The Mevlevi activities executed by this group are recognised as practices to be officially safeguarded within the candidature file of the Mevlevi Sema Ceremony for UNESCO's Proclamation of Masterpieces of the Oral and Intangible Heritage of Humanity (The International Mevlana Foundation, Forthcoming). This document was prepared by the International Mevlana Foundation, which is comprised of individuals of Turkish background or citizenship, with the exemption of one American ethnomusicologist. The candidature file was presented to and funded by the Turkish Ministry of Culture and Tourism (TMCT). Other videos mirror this uniquely male performance of officially recognised heritage. An example features a slideshow detailing participation by only men in a ceremony at the Yenikapı Mevlevi Monastery in Istanbul (Sema Ceremony Yenikapı Mevlevi Lodge in Istanbul 2010). The images in this slideshow depict a Sema performance by the group known as the Galata Mevlevi Sema and Sufi Group of the Mevlana Association of Education and Culture (Figures 1 and 2). The practices of this group have also been granted official status and safeguarded through the TMCT (The International Mevlana Foundation, Forthcoming, 5). Additional videos depict exclusively male performances outside of Turkey, such as a cultural show consisting

Figure 1. The slow procession of the dervishes around the meydan (sacred floor) at the beginning of a Mevlevi Sema Ceremony performed by the Galata Mevlevi Sema and Sufi Group of the Mevlana Association of Education and Culture in the renovated Galata Mevlevi Lodge in Istanbul (2012). © Sheenagh Pietrobruno 76 × 59 mm.

Figure 2. Male semazens (whirling dervishes) at a Mevlevi Sema Ceremony performed by the Galata Mevlevi Sema and Sufi Group of the Mevlana Association of Education and Culture in the renovated Galata Mevlevi Lodge in Istanbul (2012). © Sheenagh Pietrobruno 76 × 63 mm.

of two dervishes in Times Square in New York (Whirling Dervish 2009). This video does not present a Mevlevi Sema Ceremony in its entirety but instead employs the whirling motion of the Sema as cultural entertainment rather than as a spiritual ritual. This image of whirling dervishes as male performers isolated from the context of an actual ceremony circulates around the globe as well as within tourist sites in Turkey as a stereotypical emblem of Turkish culture. Videos can be found of male and female performances by EMAV outside of Turkey, notably in France (Derviches Tourneur d'Istanbul 2009), and there is a video uploaded by the EMAV community that depicts the spiritual practices and beliefs of this organisation (The Foundation of Universal Lovers of Mevlana Jelaluddin Rumi [EMAV] 2010). The practices of EMAV are not officially safeguarded by the TMCT primarily because they bring women and men together in their public performances. The position outlined in the candidature file is explicit in its disapproval of women performing the Sema alongside men. In reference to the activities of the EMAV community, the candidature file states that:

> In an attempt to appear more contemporary mixed male–female semazens and musicians perform together in public which is considered disrespectful to the authentic Mevlevi tradition. This community is not being selected for safeguarding in the section 5 Action Plan. (The International Mevlana Foundation, Forthcoming, 7)

A comparison of the heritage narratives that unfold within UNESCO's official video and within the video uploaded by EMAV illustrates that by storing the videos of EMAV, YouTube is capturing the varied changes that the Sema is undergoing in contemporary Istanbul through the practices of a particular community. The narrative of each video is read through the prism of layered narratives forged via actual ethnographic research on EMAV and written documentation of this ceremony.

UNESCO's official video of the Mevlevi Sema Ceremony is a shorter and revised version of a video submitted with the candidature file. This first version, entitled 'The Sacred Encounter', is funded by the TMCT, directed by Cenk Baysan and produced by Nizamettin Aykurt of Ankira Producers. 'The Sacred Encounter' can be found on YouTube, yet it was not included in the list of 275 videos tabulated under the search term 'Mevlevi Sema Ceremony' in July 2012 (Galata Mevlevi Ensemble 2009). This first version, or 'The Sacred Encounter', comprises interviews with and reports from a selection of the members of the team of advisors and experts responsible for drawing up the candidature file. These include Bârihüdâ Tanrıkorur, the director of the UNESCO project, an art historian and a Mevlevi expert; Walter Feldman, an ethnomusiologist, a Turkologist and an Ottoman music expert; and Reha Sağbaş, the director of Mevlevi musicians and a kanun player in the recordings and films for the UNESCO project and a Turkish music expert and advisor. The video initially included with the candidature file also features interviews with directors of Mevlevi groups both within Turkey and outside of the nation that have been officially recognised through this heritage document. These directors include Nail Kesova of the Galata Mevlevi Music and Sema Ensemble of the Turkish Cultural Music Association; Peter Hüseyin Cunz of The International Mevlana Foundation of Switzerland; and Ibrahim Gamard of the American Institute of Masnavi Studies. Interviews with and reports from these experts and directors of Mevlevi Sema groups have been removed from UNESCO's current official video. Yet this YouTube video draws from scenes and images in the first version to weave a similar political narrative. Along with the first version, the official UNESCO video has been funded and prepared by representatives working for the TMCT. Consequently, through its affiliation with this governmental ministry, the official UNESCO video posted on YouTube reflects the aims of the ruling Justice and Development Party (AKP) (Pietrobruno 2013, 11).

The manner in which this video emulates the goals of the governing party is embedded in the political context of the Mevlevi in Turkey. With the enactment of Law 677 on 13 December 1925, all Sufi dervish lodges were abolished, in addition to the wearing of dervish costumes and holding of religious Sufi titles (Appendix 9: Law 677, 2004, 20). This law resulted in a prohibition of the Mevlevi Sema Ceremony in 1925, after the founding of the Turkish Republic under Mustafa Kemal Atatürk in 1923. Despite this ban, the Sema has remained present in the Turkish cultural scene. It was reinstated in the 1950s under the Democratic Party, led by Adnan Menderes, with the condition that it was to be executed as a cultural show that emulated Mevlana as a great Turkish poet and thinker who realised the ideals of the secular state. It could not be performed as a religious practice linked to Islam (Aykan 2012, 49). Sema ceremonies from the 1950s onward have attracted global audiences (Aykan 2012, 50). Since the 1990s, to make the most of the Sema's potential to put Turkey on the world cultural stage, the Turkish government, under the TMCT, has arranged Sema performances and formed Mevlevi Sema groups (Aykan 2012, 51). The AKP government, according to Aykan (2012), has reinterpreted the Sema to fit its current nationalist aims. Rather than the previous emblem of secularism, this government is using visual markers of Sunni Islam to reflect the national culture of Turkey (Aykan 2012, 57). The depiction of the Sema in UNE-

SCO's video in turn realises this aim by representing the ceremony through the prism of Sunni Islam.

This video depicts the Sema as it would have existed in Ottoman times, before the policies of Atatürk transformed Turkey into a secular republic. Although the voiceover relates how the impact of secularisation has had the long-term effect of diminishing the spiritual essence of this heritage in the contemporary context, the images in the video reconstruct the Mevlevi Order and its practices prior to the time when Atatürk's secular principles governed the country. This official heritage video stages the life of a dervish at a Mevlevi monastery. This re-enactment, which takes place in the Galata Mevlevi Monastery, is performed by the Galata Mevlevi Music and Sema Ensemble under the direction of Nail Kesova. Contemporary documentation on the Sema in Istanbul indicates that this group performed at this monastery for tourists from the mid-1990s until the building's closing for renovations in 2007. Nonetheless, the video's restaging of the past depicts this contemporary Mevlevi group as though its members live in the monastery, as dervish orders would have done during Ottoman times before the abolishment of sufi lodges in 1925. This visual re-enactment of the Ottoman past conveys the desire to revive the Mevlevi Sema Ceremony as it thrived prior to 1925, which is an underlying goal of the candidature file (The International Mevlana Foundation, Forthcoming, 100). How a man would spend his 1001 days at a monastery, which was the time it took to become a dervish, is illustrated through a series of vignettes that are set in various rooms and alcoves in the building. The mounting of these short episodes resembles the depiction of the life of the dervish in Ottoman times in the Mevlana Museum in Konya, Turkey, the founding monastery and mausoleum of the Mevlevi Order. Rooms in this museum feature mannequins dressed as dervishes who perform various tasks that the men would have undertaken to become a dervish (Erol 2009, 88). The vignettes in UNESCO's video become living museum pieces that depict the past. For instance, there is a scenario that features a dervish being dressed in a ceremonial robe, or *tennure*, while other members of the order look on. Another scene features a dervish symbolically shaking the hand of the spiritual leader, or sheik, before the former leaves the monstery to return to his family after spending 1001 days there. In addition, another staged moment depicts a dervish practicing the Sema dance.

All of the participants in UNESCO's video are male. Even though there is no explicit mention that dervishes must be men to participate in this ceremony, as cited above, the exclusion of women from public performances of the Sema is supported and promoted by the government through the TMCT. The stance that women should not participate in contemporary public performances further reinstates the traditions that preceded Law 677 enacted in 1925. For instance, Tanrıkorur (2004a, 27), the director of the UNESCO project acting for this Turkish ministry, makes the following claim in the candidature file in regard to the education of women Mevlevi dervishes prior to 1925: 'They also were trained and taught the same subjects as the men but their presence was more private and publicly unnoticeable in conformation with the Islamic mystical tradition. Therefore these women dervishes would only perform the sema within their own private Mevlevi circle and never in front of male strangers'.

The video's voiceover mentions that the Sema was performed in many sites outside of Turkey during Ottoman times. Yet the video highlights the ceremony's expression within a bounded national space by depicting primarily the practices of the Mevlevi Order within the enclosed sphere of a monastery in Turkey. This visual depiction counters the standpoint outlined in the candidature file and the first video, both of which give official recognition and grant legitimacy to Mevlevi communities outside of Turkey. The candidature file specifically lists three groups in the United States as well as individual organisations in Switzerland, Germany and Iran (The International Mevlana Foundation, Forthcoming, 6).

Users are not invited to comment on this video in the posted text section, as the function of adding comments to videos has been disabled. All of the videos uploaded by UNESCO TV of the elements safeguarded under the Convention have had their comment function disabled. According to Hugues Sicard (personal communication, 4 July 2012) of the Intangible Cultural Heritage Section of UNESCO in Paris, the comment function has been disabled by UNESCO's External Relations and Information Division so that UNESCO can avoid managing the political aspects of posted text comments that could be contentious. Despite this absence of posted text comments, the lists on which this video is situated have the potential to provide alternative perspectives.

The videos on the list of suggestions that were linked to UNESCO's Sema video in July 2012 as a result of the combined effects of users and algorithms include three videos that depict the spiritual activities of EMAV. The one uploaded by the organisation itself, entitled 'The Foundation of Universal Lovers of Mevlana Jelaluddin Rumi (EMAV)' (2010) is exemplary in providing a representation of the Mevlevi Sema Ceremony that counters the one put forward by the TMCT through UNESCO. Ethnographic research reveals that this video was produced by a female dervish at EMAV who remains anonymous on YouTube. This video produced on behalf of EMAV represents the collective activities and beliefs of the community under the guidance of a spiritual leader rather than simply those of the individual dervish who created it. EMAV's video circulates on YouTube as well as on this community's website. Its English-language version along with a Turkish-language edition, both posted in the video gallery section of its website, are used to describe and promote the activities of this community (EMAV Video Gallery 2010).

On YouTube, the contents of EMAV's video provide a contrast to the depiction of the Mevlevi Sema Ceremony in UNESCO's official video. Ethnographic research reveals that EMAV is not actively seeking to counter the parameters of the Mevlevi Sema Ceremony sanctioned by the ruling government of the Turkish nation-state. As a Mevlevi community, EMAV is concerned with performing this ceremony in a manner that reflects its spiritual vision. In contrast, within the candidature file, the TMCT does explicitly contest the way that EMAV performs the Mevlevi Ceremony. On four separate occasions, this document takes issue with the joining of women and men in public Sema performances (Tanrıkorur, 2004a, 31, 2004b, 75; The International Mevlana Foundation, Forthcoming, 4,7). Contestation by EMAV of the official national version of the Mevlevi Sema Ceremony is performed instead by YouTube, which lists this community's video under the search heading 'Mevlevi Sema Ceremony' within a stream of videos that includes the one uploaded by UNESCO through the Turkish nation-state. By means of the combined efforts of algorithms and user-generated content, YouTube archives videos of EMAV performances along with UNESCO's official video under the same search term. The archiving produced by the workings of this video-hosting service juxtaposes this community's practices with the representation of the Mevlevi Sema Ceremony sanctioned by the Turkish government.

EMAV's video, which is listed under the search heading 'Mevlevi Sema Ceremony', offers a narrative of this ceremony that challenges the depiction featured in the video uploaded by UNESCO TV through the TMCT. The voiceover relates how women should be and are active participants in ceremonies. The justification for women's involvement is based on the ideas of Rumi, who advocated complete equality and tolerance among all human beings. The voiceover reflects the teachings of Rumi by announcing that 'On the path of lovers, it is necessary to love and accept all creation' (The Foundation of Universal Lovers of Mevlana Jelaluddin Rumi [EMAV] 2010). Research on popular documentation of this community, which was first founded in 1982, reveals that its spiritual guide, Hasan Dede, has allowed women to take part in ceremonies alongside men since 1993. Ethnographic research shows that women do take part in public ceremonies that are held every Thursday at the Silivrikapı Mevlana Cultural Centre; performances at this centre, which opened in 2006, are featured in EMAV's YouTube video. In these ceremonies, women whirl alongside men in coloured or white robes (Figure 3). Popular Turkish documentation has described Hasan Dede as a 'Kemalist Mevlevi' since he incorporates the secular ideas of Mustafa Kemal Atatürk, including greater equality between men and women in the spiritual practices of the community (Ayman 2004, 48). The video's voiceover recounts that Atatürk's constitututional precepts and principles are also incorporated in expressions of the Sema by EMAV. This connection to Atatürk is visually demonstrated through a close-up of his face that is superimposed over a contemporary Mevlevi Sema Ceremony performed by members of EMAV at their cultural centre in Istanbul. Furthermore, in the final prayer that marks the end of the ceremony, a litany of saints is invoked by the head dervish. All Sema ceremonies in Turkey include the Turkish nation-state in this prayer, but EMAV takes this blessing of the nation-state further by calling on Atatürk in an address that combines his first names, 'Mustafa Kemal', with the honorific title of 'Hazret', which means 'Exalted'. The summoning of 'Hazreti [the Exalted] Mustafa

Figure 3. A woman semazen (whirling dervish) at a Mevlevi Sema Ceremony at the Silivrikapı Mevlana Cultural Centre in Istanbul (2012). © Sheenagh Pietrobruno 76 × 57 mm.

Kemal' is included in the final prayer along with the invocation of other Sufi saints, who are also referred to as 'Exalted'. The veneration of Atatürk in the video and in actual Sema ceremonies of this community as ascertained through ethnographic research reflects the way that the Mevlevi Sema Ceremony is being recreated by this contemporary Mevlevi Sufi group. In contrast to UNESCO's video, which makes a distinction between secularism and Mevlevi Sufism, this video visually and textually interconnects the two, establishing that spirituality, religion and secularism can coexist.

EMAV's video of the Sema further differs from UNESCO's video by transporting this ceremony beyond the borders of Turkey and combining it with other religious traditions within Islam. The narrator states that the activities of this community have reached nations and peoples outside of Turkey: 'The universal enlightment of Mevlana is spreading from Turkiye to America, Asia and Europe through the presentation of the Sema ceremony, [and] Sufi mystic concerts' (The Foundation of Universal Lovers of Mevlana Jelaluddin Rumi [EMAV] 2010). Ethnographic research has uncovered that EMAV performs non-profit ceremonies in countries around the world. The community also incorporates the religious practices of other communities in Turkey. For instance, EMAV's video includes a clip of a documentary that features members of the EMAV community performing the Sema alongside a group of women performing the Semah, a ritual dance of the Alevi-Bektashi. The Semah is part of the Cem Ceremony of the Alevi community, whose members situate themselves within Islam despite the syncretic roots of their beliefs and culture, which combine Christianity, shamanism, Buddhism, Manichaeism and prehistoric Anatolian religions. The Semah is linked to the Alevi-Bektashi since the beliefs of the Alevi are the same as those of the the Bektashi Sufi Order. The only difference between these two communities is that one has to be born an Alevi to become a member, whereas anyone who chooses to and is deemed deserving can become a Bektashi (Erol 2010, 376). Ethnographic research has shown that on the

Figure 4. A unity ceremony at the Silivrikapı Mevlana Cultural Centre in Istanbul that combines the Mevlevi Sema Ceremony with the Semah of the Alevi-Bektashi (2011). © Sheenagh Pietrobruno 76 × 57 mm.

first Thursday of each month a unity ceremony is performed that combines the Mevlevi Sema Ceremony with the Semah (Figure 4). An interview with a female dervish at EMAV in 2012 revealed that some of the members of this community are Alevis and that one of them is responsible for teaching the Sufi dervishes how to perform the Semah. The representation of the Mevlevi Sema Ceremony in EMAV's video captures the contemporary practices of a specific community not officially recognised by UNESCO through the TMCT. This community recreates this practice by incorporating female dervishes, integrating secular principles with religious precepts, promoting this spiritual practice to the world and combining Mevlevism with the religious performance of the Alevi-Bektashi.

Conclusion

Whereas the UNESCO video put forward by the TMCT reproduces the way that the Sema was embodied before secularisation during Ottoman times, the video by EMAV captures how this practice is revived in the contemporary context though the performances of a specific community. Certain YouTube videos uploaded by non-official heritage agents can potentially embody the spirit of the Convention by showing how intangible heritage can continuously transform and alter in accordance with changes in contemporary societies. According to print documentation produced by EMAV, the incorporation of women dervishes in this community's public Sema performances reflects the reshaping of Turkish society:

> Throughout history there was cultural and religious pressure which made it necessary for women to hold their Sema separately. Today women and men work in every occupation together, ride buses [sic] and trains together, and perform the rites of the pilgrimage together. Thus the Sema is an appropriate place for them to worship together. (Özalp 1991, viii)

Moreover, popular media in Turkey have envisioned the Silivrikapı Mevlana Cultural Centre not merely as a cultural centre but in fact as a modern Mevlevi lodge. (Biçer 2011).

Videos of EMAV performances posted on YouTube document the changes that are taking place in current expressions of intangible heritage. That YouTube may enable the storing of heritage as it emerges in lived practices brings Taylor's (2003) concept of the repertoire slightly closer to her vision of the archive as the recording of performance in documentation. Because YouTube is produced to a large extent by users, it can counter official heritage narratives put forward by nation-states through UNESCO. The system of YouTube brings divergent video representations of intangible heritage under the same search heading and within the same list, potentially producing through visual and textual juxtapositions conflicting heritage narratives. This video-hosting service challenges the freezing of intangible heritage by national governments through the stories related in videos as well as through the lists produced by algorithms and user-generated content on which particular videos are situated. Once a video is uploaded onto YouTube, a combination of cultural forms comes into play – narratives and lists – whose potential to document and shape intangible heritage is forged through human subjectivity and interpretation. Intangible practices transmitted through YouTube's online narratives and lists re-enact heritage through the continous circulation of mediated performances, capturing the renewal and recreation that lies at the heart of intangible heritage.

Acknowledgements

I would like to thank Bahar Aykan, Mercan Dede, Burcu Gurkan, Defne Karaosmanoğlu, Kerem Karaosmanoğlu, Britta Timm Knudsen, Verena Laschinger, Marcella Özenç, Joshua Parker, Ralph Poole, Marc Raboy, Ingrid Schmutzhart, Laurajane Smith and William Straw as well as audiences in Seattle, Montreal, Paris and Salzburg for their comments on earlier versions of this article.

References

Aikawa-Faure, N. 2009. "From the Proclamation of Masterpieces to the Convention for the Safeguarding of the Intangible Cultural Heritage." In *Intangible Heritage*, edited by L. Smith and N. Akagawa, 1–44. London: Routledge.

Appendix 9: Law 677. 2004. *Candidature File of the Mevlevi Sema Ceremony for UNESCO's Proclamation of 'Masterpieces of the Oral and Intangible Heritage of Humanity, 20*. Unpublished Manuscript.

Auslander, P. 2006. "The Performativity of Performance Documentation." *Performing Arts Journal* 28 (3): 1–10.

Aykan, B. 2012. "Intangible Heritage's Uncertain Political Outcomes: Nationalism and the Remaking of Marginalized Cultural Practices in Turkey." PhD diss., City University of New York.

Ayman, O. 2004. "Kadın Semazenler [Women Semazens]." *National Geographic Türkiye*, April, 46–60.

Bastian, J. A. 2003. *Owning Memory: How a Caribbean Community Lost Its Archive and Found Its Memory*. Westport, CT: Libraries Unlimited.

Biçer, B. 2011. "Kadın Semazenler" [Women Semazens]. Sabah, 13 September. Accessed February 15, 2013. http://www.sabah.com.tr/fotohaber/yasam/kadin-semazenler

Burgess, J., and J. Green, with contributions by H. Jenkins, and J. Hartley. 2009. *YouTube: On Video and Participatory Culture*. Cambridge, UK: Polity.

Chun, W. H. K. 2011. *Programmed Visions: Software and Memory*. Cambridge, MA: MIT Press.

Derviches Tourneur d'Istanbul – 5 – www.cafeturc.com. 2009. Accessed August 4, 2012. http://www.youtube.com/watch?v=9VLEw6Ucrvw

EMAV Video Gallery. 2010. Accessed February 12, 2012. http://www.emav.org/en/home/video-gallery

Ernst, W. 2006. "Dis/continuities: Does the Archive Become Metaphorical in Multi-media Space?" In *New Media, Old Media: A History and Theory Reader*, edited by W. Chun and T. Keenan, 105–123. New York: Routledge.

Erol, E. 2009. "The Mawlana Museum." In *Rumi and His Sufi Path of Love*, edited by M. F. Çıtlak and H. Bingül, 83–88. Clifton, NJ: Tughra Books.

Erol, A. 2010. "Re-imagining Identity: The Transformation of the Alevi Semah." *Middle Eastern Studies* 46 (3): 375–387.

Galata Mevlevi Ensemble – 'Sacred Encounter': UNESCO Proclamation Masterpieces. 2009. Accessed August 4, 2012. http://www.youtube.com/watch?v=hLe2CEfE3IE

Galloway, A. 2010. "What You See is What You Get?" In *The Archive in Motion: New Conceptions of the Archive in Contemporary Thought and New Media Practices*, edited by E. Røssaak, 155–179. Oslo: Novus.

Goody, J. 1977. *The Domestication of the Savage Mind*. London: Cambridge University Press.

Gracy, K. F. 2007. "Moving Image Preservation and Cultural Capital." *Library Trends* 56 (1): 183–197.

Hafstein, V. Tr. 2009. "Intangible Heritage as a List: From Masterpieces to Representation." In *Intangible Heritage*, edited by L. Smith and N. Akagawa, 93–111. London: Routledge.

Halavais, A. 2009. *Search Engine Society*. Cambridge, UK: Polity.

Hartley, J. 2012. *Digital Futures for Cultural and Media Studies*. Chichester, UK: Wiley.

Hayles, K. N. 2007. "Narrative and Database: Natural Symbionts." *PMLA* 122 (5): 1603–1608.

Jones, A. 1997. "'Presence' in Abstentia: Experiencing Performance as Documentation." *Art Journal* 56 (4): 11–18.

Kirshenblatt-Gimblett, B. 1998. *Destination Culture: Tourism, Museums, and Heritage*. Berkeley: University of California Press.

Kozinets, R. V. 2009. *Doing Ethnographic Research Online*. Thousand Oaks, CA: Sage.

Lenzerini, F. 2011. "Intangible Cultural Heritage: The Living Culture of Peoples." *European Journal of International Law* 22 (1): 101–120.

Lixinski, L. 2011. "The Interplay of Art, Politics and Identity." *European Journal of International Law* 22 (1): 81–100.

McPherson, T. 2012. "Why are the Digital Humanities so White? Or Thinking the Histories of Race and Computation. In *Debates in the Digital Humanities*, edited by M. K. Gold, 139–160. Minneapolis: University of Minnesota Press.

Özalp, A., ed. 1991. *Rumi Discourses from the Tongue of Hasan Dede*. Translated by Carole J. Douglas. Istanbul: Foundation of Universal Lovers of Mevlana (EMAV).

Parikka, J. 2011. "Operative Media Archaeology: Wolfgang Ernst's Materialist Media Diagrammatics." *Theory, Culture and Society* 28 (5): 52–74.

Parikka, J. 2012. "Archives in Media Theory: Material Media Archaeology and Digital Humanities." In *Understanding Digital Humanities*, edited by D. M. Berry, 85–104. Houndsmills, UK: Palgrave Macmillan.

Phelan, P. 1993. *Unmarked: The Politics of Performance*. London: Routledge.

Pietrobruno, S. 2013. "YouTube and the Social Archiving of Intangible Heritage." *New Media and Society*: 1–14. Accessed February 15, 2013. doi: 0.1177/1461444812469598

Sema Ceremony Yenikapı Mevlevi Lodge in Istanbul. 2010. Accessed August 4, 2012. http://www.youtube.com/watch?v=s5pC5ccHpFY

Smith, L. 2006. *The Uses of Heritage*. London: Routledge.

Tanrıkorur, B. S. 2004a. "Mevlevihanes: Their Organization and Function." In *Candidature File of the Mevlevi Sema Ceremony for UNESCO's Proclamation of 'Masterpieces of the Oral and Intangible Heritage of Humanity'*, 25–34. Unpublished Manuscript.

Tanrıkorur, B. S. 2004b. "Sustainability and Possible Risks of Disappearance, Pressures or Constraints Due to: The Risk of Its Disappearing, Due Either to the Lack of Means for Safeguarding and Protecting It or to Processes of Rapid Change, or to Urbanization, or to Acculturation." In *Candidature File of the Mevlevi Sema Ceremony for UNESCO's Proclamation of 'Masterpieces of the Oral and Intangible Heritage of Humanity'*, 71–75. Unpublished Manuscript.

Taylor, D. 2003. *The Archive and the Repertoire: Performing Cultural Memory in the Americas*. Durham, NC: Duke University Press.

The Foundation of Universal Lovers of Mevlana Jelaluddin Rumi (EMAV). 2010. Accessed August 4 2012. http://www.youtube.com/watch?v=PhniyfaSOJo

The International Mevlana Foundation. Forthcoming. "Candidature File of the Mevlevi Sema Ceremony for UNESCO's Proclamation of 'Masterpieces of the Oral and Intangible Heritage of Humanity'." Unpublished Manuscript.

The Mevlevi Sema Ceremony. 2009. Accessed August 4, 2012. http://www.youtube.com/watch?v=_umJcGodNb0

UNESCO. 2001. "Action Plan for the Safeguarding of the ICH as Approved by the International Experts on the Occasion of the International Round Table on 'Intangible Cultural Heritage-Working Definitions.'" Turin, March 2001.

UNESCO. 2003. *Convention for the Safeguarding of the Intangible Cultural Heritage.* Accessed September 8, 2012. http://www.unesco.org/culture/ich/index.php?pg=00006

UNESCO. 2012. *Intangible Heritage Lists.* Accessed August 4, 2012. http://www.unesco.org/culture/ich/index.php?pg=00011

Whirling Dervish – Mevlevi Sema Ceremony – Times Square Turkish Days in New York. 2009. Accessed August 4, 2012. www.youtube.com/watch?v=Yhe1lc5VJvc

Performing heritage (studies) at the Lord Mayor's Show

Duncan Grewcock

Nottingham Trent University

A response to conceptions of heritage as process, this paper puts forward a (re) enactment of heritage (studies) in which the lively materiality, temporality and mobility of an event become entangled with the performance of its research. The event in question is the Lord Mayor's Show in London. First established eight centuries ago, the Show is an annual ritual and touristic performance of The City; London's historic heart and today's global financial centre. One day each year, City life is temporarily suspended by the passing of the new Lord Mayor in his State Coach accompanied by a procession of well over one hundred participating organisations with an audience of tens of thousands lining the route. 2011 was a particularly event-ful year for the Show taking place as it did amidst a global financial crisis and the Occupy London Stock Exchange protest movement camped outside St Paul's Cathedral, disrupting the regular processional route. In drawing on aspects of non-representational theory from human and cultural geography, a more performative sense of doing heritage studies emerges that attends to the lived process and actions of heritage.

Openings

I'm standing on the steps of St Paul's Cathedral. Central London. Heart of the City. To my left, the formal processional route of the Lord Mayor's Show. To my right, Occupy London, an informal tented community of protest and performance. Police, public and protestors co-creating a new space of betweeness. A porous edge where indifferences and inequalities meet and mingle. Differences in the making.

The Occupy encampment is an inhabited exhibition. Adhering to the surfaces of this fragile territory is a messy assemblage of words and images. Slogans and information are posted and pasted by invisible curators. The encampment is a collaborative, cumulative piece of insurgent programming always in a state of re-dress. But this is not my reason for being here. I'm here for the Lord Mayor's Show.

All photographs taken by the author.

This paper argues for and enacts new ways of doing heritage studies in response to the understanding of heritage as process (Smith 2006, 2011). It does this through the particular challenge of researching performance and events. As a step towards new ways of doing heritage studies, my approach begins by taking responsibility for the positionality of the researcher and the situatedness of the research produced. In so doing, I take forward aspects of non-representational theory (NRT) (Anderson and Harrison 2010b; Thrift 1996, 2004, 2008) through three 'brief encounters'. Here, questions of situation and research *as* performance are foregrounded to focus attention on the affective and embodied actions and practices of heritage studies. This leads to experimentation with the forms and expressive registers of presentation that aspire to be *more-than*-representational (Lorimer 2005). It is hoped that from this engagement and enactment, new insights and perspectives might be generated towards alternative ways of doing heritage studies that respond to heritage as process and to the field's ability to research performance and events more broadly.[1] At the level of this paper, these ideas are performed by locating and entangling my argument within an episodic (re)enactment of the Lord Mayor's Show, a hybrid form of commemoration, re-enactment and live interpretation.

Positioning

I arrived in the area early. I walked from Bank underground station and its financial nexus of Royal Bank of England, Royal Exchange and Mansion House and along to St Paul's Cathedral, taking the route the procession would follow later that morning. Occupy London Stock Exchange (Occupy LSX) had set up camp outside St Paul's Cathedral the previous month.[2] This disruption presented a new position from which to view the procession. In previous years, I had witnessed the Lord Mayor's Show from Ludgate Hill, the street looking back up towards St Paul's, or from outside the Guildhall where the procession begins to take shape. The main steps in front of the Cathedral usually provide a pause in the procession as that year's incoming Lord Mayor is blessed by the Dean of St Paul's. In 2011, this part of the Show's ceremony would be relocated by Occupy LSX to the south doors of the Cathedral.

As my physical position has changed over the years, so has my intellectual one. Those first experiences were part of my doctoral research. Since then, my presence at the event has changed; as part of a family day out with my girlfriend, brother, sister-in-law and two nieces and then again with postgraduate students of museums, galleries and heritage. Our positions in relation to an event can and do change, particularly when that event takes place regularly, if only once a year. These positions matter. They make material differences to our research and our efforts at representation. Making more of the positionality of the researcher and situatedness of research is an important first step in recognising and responding to heritage as process in our research projects and particularly when researching performance and events given the mobile yet locatable nature of these experiences. The positionality of the researcher and the situatedness of research is little commented upon in the field of heritage studies although examples are appearing that indicate a possibly richer sense and feeling of researching heritage that might emerge from more partial and locatable research projects.

In Carman and Sørensen's useful introduction to heritage studies, their sketch of the field convincingly traces its major themes and concerns; its subject matter (Carman and Sørensen 2009). What then follows are chapters exploring different methods and approaches that, to varying degrees of critical reflection, account for the positionality of the researcher and the situatedness of the research produced. It is perhaps not surprising that those chapters addressing these issues most directly are concerned with 'investigating people' and mainly through adapted anthropological approaches (Andrews 2009; Keitumetse 2009; Kersal 2009; McDavid 2009; Palmer 2009; Sørensen 2009). This is a broad acknowledgement of the academy's wider 'crisis of representation' and its implications for researching human subjects. However, for the most part, the book is concerned with approaches to researching heritage as product rather than heritage as process (after Smith 2006, 2011). Researching heritage as process requires different ways of thinking and doing heritage studies in practice. This need is brought into sharper relief by the challenge of researching performance and events.

In researching performance informed by an understanding of heritage as process, the questions asked of our approaches to research and representation multiply. What happens when things move, when our subjects of research *take place*? What difference is made? What changes? What claims and questions does it make of our research practices and our ability to communicate an event that takes place somewhere else, sometime else? How, where and when does *research* take place? To move before and beyond heritage as product to heritage as process raises questions of our research projects and their ability to adapt to alternative, more open and contingent ways of knowing and performing heritage.

Laurajane Smith provides a cogent argument for understanding heritage as process (Smith 2006, Chap. 2). Heritage as process is something that is done. It is not an essential attribute of an object, building or site, not something 'out there' waiting to be discovered, examined, contained and labelled. In making the case for heritage as process, Smith combines a series of familiar elements of heritage from the literature: experience, identity, intangibility, memory and remembering, performance, place and dissonance (ibid). The most important issue for the current discussion is how these elements are combined and how they speak to questions of representation and the temporality and materiality of the event. The fundamental concern of Smith's conception of heritage as process is the *act* of heritage. If meanings and values are located within doing as Smith suggests, then all heritage is in fact intangible and affective in the sense that attention is now directed at the personal, social, emotional and embodied doing of heritage rather than its material representations. The implication of this is that heritage is porous and therefore always in a state of becoming as new interpretations and encounters meet and mingle in its performance. Being time and place specific, these actions are locatable (if only temporarily) and manifest themselves differently on different occasions. These assumptions destabilise any attempt to maintain 'authorised heritage discourses' and effectively resets heritage as something that is contested locally by critical participants rather than more distanced, passive consumers. As Smith concludes:

> Heritage is something vital and alive. It is a moment of action not something frozen in material form. It incorporates a range of actions that often occur at places or in certain spaces ... There is an interlinked relationship between the activities that occur at places and the places themselves – but it is the tension between action and material representation that is an important element of heritage. The tension may at once be about creating and maintaining historical and social consensus, but simultaneously it can also be a process of dissent and contestation. (Smith 2006, 83)

In the context of heritage as process outlined by Smith, performance is being considered in at least two registers; performance as 'the art of producing the now' (Thrift 2000a, 577), and performance as a 'sense of occasion' (Smith 2006, 46). More specifically, Smith characterises performance as the choreographed events of commemorations, historical re-enactments and live interpretation (ibid., 69). Interestingly, the Lord Mayor's Show is neither commemoration, historical re-enactment or live interpretation although one might suggest it contains elements of all three. Although performed hundreds of times over the centuries, it is not strictly speaking a *re*-enactment. Rather, the Show is a contemporary *action* or better still *en*actment.[3] It *does* something, now. It is an annual ritual passage marking the arrival of a new Lord Mayor, a performance of the office of Lord Mayor of London and of the City of London. But, the 2011 Show happened differently. It was a rare moment of insurgent action and critical participation where dissent and contestation became overtly entangled within the performance of the 'main event'. It made a difference.

Happening differently

Occupy is stubbornly about the physical reality of space. (Fraser 2012, 1)

Occupy had set up camp outside St Paul's Cathedral in October, less than a month before the Lord Mayor's Show was due to take place. It created a different atmosphere and a different feeling about the Show that year. What might happen? What protests might greet the new Lord Mayor who represents the 'Square Mile' of The City that so many of the protesters and others hold responsible for the global financial crisis and the inequalities of a wider system based on profit and growth?[4]

I meet up with some of my students outside St Paul's underground station. Before us a number of the Show's participants are waiting, hanging out. Final preparations. Grabbing a coffee. Gathering. They will find their place within the Show soon enough as it snakes around to collect the new Lord Mayor in his Coach at the Guildhall. I learn that some of my American students have received emails from their embassy advising them not to get caught up in any protests.

We disperse to different points along the route. I have already chosen mine. Back to the steps of St Paul's. More people are arriving around me to occupy this new space in the middle of things that normally forms part of the Show. Not today. A space has been taken and a new place created. From this vantage point the Show will emerge from the side of the Cathedral to my left. Occupying a space between Yo Sushi and Strada a surveillance camera rises high from a white van pointing directly at the encampment to my right. Watching. Waiting. What will happen? Cameras and video cameras, not simply in the hands of onlookers there to see the Show but in the hands of protesters and police. Everyone is documenting and recording the event. Different positions. Gathered together. Looking on silently. Police watchful. The uncertainty of an event. Anticipation.

It is in the intersections of performance and heritage as process that NRT presents alternative and potentially productive ways of thinking and doing.

Brief encounters (1)

Although this paper cannot provide a detailed account of NRT, which does not exist as any 'singular thing' (Wylie 2007, 164),[5] in attempting to briefly sketch out some of its core ontological assumptions of particular relevance to questions of heritage (studies) as process, I hope to create a local starting position as an encouragement towards the ongoing entanglement of NRT and heritage studies.[6]

NRT is relational and based on a series of ontological assumptions that the world and its meanings happen together through always ongoing encounters and association, not through separation (Anderson and Harrison 2010a). The encounters through which the world and its meanings emerge are heterogeneous assemblages of materials, bodies, things and *affects* that move and take place through the idea of the *event*.

> The NRT focus on the idea of the event attempts to undo a sense of finishedness in the world and refocus our attention on a constant state of becoming … the idea of the event is at its strongest when it is applied to those very things that do appear to be 'finished'. (Creswell 2013, 229)

The affective dimension of the world and its becoming is another important element of NRT in that affect is conceived of as embodied and pre-cognitive and therefore pre-representational, coming as it does *before* emotion which is often characterised as our way of making sense of affects. Affect, when seen as a 'force that proceeds processes of cognition' offers an 'opportunity to explore the movements and consequences of these forces' (Bissell 2010, 81) and, in this case, how they impact on and make the Lord Mayor's Show happen. Affect and affects flow between the various participants, spectators, protestors, materials, objects, spaces, sounds and senses. It cannot be stilled, and most of it was lost on the day. This is the affective dimension of the Show which 'always exceeds understanding and conceptualisation' because 'so much is going on here that cannot be squeezed into knowable or representational form' (ibid.).

In recognising the world as open-ended, as always being 'more excessive than we can theorise' (Dewsbury et al. 2002, 437), our attempts at representation are therefore inevitably always incomplete and impossible because we can only ever be slap bang in the messy middle of things, *with* the world. Recognising this 'failure' and exploring how things might be other-wise and done differently are a central observation and opportunity of NRT (Dewsbury 2009). It follows that this 'desire to think of the world as *lively* and in a state of *becoming*', is a desire that operates before and beyond text and 'looks instead to moments of creativity and surprise in the way the world is performed' (Creswell 2013, 227 and 228 original emphasis). Followed and employed in this way, NRT often encourages, perhaps even requires, experimentation in our attempts to know the world and make that world knowable through our research (Dewsbury 2009). Hence, the attempt to *enact* rather than represent the Show in this paper is through its approach to *presentation* (Dewsbury et al. 2002). The relational ontology of NRT can therefore be felt by how the distinctions between Show and Occupy become blurred. Both were performed together through excessive, lively encounters, on this one day and over the space of little more than an hour or so.

Performance is often used to do both practical and metaphorical work in accounts and expressions of NRT (Latham 2003a, 2003b; Nash 2000; Thrift 2003; Thrift and Dewsbury 2000). An understanding of performance as that which is productive of life (and of research) has particular meaning when employed along with ideas of the event and affect. Here, NRT can be seen as 'a means of *valuing* and *working with* everyday practical *activities* as they occur' (Thrift 2000b, 216 original emphasis). The 'with' is significant. Not 'about' but 'with'. The relevance of these concerns to heritage (studies) as process starts to emerge when one considers them in the context of performance, both in the sense of producing the now and as a sense of occasion, and the events and encounters that make things happen, that perform. This performative concern has something to offer understandings of heritage as process and the work(ings) of heritage studies in relation to performance and (re)enactment. In this paper, I am not attempting to *apply* NRT to heritage studies.[7] Instead, approached as a 'style of work' (Thrift 2000b, 216), NRT is suggestive of new ways of performing heritage (studies) as process and of reframing research *as* performance, responding to the lively complexity of events and our encounters with them.

Brief encounters (2)

NRT, and research informed by it, therefore recognises research – its questions, methods and representations – as themselves performances and performative (Thrift and Dewsbury 2000). In part a strategy to address the seemingly impossible task of being non-representational in the representational universe of the academy, approaching research in this way supplements and significantly expands understandings of researcher as positioned and knowledge as situated. The resetting of academic practice as performance encourages an ongoing critical and reflexive questioning of methods and forms of expression and communication. It encourages experimentation. Although NRT has had very little explicit impact on heritage studies to date (although see Crouch 2010; Smith 2006), attending to research as performance opens new possibilities for the field.[8] Some of these possibilities can be briefly outlined by a consideration of recent examples from the literature of human and cultural geography and that help to contextualise my own approach to performing heritage (studies) with the Lord Mayor's Show.

Something that many geographies enacting or found moving along non-representational trajectories have in common is a commitment to experimentation; to explore and expand the boundaries of academic practice, to access other ways of knowing and telling materials and actions that bring into being, and constitute, different spaces and places. Examples from the growing literature include music and dance (McCormack 2004; Revill 2004), caravanning (Crouch 2001), gardening (Hitchings 2003), and encounters in cafés (Laurier and Philo 2006).[9] The work of John Wylie is particularly suggestive of the possibilities of NRT for heritage studies. Wylie experiments with the performance of academic research through writing and photography (Wylie 2002a, 2002b, 2005, 2006, 2009, 2010); 'My own personal ambition … involves writing specifically: to practice cultural geography as a form of writing at once both critical and creative, at once scholarly and story-like' (Wylie 2010, 212). Wylie has practised his cultural geography as writing in different ways, often through a perambulatory aesthetic of encounter with the environment. For example, in 'A single day's walking: narrating self and landscape on the South West Coast Path' (2005), Wylie narrates a phenomenological walk along a stretch of an 'official' signposted route, reflecting on academic sources and environmental encounters as he goes, presenting an engaging and critically engaged sense of being there, then. Photographs within the text hold out specific moments in time for our attention. Fragments of his moving and mobile everyday experience of walking are stilled by the photograph, at least momentarily, and through their juxtaposition with the written text one can feel something of the walk's temporality and materiality emerging from within and between, locating the research and researcher amidst the field.

> Limbs and lungs working hard in haptic, step-by-step engagement with nature-matter. Landscape becoming foothold … This is one possible account of coastal walking: a self forgotten in unintentional corporeal *hexis*, a landscape inhabited and processed rather than beheld. Ingold's (1993, 1995) articulation of a phenomenological understanding of landscape as a *milieu* of embodied, quotidian dwelling perhaps points in this direction. (Wylie 2005, 239 original emphasis)

Experimenting further with the form of his narratives, in 'Smoothlands: fragments/landscapes/fragments' (2006), a three-day exploration of a particular landscape on the north Devon coast opens up 'methods of watching and picturing dovetailed with reading and reflection on the topics of landscape and subjectivity' (ibid., 458). Brief textual fragments, often taken from other writers, are juxtaposed and found between small photographs of the coast, some in close up and others at a distance. This changes our sense of engagement with the landscape; 'landscape is tension' in this work, 'only landscape works amidst and through both of them [space and place]: presence/absence – tear things apart and even thread them together again' (ibid., 465). And finally, a more recent collaboration with Hayden Lorimer, 'Loop (a geography)' published in *Performance Research* (Lorimer and Wylie 2010), two geographers craft a combined narrative of walking:

> The walkers each carried some books and bits of writing, and some pre-conceived ideas to play with by means of perceptive experiment … Though this excursion on foot is figured as an open-ended investigation, it is the possibility of adventures in sound that supplies your sense of mission … To walk is one version of personhood, figuring a learning body as a centre of activity and awareness in the world. (ibid., 6 and 8)

Wylie's work is clearly not *anti*-representation. But, by expanding the creative and critical possibilities of writing and working visually, a 'geopoetics' (Lorimer 2007, 90) is performed from an assemblage of expressive practices that more partially and therefore convincingly communicate the materiality, temporality and story of his subjects; tales of movement and being moved, and of moving through, moving with and living with. Wylie's use of NRT takes representation seriously within his accounts of the world.

There is currently little evidence of such experimentation in the doing of heritage studies. A recent volume of essays brought together through the Performance, Learning and Heritage project led by the University of Manchester is a revealing case in point (Jackson and Kidd 2011). The book offers a thoughtful survey of approaches to 'innovation in museum theatre and live interpretation' that is interesting as far as it goes.[10] But, it does not go as far as to employ innovation or experimentation in how these accounts are *made* at the level of their making and their showing and telling. What is often lacking in research *about* performance is the liveliness, smell, thrill, or even plain boredom of the actual event itself. A sense of being there, then. This liveliness can be glimpsed at within the book, particularly Kershaw's attempt to visualise a sense of performance (Kershaw 2011), but for the most part it is missing. In the context of heritage studies, which needs to contend with the still dominant material representations of heritage as well as heritage as process, it is perhaps more helpful to adopt a 'more-than-representational' approach (Lorimer 2005; Rose 2010)[11]. Lorimer offers the *more-than*-representational in response to the expanded ideas of knowing and doing opened up by NRT whilst recognising the still significant poetics and politics of representation. It is this doubled-lens that I am working with in my enactment of the Lord Mayor's Show.

Prologue

> The point is now to engage in the research and move towards creating presentations of the experience that we encounter and create. (Dewsbury 2009, 328)

From earlier accounts of the pre-Show and its gathering anticipation and apprehensions, we have come to the 'main event'. The waiting is over. The band begins to play. But, how to respond to the injunctions and encouragements to experiment and really perform? My approach is to attempt a presentation of the tensions of that day and at play at that event, of encounters and affects emerging from the page that are performative of both Show and Occupy. Where Show and Occupy are performed and take place, together. This is done through the simple conceit of juxtaposing photographs with text. Photographs taken by the author of Occupy appear alongside a complete list of all 153 participants in the 2011 Show. What follows clearly does not attempt to present anything that might be thought of as a 'complete' account of the Show, which NRT would argue is impossible. It is hoped that affects may flow between images and text as elements and encounters of the Show-Occupy assemblage. The presentation is positioned as a third 'brief encounter' with the possibility and promise of NRT, this time more specifically for heritage studies.

The list is practical, finite (Eco 2011, 122). All participants are faithfully recorded, represented. But, it fails. It fails to communicate the Show, of being there that day, not least (but certainly not only) due to the co-presence of Occupy. It also fails within itself. The Show did not process passed spectators at regular, uniform intervals. There were some long delays. Pauses. Shuffling of feet. Waiting. But, the list does slow the reader, perhaps even boring the reader, as the verticality of the list is followed. But, on each page, the list is read across as it (en)counters the chaotic, informal (co)presence of Occupy participants. Occupy also moved the researcher, forcing a more mobile participation, walking and jostling through crowds gathered in the newly created space outside St Paul's Cathedral, responding to surprising encounters with Occupy's messy assemblage, 'alive to change and chance' (Dewsbury 2009, 324). Photographs are taken and presented at different distances from different subjects, reflecting the mobility of the researcher and the closeness to the action at hand, right in the middle of things. In this (re)enactment, photographs and list are together performative of Show and Occupy, materials of an empirical site of research that does not attempt a representation of that site but rather a presentation of it. The band begins to play.

Brief encounter (3)

1. Band of the Irish and Welsh Guards[12]

2. Assistant Commissioner, City of London Police, and Deputy Commander London District

3. Bradford Grammar School

4. The Lord Mayor's Appeal 2012 Fit for the Future

5. Allen & Overy and Bethnel Green Technology College

6. Bromley by Bow Centre

7. Langbourn Ward Club

Langbourn Ward Club, founded in 1890, is proud to honour its Alderman, David Wootton, the 690th Mayor of London… Its entry reflects one of David's passions as Chairman of Trustees of the Dickens Museum.

8. Worshipful Companies of Fletchers and Bowyers

9. Society of Young Freemen/Gog and Magog/RA100

…Gog and Magog, the mythical giant protectors of the City of London.

10. Romford Drum & Trumpet Corps

11. Trafalgar 200 Past Masters' Association

12. Westridge Carriages

13. Worshipful Company of Woolmen

14. Worshipful Company of Lightmongers

15. Worshipful Company of Clockmakers

16. Worshipful Company of Gunmakers

17. Worshipful Company of Masons

18. Worshipful Company of Glovers

19. Band of the RAF

20. RAF

21. 600 (City of London) Sqn RAuxAF

22. Institute of Directors

23. Welcome to Yorkshire

24. London's Air Ambulance

25. Worshipful Company of Paviors

26. Thomson Reuters

It believes that the right information in the right hands leads to amazing things. That's the Knowledge Effect.

27. The Air Training Corps Band

28. The Air Training Corps

29. Army Cadet Force (NW London)

30. Worshipful Company of Glaziers

31. Army Cadet Force (SE London)

32. University of London Officers Training Corps

33. 3 MI Battalion

34. National Youth Marching Band

35. Volunteer Police Cadets

36. Admiral Scaffolding Group

37. One New Change

One New Change is the City of London's largest shopping and leisure destination, open seven days a week.

38. Hong Kong Government

39. Fireman Sam

40. Kellswater Flute Band

41. City of Stoke-on-Trent

42. DARE City of London

43. Kerala – Incredible India

44. Paramount Theatrical: Puss in Boots

45. Elizabeth the Whitby Steam Bus

46. The London Regiment

47. B Company, 4 Para

48. F & G Companies 7 Rifles

49. 256 Field Hospital RAMC (V)

50. 135 Independent Geographic Squadron RE (V)

51. 41 (PLK) Signal Squadron (V)

52. 151 (London) Transport Regiment (V)

53. 1st Hook Scout & Guide Band

54. Guild of the Royal Hospital of St Bartholomew – Centenary Year

55. Metropolitan Grand Lodge

56. Worshipful Company of Loriners, 1261-2011

57. Square Mile Salute

58. Automobile Association

59. The Pipes & Drums of the Royal Corps of Signals

60. Hammersmith Academy

61. Jack Petchey Foundation

62. Jack Petchey Foundation

63. Jack Petchey Foundation

64. Canary Wharf

65. Worshipful Company of Broderers

66. Royal Yeomanry Band (IC & CY)

67. 71st (CoL) Yeomanry Signal Regiment Riding Detachment – 68 Sig Sqn (V)

68. FANY

69. Guilds of Zurich

70. Royal Yeomanry

71. 265 (Home Counties) Battery 106 (Y) Regt RA (V)

72. 217 Field Squadron RE (V)

73. Royal British Legion Band & Corps of Drums, Romford

74. City of London Solicitor's Company

75. Modern Livery Companies

Walkers represent 24 Livery Companies: Actuaries, Air Pilots, Arbiters, Art Scholars, Accountants, Architects, Constructors, Educators, Engineers, Environmental Cleaners, Farmers, Firefighters, Fuellers, Furniture Makers, Insurers, Launderers, Marketors, Secretaries & Administrators, Scientific Instrument Make rs, Security Professionals, Surveyors, Tobacco Pipe Makers, Water Conservators and World Traders.

76. Classic Motor Cars

77. Girlguiding LaSER

....comprising girls and leaders from Kingston, Merton, Richmond and Sutton boroughs....

78. Mexican Chamber of Commerce (MCC)

79. Household Troops Band of the Salvation Army

80. Figaro Masters

81. Pimlico Plumbers

82. Worhipful Company of Gardeners

83. CCA He' Art Bus

....rock 'n' roll tour bus designed by Sir Peter Blake.....

84. City University London

85. Royal Marines Band (HMS Collingwood)

86. Royal Navy

87. Royal Marines

88. RNR London District (HMS President)

89. Royal Marines Reserve (City of London)

90. 131 Independent Commando Squadron RE (V)

91. Lloyd's Register

92. Sea Cadet Corps Band

93. Sea Cadet Corps Band (London area)

94. St John Ambulance

95. Taf Valley Youth Choir

96. ASDAN Education

97. City Bridge Trust working with Heart n Soul

98. Worshipful Company of Merchant Taylors

99. London Massed Bugle Band

100. Livery Olympians

101. Lions Club International

102. Radio Taxis

103. Pan Nation.

....the newest steel band to erupt from North London....

104. Vauxhall Motors

105. Dogs Trust

106. Surbiton Royal British Legion Youth Marching Band

107. Royal British Legion

108. Colours of the Philippines

109. Coming Home

110. Paraiso School of Samba

111. British Red Cross Society

112. St Dunstan's CCF Band

113. Worshipful Company of Marketors

114. Worshipful Company of Tin Plate Workers

115. Variety Club of Great Britain

116. HNT Cancer Support

117. Community Policing Cycle Team

118. Corps of Drums Society

119. The King's Troop RHA

120. United Wards' Club, Guild of Freemen, City Livery Club, Royal Society of St George (City of London branch)

121. Worshipful Company of Pattenmakers

122. The Great Twelve

There are 108 Livery Companies, the first 12, according to an order established in 1515, are: Mercers' Company, Grocers' Company, Drapers' Company, Goldsmiths' Company

123. Worshipful Company of Glovers

124. Worshipful Company of Fishmongers

125. Worshipful Company of Fletchers

The Mother Company of the new Lord Mayor.....

126. Christ's Hospital School Band

127. Deputation of the Lord Mayor and Sheriffs' Committee

128. Chief Commoner and Secondary

129. City High Officers

130. Town Clerk and Aldermen below the Chair

131. Aldermen below the Chair

132. Aldermen below the Chair

133. Recorder and Aldermen below the Chair

134. Aldermen past the Chair

135. Aldermen past the Chair

136. HAC

The Honorable Artillery Company, HAC, formed in 1537 by King Henry VII, is the oldest regiment in the British Army.

137. Sheriff

138. Aldermanic Sheriff

139. Late Lord Mayor

140. Pageantmaster

141. Lady Mayoress

142. Light Cavalry, HAC

143. Commissioner, City of London Police

144. Household Cavalry Mounted Regiment Band & Division

145. City Marshall

146. The Rt. Hon. the Lord Mayor of London, Alderman David Wootton.

The Lord Mayor rides in the 18th century gold State Coach drawn by six shire horses, and preceded by Doggett's Coat and Badge Men. His personal standard and the standard of his Mother Livery Company, The Worshipful Company of Fletchers, are carried by members of the Company of Pikemen and Musketeers of the Honourable Artillery Company. The Lord Mayor is attended by his Chaplain and two of his Esquires, or personal staff officers.

Chaplain:

The Reverend Andrew Walker

Swordbearer: Colonel Richard Martin

Common Cryer and Sergeant-at-Arms:

Colonel Geoffrey Godbold, OBE, TD DL

147. Pikemen and Musketeers, HAC

The soldiers which follow the State Coach are the Lord Mayor's personal bodyguard and parade under Royal Warrant.

148. Federation of Old Comrades

149. Tack Vehicle

150. The King's Troop RHA

151. Support Taxis

152. (GL) Tpt Regt (V)

153. City of London Cleansing Department

The City of London is a place full of contradictions.[12]

Epilogue

Tuesday 28th February 2012. I'm travelling up to the Museum of London on a train through the city's southern suburbs. A session is planned there for my MA students: Mapping the Global City: Materials and Mobilities. My smartphone updates its news app to confirm that in the early hours of the morning the Occupy encampment had been forcibly removed from outside St Paul's Cathedral. I make an unscheduled detour to witness the scene. Turning into St Paul's Churchyard I see men in fluorescent jackets spraying the pavement with high powered jets of water. The public are fenced off from the clean up. There is no immediate sign of Occupy save for the process of its cleansing. 'Chewing Gum Removal. We are working to remove chewing gum and staining from this area of the pavement today.'

And then the traces. Lines of gummy adhesive form empty frames. Remnants of tape on corners. Slowly drying pavements. Small, hand-written graffiti. 'Your heart is a weapon the size of your fist'. Police are milling about, maintaining a presence. 'Essential City streetworks'. Other unnamed individuals are being filmed giving interviews to camera. 'Intensive Street Cleansing'. The pavement of St Paul's Churchyard has been inscribed by its now departed temporary inhabitants. Slogans and messages are written in chalk, that most fragile of scriptive materials. No need for street cleansing. Rainfall will wash them away.[13]

- - - - - - - - - - -

... don't fret about the risks of experimenting, it is a justifiable way of proceeding that works better if you really embrace it. (Dewsbury 2009, 321–322)

As with any experiment, there is the risk of failure. And, this is something I fret about. If experimentation is indeed central to the employment of NRT as an approach to research, then perhaps I should fret less. To go ever further, much further than I have attempted here. In presenting my work in this way, the risk of failure – whatever that might look like – seems less worrying than not performing an experiment in the first place, of not following NRT all the way through into the performative, problematic potential of the enactment. The reader will have to be the judge of what the author has achieved or contributed in this regard. Indeed, working in this way recognises and hopes to enfold the creative agency of the reader and their encounter with the material. The broader gains for heritage studies that might be achieved through ongoing experimentation are potentially substantial. At the very least, NRT proves to be an effective 'machine for multiplying questions' (of heritage studies), 'and thereby *inventing new relations between thought and life*' (Thrift 2004, 82, original emphasis).

More-than-heritage studies

Representation has been and continues to be a central concern of heritage studies (e.g. Boswell and Evans 1999; Walsh 1992; Waterton and Watson 2010). It would be wrong to suggest that our work in engaging with representation is over, or perhaps ever could be. Conceiving of heritage as process does not ignore the products and material representations of heritage. But, reframing heritage as performed, as process, requires a similar response in the doing of heritage studies. Here, working more-than-representationally offers new ways of performing heritage (studies) as process. Working productively with NRT as a style of work, performing heritage (studies) emerges as a complex, uncertain and creative series of encounters, actions and (re)enactments. A more-than-heritage studies. NRT opens up new lines of enquiry, trajectories of thought and strategies of expression; not research *about* performance, but research *with* performance and *as* performance.

I do not put forward a more-than-representational approach as an attempt to accommodate 'opposed factions who require a neutral middle' (Wylie 2010, 215). Anyone who has ever reflected on the 'spurious neutrality' (INTERCOM 2011) of the museum will know that occupying a middle ground is never a neutral position. Rather, the being in the middle of things can be more productively treated as an ongoing series of abrasive moments of possibility and engagement where things happen and differences are made. At St Paul's Churchyard, a new place was created from alternative visions of life and living; a place of protest and engagement the edges of which were amplified for a time by the passing Lord Mayor's Show. Heritage as process and NRT together encourages the emergence of a new poetics and politics of research in heritage studies that works with the moments, encounters

fragments and gaps of the world and its meanings, towards more locatable and possibly progressive practices.

Notes

1. Included within my definition of heritage and heritage studies are museums, galleries and curating. However, this category work is done in the knowledge that these are all distinct fields in their own right and should be recognised as such, each operating within and through different if related institutional, operational and academic contexts. A criticism I have with much of 'heritage' as a broad field of academic enquiry is the lack of responsibility taken for these and other points of difference, which *make* a difference to our research projects.
2. For a useful chronology of Occupy London Stock Exchange, see Guardian Online http://www.guardian.co.uk/uk/occupy-london and the Occupy LSX website http://occupylsx.org/ both last accessed 23 March, 2012.
3. This difference accounts for my use of (re)enactment when discussing how I have chosen to perform the Lord Mayor's Show within this paper. The Show itself on the day was an enactment, and my performance of it within this paper its (re)enactment.
4. The Lord Mayor of London is an entirely different position to that of the Mayor of London. The Lord Mayor is responsible for the City of London, the Square Mile, and a new Mayor is not democratically elected by the people of the City. The Mayor London is a democratically elected office, voted for by all registered voters of London, and whose term is usually four years. The Mayor of London has a responsibility that stretches across the city of Greater London.
5. For a thorough-going introduction to and discussion of the main concerns and trajectories of non-representational theory see Anderson and Harrison's opening chapter of their book, (Anderson and Harrison 2010a). In their introduction, Anderson and Harrison make a convincing case for a plural reading of non-representational *theories*; that it cannot be reduced to a single position, perspective or approach. See also the introduction to Thrift 1996 and 2008.
6. Non-representational theory can be located within a far broader context of performative forms of research practice and representation emerging from the intersection of a range of related disciplines, including heritage (e.g. Bishop 2012; Butt 2005; Carter 2004;

Kirshenblatt-Gimblett 1997, 2001; Muncey 2010; Pink 2009;Rendell 2010; Schneider and Wright 2006; Whybrow 2011).

7. Whether or not non-representational theory does in the end still amount to a theory notwithstanding the claims made against this, and the potential contradictions that raises, is beyond the scope of this paper (but see e.g. Castree and MacMillan 2004; Creswell 2012; Olwig 2011).

8. It should be noted that human and cultural geography does engage with heritage broadly interpreted but these accounts have yet to fully engage with heritage through non-representational theory. Those most closely associated with new forms of approaches place within a heritage context include Crang and Crouch, particularly their work in tourism. See for example Crang 1994, where an earlier version of the performance of heritage is articulated, and Crouch 2002 and 2010.

9. This selection is taken from a much wider literature than can be meaningfully summarised here.

10. 'Museum theatre and live interpretation' forms the book's subtitle but reveals a lack of specificity between museums and heritage that I believe are important to account for. See also Kidd 2011.

11. Nigel Thrift, the originator of non-representational theory has conceded that the 'non' prefix has unhelpfully impeded understanding and acceptance of his ideas (Thrift 2004).

12. The first sentence of the main introductory panel of the Museum of London's City Gallery, last visited 28 February 2012.

13. Newspaper reports on the day suggested that the Occupy LSX encampment would relocate to another site of occupation elsewhere in the City of London.

References

Anderson, B., and P. Harrison. 2010a. "The Promise of Non-representational Theories." In *Taking Place: Non-representational Theories and Geography*, edited by B. Anderson and P. Harrison, 1–34. Farnham: Ashgate.

Anderson, B., and P. Harrison, eds. 2010b. *Taking Place: Non-Representational Theories and Geography*. Farnham: Ashgate.

Andrews, C. 2009. "Heritage Ethnography as a Specialised Craft: Grasping Maritime Heritage in Bermuda." In *Heritage Studies. Methods and Approaches*, edited by M. L. Sørensen and J. Carman, 140–164. London: Routledge.

Bishop, C. 2012. *Artificial Hells. Participatory Art and the Politics of Spectatorship*. London: Verso.

Bissell, D. 2010. "Placing Affective Relations: Uncertain Geographies of Pain." In *Taking Place: Non-representational Theories and Geography*, edited by B. Anderson and P. Harrison, 79–99. Farnham: Ashgate.

Boswell, D., and J. Evans, eds. 1999. *Representing the Nation: A Reader. Histories, Heritage and Museums*. London: Routledge.

Butt, G., ed. 2005. *After Criticism. New Responses to Art and Performance*. Oxford: Blackwell.

Carman, J., and M. L. Sørensen. 2009. "Heritage Studies: An Outline." In *Heritage Studies. Methods and Approaches*, edited by M. L. Sørensen and J. Carman, 11–29. London: Routledge.

Carter, P. 2004. *Material Thinking. The Theory and Practice of Creative Research.* Melbourne: Melbourne University Press.

Castree, N., and T. MacMillan. 2004. "Old News: Representation and Academic Novelty." *Environment and Planning a* 36: 469–480.

City of London Corporation. 2011. *The Lord Mayor's Show 2011. Official Commemorative Programme in Aid of the Lord Mayor's Appeal.* London: City of London Corporation.

Crang, M. 1994. "On the Heritage Trail: Maps of and Journeys to Olde Englande." *Environment and Planning D* 12: 341–355.

Creswell, T. 2012. "Non-representational Theory and Me: Notes of an Interested Sceptic." *Environment and Planning D: Society and Space* 30 (1): 96–105.

Creswell, T. 2013. *Geographic Thought. A Critical Introduction.* Chichester: Wiley-Blackwell.

Crouch, D. 2001. "Spatialities and the Feeling of Doing." *Social and Cultural Geography* 2 (1): 61–75.

Crouch, D. 2002. "Surrounded by Place: Embodied Encounters." In *Tourism: Between Place and Performance*, edited by S. Coleman and M. Crang, 207–218. London: Berghahn Books.

Crouch, D. 2010. "The Perpetual Performance and Emergence of Heritage." In *Culture, Heritage and Representation. Perspectives on Visuality and the past*, edited by E. Waterton and S. Watson, 57–75. Farnham: Ashgate.

Dewsbury, J.-D. 2009. "Performative, Non-representational, and Affect-based Research: Seven Injunctions." In *The Sage Handbook of Qualitative Geography*, edited by D. DeLyser, S. Herbert, S. Aitken, M. Crang, and L. McDowell, 321–334. London: Sage.

Dewsbury, J.-D., P. Harrison, M. Rose, and J. Wylie. 2002. "Enacting Geographies." *Geoforum* 33: 437–440.

Eco, U. 2011. *Confessions of a Young Novelist.* Cambridge, MA: Harvard University Press.

Fraser, G. 2012. "From a Colourful Camp to a Dismal Metal Fence: The End of Occupy St Paul's." *The Guardian*, 1–2.

Hitchings, R. 2003. "People, Plants and Performance: On Actor Network Theory and the Material Pleasures of the Private Garden." *Social & Cultural Geography* 4 (1): 99–113.

Ingold, T. 1993. "The Temporality of the Landscape." *World Archaeology* 25: 152–171.

Ingold, T. 1995. "Building, Dwelling, Living: How People and Animals Make Themselves at Home in the World." In *Shifting Contexts: Transformations in Anthropological Knowledge*, edited by M. Strathern, 57–81. London: Routledge.

INTERCOM (International Committee on Management, International Council of Museums). 2011. "Intercom Declaration of Museums and Politics". Accessed March 31, 2012. http://www.intercom.museum/index.html last.

Jackson, A., and J. Kidd, eds. 2011. *Performing Heritage. Research, Practice and Innovation in Museum Theatre and Live Interpretation.* Manchester, NH: Manchester University Press.

Keitumetse, S. 2009. "Methods for Investigating Locals' Perception of a Cultural Heritage Product for Tourism." In *Heritage Studies. Methods and Approaches*, edited by M. L. Sørensen and J. Carman, 201–217. London: Routledge.

Kersal, M. M. 2009. "Walking a Fine Line: Obtaining Sensitive Information Using a Valid Methodology." In *Heritage Studies. Methods and Approaches*, edited by M. L. Sørensen and J. Carman, 178–201. London: Routledge.

Kershaw, B. 2011. "Nostalgia for the Future of the Past: Technological Environments and the Ecologies of Heritage Performance." In *Performing Heritage. Research, Practice and Innovation in Museum Theatre and Live Interpretation*, edited by A. Jackson and J. Kidd, 123–144. Manchester: Manchester University Press.

Kidd, J. 2011. "Performing the Knowing Archive: Heritage Performance and Authenticity." *International Journal of Heritage Studies* 17 (1): 22–35.

Kirshenblatt-Gimblett, B. 1997. "Afterlives." *Performance Research* 2 (2): 1–10.

Kirshenblatt-Gimblett, B. 2001. "Performing Live. An Interview with Barbara Kirshenblatt-Gimblett." *Tourist Studies* 1 (3): 211–232.

Latham, A. 2003a. "Research, Performance, and Doing Human Geography: Some Reflections on the Diary-photograph, Diary-interview Method." *Environment and Planning a* 35 (11): 1993–2017.

Latham, A. 2003b. "The Possibilities of Performance." *Environment and Planning a* 35: 1901–1906.

Laurier, E., and C. Philo. 2006. "Possible Geographies: A Passing Encounter in a café." *Area* 38 (4): 353–363.

Lorimer, H. 2005. "Cultural Geography: The Busyness of Being 'More-than-representational." *Progress in Human Geography* 29 (1): 83–94.

Lorimer, H. 2007. "Cultural Geography: Worldly Shapes, Differently Arranged." *Progress in Human Geography* 31 (1): 89–100.

Lorimer, H., and J. Wylie. 2010. "Loop (a Geography)." *Performance Research* 15 (4): 6–13.

McCormack, D. 2004. "Drawing out the Lines of the Event." *Cultural Geographies* 11 (2): 211–220.

McDavid, C. 2009. "The Public Archaeology of African America: Reflections on Pragmatic Methods and Their Results." In *Heritage Studies. Methods and Approaches*, edited by M. L. Sørensen and J. Carman, 217–235. London: Routledge.

Muncey, T. 2010. *Creating Autoethnographies*. London: Sage.

Nash, C. 2000. "Performativity in Practice: Some Recent Work in Cultural Geography." *Progress in Human Geography* 24 (4): 653–664.

Olwig, K. 2011. "Book Review: Taking Place: Non-representational Theories and Geography." *Progress in Human Geography* 35 (6): 803–805.

Palmer, C. 2009. "Reflections on the Practice of Ethnography within Heritage Tourism." In *Heritage Studies. Methods and Approaches*, edited by M. L. Sørensen and J. Carman, 123–140. London: Routledge.

Pink, S. 2009. *Doing Sensory Ethnography*. London: Sage.

Rendell, J. 2010. *Site-writing. The Architecture of Art Criticism*. London: I.B. Tauris.

Revill, G. 2004. "Performing French Folk Music: Dance, Authenticity and Nonrepresentational Theory." *Cultural Geographies* 11 (2): 199–209.

Rose, M. 2010. "Envisioning the Future: Ontology, Time and the Politics of Non-representation." In *Taking Place: Non-representational Theories and Geography*, edited by B. Anderson and P. Harrison, 341–361. Farnham: Ashgate.

Schneider, A., and C. Wright, eds. 2006. *Contemporary Art and Anthropology*. London: Berg.

Smith, L. 2006. *The Uses of Heritage*. London: Routledge.

Smith, L. 2011. "The 'Doing of Heritage': Heritage as Performance." In *Performing Heritage. Research, Practice and Innovation in Museum Theatre and Live Interpretation*, edited by A. Jackson and J. Kidd, 69–82. Manchester, NH: Manchester University Press.

Sørensen, M. L. 2009. "Between the Lines and in the Margins: Interviewing People about Attitudes to Heritage and Identity." In *Heritage Studies. Methods and Approaches*, edited by M. L. Sørensen and J. Carman, 164–178. London: Routledge.

Thrift, N. 1996. *Spatial Formations*. London: Sage.

Thrift, N. 2000a. "Performance." In *The Dictionary of Human Geography*, 4th ed., edited by R. J. Johnston, D. Gregory, G. Pratt, and M. Watts, 577–577. Oxford: Blackwell.

Thrift, N. 2000b. "Afterwords." *Environment and Planning D: Society and Space* 18: 213–255.

Thrift, N. 2003. "Performance and… ." *Environment and Planning a* 35: 2019–2024.

Thrift, N. 2004. "Summoning Life." In *Envisioning Human Geographies*, edited by P. Cloke, P. Crang, and M. Goodwin, 81–104. London: Arnold.

Thrift, N. 2008. *Non-representational Theory. Space, Politics, Affect*. London: Routledge.

Thrift, N., and J.-D. Dewsbury. 2000. "Dead Geographies – and How to Make Them Live." *Environment and Planning D: Society and Space* 18: 411–432.

Walsh, K. 1992. *The Representation of the past: Museums and Heritage in the Post-modern World*. London: Routledge.

Waterton, E., and S. Watson, eds. 2010. *Culture, Heritage and Representation. Perspectives on Visuality and the past*. Farnham: Ashgate.

Whybrow, N. 2011. *Art and the City*. London: I.B. Tauris.

Wylie, J. 2002a. "An Essay on Ascending Glastonbury Tor." *Geoforum* 33: 441–454.

Wylie, J. 2002b. "Becoming-Icy: Scott and Amundsen's South Polar Voyages, 1910–1913." *Cultural Geographies* 9 (3): 249–265.

Wylie, J. 2005. "A Single day's Walking: Narrating Self and Landscape on the South West Coast Path." *Transactions of the Institute of British Geographers* 30: 234–247.

Wylie, J. 2006. "Smoothlands: Fragments/Landscapes/Fragments." *Cultural Geographies* 13: 458–465.

Wylie, J. 2007. *Landscape*. London: Routledge.

Wylie, J. 2009. "Landscape, Absence and the Geographies of Love." *Transactions of the British Association of Geographers* 34: 275–289.

Wylie, J. 2010. "Cultural Geographies of the Future, or Looking Rosy and Feeling Blue." *Cultural Geographies* 17 (2): 211–217.

The time travellers' tools of the trade: some trends at Lejre

Cornelius Holtorf

Linnaeus University

This paper is about how the emphasis of the archaeological open-air museum at Lejre, Denmark, has been shifting from a research institution towards an archaeological theme park. I am discussing how material culture and associated skills and perceptions have been facilitating time-travel experiences at Lejre from 1964 until today. My main focus is on the prehistoric families who each summer have been inhabiting the full-size model of the Iron Age village known as Lethra. In 2011, I conducted participant observation in the village. This paper presents some of my observations and insights. I am also asking what the discernible trends and transformations over time, imply for how we are to understand contemporary forms of living history and related genres. The discussion explores some implications of my study regarding the nature of authenticity and how the past 'comes to life' at Lethra. I conclude by exploring some important trends for cultural heritage and heritage tourism in our age that arise from my study.

Introduction to the Iron Age

Founded in 1964, the archaeological open-air museum at Lejre, Denmark (formally called Land of Legends) has long been combining scientific research in experimental archaeology and the reconstruction of prehistoric technologies with public interpretation and education. The site has become an institution in Denmark, features in school books and according to one survey it was known among 43% of the Danish population (Land of Legends 2009). Lejre attracts every year about 55,000 visitors, most of which are families with children. In this paper, I discuss how at Lejre, over recent decades, the emphasis of the site has been shifting from a research institution towards an archaeological theme park.

My argument is based, in parts, on available documents and relevant academic literature and, in other parts, on my own experiences gained in August 2011 from participant observation in the reconstructed Iron Age-village of Lethra at Lejre. I considered carefully the previous research published on this topic and on various occasions I received documents and insightful commentary from the Centre's leadership, notably its Director Lars Holten. Many insights discussed in this paper derive, however, from a limited empirical study. Adopting an ethnographic research approach, I immersed myself for one week in Lethra, together with my son Tom (then 10) and accompanied by two Danish families (together 5 adults and 4 children aged 3–8). During the week, as well as during a couple of later reunions with the other families, I did not carry out structured or semi-structured interviews but confined myself to keeping eyes and ears open while fully participating in the various activities. Occasionally, I encouraged the other families and visitors to tell me more about relevant topics and opinions. Whenever possible I took notes. I also kept a diary in the evenings and had a camera hidden away for occasional snapshots. My research interest was known (and approved) both by the other families and by the leadership of the site, but it was unknown to the visitors who strolled through the village and our houses during opening hours.

In the future, additional light on some of my rather preliminary observations may be thrown by a systematic data collection among visitors and families over a longer period of time and from different sites, followed by a more formal analysis of the data gained. In particular, I am aware that I am glossing over many potentially relevant distinctions between different kinds of visitors – and indeed different kinds of prehistoric families – that invariably exist. Another interesting angle to be investigated in the future concerns the role of wild and domestic animals in evoking the past, as animals are an important part of archaeological open-air museums in general and of Lethra, specifically (see also Fenske 2007, 101–102). Nevertheless, I hope that my present discussion will meet wider interest, partly because of the paradigmatic character of the open-air museum at Lejre, which is the oldest of its kind and a site that has long been inspiring other centres and museums (Petersson 2003, 140–142), and partly because my observations are linked to wider discernible trends in society concerning cultural heritage and heritage tourism.

The present research forms part of a larger project investigating the nature of contemporary time-travel experiences. That project, jointly led with Bodil Petersson, has been investigating various time-travel phenomena and techniques, including virtual realities, from the perspective of several disciplines (Holtorf and Petersson 2010). It contributes to an emerging field of research investigating a wide variety of sensual evocations of the past, stretching from meticulously researched re-enactment to TV docu-soaps and from educational living history to entertaining role-play and games (e.g. Crang 1996; Gustafsson 2002; Hjemdahl 2002; Drieschner 2005; Kansteiner 2005; Fenske 2007; Dreschke 2010; Melotti 2011; Kalshoven 2012; Lowenthal 2013). I discussed elsewhere the general nature of how time travel in its various manifestations is transforming the way in which many of us today appreciate and perceive the past (Holtorf 2007, 2010, 2012). In the present paper, I am asking how material culture and associated skills and perceptions have been facilitating time-travel experiences at Lejre and I thus aim to extend previous studies of visitors and prehistoric families in archaeological open-air museums (e.g. Steenstrup 1999; Svendsen 2010). I discuss specifically what discernible trends and transformations over time imply for how we are to understand contemporary forms of living history and related genres. In this way, my paper complements previous research investigating the general trend to engage with the past by time-travelling and outdoor-sensual experiences, rather than by visiting conventional museums (Kristiansen 2001; Petersson 2003; Keefer 2006; Samida, n.d.).

Since 1974, families have been able to inhabit for one week at a time, during the summer months, the full-size model of the Iron Age village known as Lethra. The families are both to experience and to perform life in the past. Initially, they were considered part of the experiment of a complete village as it were, and they were even to engage in some practical work linked to experiments (Rasmussen 2011, 159–160). A change took place around 1980, when the families became seen more and more as a tourist attraction and became in their own right a learning possibility for visitors (Steenstrup 1999, 21–22, 29–31). Either way, both the roles as an attraction and as a pedagogical tool meant that the families were de facto considered as employed staff. Consequently they stayed for free on a full board basis (Steenstrup 1999, 38). Today, the families' role has changed even more. This is visible not the least in the fact that they are now being charged in order to be able to live in the Iron Age (in 2012, 1500 DKK = ca € 200 per adult and week, food included). My paper is about this change in the role and perception of prehistoric families at Lejre.

In the laboratory

The *Historical-Archaeological Experimental Centre* was initially conceived and set-up by Hans-Ole Hansen during the early 1960s (Hansen 1964, Chap. 1; Paardekooper 2006). It was intended as a scientific field station and laboratory for archaeological experiments and reconstructions that would bring to life for a large public the foreign culture that was Iron Age Denmark. This purpose followed naturally from the common idea that one of archaeology's major aims is to understand prehistoric living conditions based not only on archaeological finds and features, but also on ethnographic analogies and on contemporary experiments (see also Keefer 2006; Rasmussen 2011, 149). In addition to specifically archaeological experiments, the Centre initially also supported many projects derived from the natural sciences and ethnology (Rasmussen 2011, 149). In this scientific context, the material culture present on the site served experimental purposes as heuristic devices in closing in on a past reality. The issues to be investigated ranged from techniques of manufacturing and using ancient types of tools to functional reconstructions of Iron Age buildings, and from daily life under conditions of the distant past to taphonomic processes that inform archaeological methodology (Hansen 1964; Meldgaard and Rasmussen 1994).

At the centre of attention were initially research questions concerning the design and construction of the full-scale models of Iron Age houses in Lethra and the living conditions inside and around them (Sagnlandet Lejre 2010, 15–23). The prehistoric families conducted their own experiments and formed an integral part of the experimental character of the village at large (Steenstrup 1999, 29–30). As the former Head of Research at the Centre, Rasmussen (2011, 159), explained:

> Originally the Iron Age village … was intended as a kind of total experiment, where living in and using the houses was seen as a comparative experiment which could open up a new interpretative potential for archaeology.

This agenda is not only widely known, especially through the Centre having long featured in Danish school textbooks about history, but it is also intuitive as you enter the village with its prominent buildings and living inhabitants. Accordingly, visitors typically ask questions about what life was like in and around the houses, such as why the doors are so low, if the animals in the houses provided natural heating during the winter and why there is no chimney (Sagnlandet Lejre 2010, 9). Other questions in this genre which I heard myself concerned the exact way our oven worked and how fast the wooden supports sustaining the heavy roof were rotting and therefore requiring replacement.

   Besides their scientific purpose, the houses and other material objects thus fulfilled even important didactic purposes for a curious public visiting the Centre. They visualised and exemplified scientific methodology and eventually scientific knowledge about prehistoric living conditions. The Centre was keen to foster a dialogue between craftspeople and researchers, students and teachers, professionals and amateurs, and between visitors and their ancestors (Meldgaard and Rasmussen 1994, 129). These ambitions are still today expressed very clearly in § 2 of the Statutes of the Land of Legends that have remained unchanged since 1964:

> The Experimental Centre's purpose is to run a research centre for the carrying out of ethnological, historical and archaeological experiments, execution of associated research tasks and dissemination of the results through scientific channels and through active communication and instruction. (cited after Land of Legends, n.d. (a))

In this context of scientific experimentation and visitor didactics, the body became a tool in the process of re-doing past practices and thus learning about the past. As the researcher learned how to 'handle' objects in the best way and gradually 'picked up' prehistoric living conditions, visitors were given information in order to 'grasp' the nature of the investigations and thus get a 'grip' on the past (see Hansen 1964). It is significant that even though the intention was very much focused on objects and material culture, the main aim was nearly entirely cognitive. The Centre initially wanted to contribute to scientific knowledge about the past and its dissemination to the visitors. The kind of knowledge to be gained was cerebral, rational and verbal, corresponding to the conventions used in academic publications. This is reflected in the Mission statement which states under the motto of 'Let me try and I will understand!' that

> The Land of Legend Lejre's mission is to create and spread knowledge and astonishment about prehistoric ways of life through research in experimental archaeology, practical demonstrations and educational programmes based on active participation. (my translation from Land of Legends, n.d. (b))

The educational side of the activities at the Centre has been significant all along also in economic terms as a substantial part of its budget derives from the Danish Ministry of Education in relation to the service provided for school classes. Since the 1990s, this important source of income has not been given as a longer-term subsidy, but is awarded annually in competition with other educational science centres that fulfil certain minimum criteria related to the activities provided, overall visitor numbers and economic viability. As the character of such centres, in Denmark and elsewhere, has been changing over recent years in line with increasing competition, new conditions of funding and evolving expectations of children and adults alike, the *Historical-Archaeological Experimental Centre* at Lejre has been changing too (Holten, personal communication, March 11, 2013).

On stage

Today, full-scale models and most other material cultures at Lejre have to some extent assumed new roles. Instead of mostly facilitating scientific experiments, they are increasingly facilitating embodied and narrated performances through which the prehistoric past is staged (Steenstrup 1999, Chap. 4). Ironically, therefore, the activities at Lejre, which once had pioneered a modern way of researching, teaching and presenting the past to a wide audience, now appear to hark back to a far earlier tradition of constructing evocative and somewhat romanticised sceneries of the past (Schöbel 2004). This does not mean, however, that the Centre has been developing backwards or into an inappropriate direction. In effect, the scientific field station at Lejre has been turning, to some extent, into a modern theme park. By using this term, I do not mean to make a negative value judgement like other heritage critics following Robert Hewison's (1987) biting critique of the Heritage Industry in 1980s Britain. Historical theme parks provide experiences that have proven to be well suited to attract visitors in contemporary society (Hjemdahl 2002). They are large outdoor areas where people engage in activities rendered meaningful by linking them to a unifying idea such as a particular historical period. Today, some historical museums, for example Jamtli in Sweden (Zipsane 2012), are calling themselves theme parks.

This timely transformation at Lejre was not due to a review of the Centre's main purpose and mission which remain unchanged (as quoted earlier), but rather due to a new public relations strategy based on an analysis of what visitors demand from attractions in the Experience Economy and why (Holten 2010). After conducting their own visitor-studies, time-travel experiences and story-telling had been identified by the Land of Legends management as two significant realms for further development. One outcome of this process was the recent name change and re-branding from *Historical-Archaeological Experimental Centre* to *Land of Legends Lejre. Centre for Historical-Archaeological Research and Communication* (the second part of this title has now been scrapped). Market research commissioned by the Centre had led to the insight that terms like antiquity, prehistory and history are widely associated with something that is dusty, boring and passive. The new term 'Land of Legends' on the other hand was found to be associated with a place that is far away, fantastic and full of activities, thus creating curiosity and interest (Land of Legends 2009). It seemed to correspond perfectly to an Iron Age village inhabited by families who can tell visitors fascinating stories about life in the past. Whereas, previously the Centre educated visitors about the past in an exciting way, now it wants to tell exciting stories that also educate about the past. The fact that many of the stories and experiences to be gained in the Land of Legends have a direct connection to academic research is now considered as an additional strength of the overall package offered to visitors making the entertainment meaningful and endowing the attraction with 'a wonderful authenticity', as the official translation has it (Land of Legends 2009).

In practice, previously important historical veracity gained by tightly controlled scientific experiments and manifested in full-scale models and reconstructions was replaced by sensual evocations of a different time period brought about by applying 'creative imagination' to support 'the magic of make-believe' (Hjemdahl 2002, 116). Although sensory and emotional dimensions are gradually entering experimental archaeology generally and arguably could be accommodated in a broader view of what qualifies as a legitimate experiment (Petersson and Narmo 2011; Daugbjerg, n.d.), the approach that becomes manifest at Lejre is another one. Visitors and prehistoric families alike are invited and appear to be more than willing to experience Lethra holistically 'as if' it was something other than the patchwork of various assumptions and interpretations by several generations of archaeologists, which it actually is (Rasmussen 2011, 162–163). Following the sociologists Beardsworth and Bryman (1999, 249), I, therefore, like to describe the prehistoric village as a quasification which results from 'processes which allow consumers to "pretend" that they are embroiled in an experience that is *outside* the modern context, but which is in fact firmly and safely rooted in it'. This sense of pretence became very tangible one day when a visitor asked me to climb up a ladder leaning against the roof of one of the houses with the instruction to 'look busy' for her photograph. I did not feel I was cheating anybody as her instructions had indeed made me busy at that moment. Balancing precariously on that ladder, surely I was not cheating myself either.

Significantly, this prehistoric past being staged at the Land of Legends is a past in which chronological differences in practice seem to be largely irrelevant, both for the visitors and for the Centre itself. There are big chronological differences of several centuries between the various house models which date to the period of ca 200 BC – AD 200 (Sagnlandet Lejre 2010, 15), but not much time is wasted on explaining this in detail, either to the prehistoric families or to the visiting tourists. I share the view of Director Lars Holten (personal communication, March 11, 2013) that in the light of the difference of the entire prehistoric village to the present, any chronological distinctions within Lethra will remain abstract and are not very significant to the visitor experience. Indeed, on the introductory day for all the families of the season, held in Lejre on 16 April 2011, when one family father suggested to the responsible staff member that Lethra belonged to 'Asterix time', the latter was more than happy to agree and continue with his lecture describing the features of each house. Another staff member, assisting the Iron Age families during opening hours, happily declared one morning that today she was actually wearing shoes resembling Viking age originals and she went on to suggest that, really, it made no difference to the overall experience of the Iron Age. Regarding visitors, Johanne Steenstrup observed a mother discovering a person in Iron Age garments, only to advise her daughter: 'Look dear, here comes a woman from the Stone Age!' (1999, 57, my translation). Similarly, a prehistoric father expressed to me that it made no difference to him whether he was spending his holidays in the Iron Age or in the Stone Age; to him, the 'prehistoric' experience was the same either way. In Lethra, all periods are thus merging into one generic, prehistoric past. Whether or not all archaeologists and other experts approve of this development, at Lejre the holistic experience of pastness, which is the perceived quality or condition of something to be 'of the past' appears to have become more significant than chronological correctness (Holtorf 2013).

Even fictional pasts are included into the prehistoric pastiche being created. Some prehistoric families stated frankly that they had been inspired by Jean Auel's global bestseller *The Clan of the Cave Bear* and its sequels, among other fiction (Steenstrup 1999, 36, 58), the Land of Legends itself makes ample reference in its weekly programmes to Beowulf and the Nordic Gods, even offering a Ghost Tour. Elsewhere, at the archaeological open-air museum of Eketorp in Sweden, nightly screenings of the film *The Lord of the Rings* were scheduled during the summer of 2009 as if it was the most natural thing in the world to connect prehistory with contemporary fantasy. As these examples illustrate, at the foreground are no longer scientific research or visitor learning about the past but holistic time-travelling experiences of a creatively adapted, generic prehistory. This change has been aptly described by Daugbjerg (n.d., 5) who wrote that the experimental ventures of yesteryear, when tests, facts and scientific rigor were higher on the public agenda, have today merged with, and to some degree been super- seded by, vaguer but also perhaps more alluring and individualistically pitched invita- tions to immerse oneself in landscapes and milieus of experience, legend and fantasy.

Part of the appeal of experiencing such a past results from an often observed grow- ing desire of people to appreciate the past in 3-D, fully embodied and with all the senses (Hjemdahl 2002; Drieschner 2005; Fenske 2007; Schöbel 2010; Kalshoven 2012). The human body is thus no longer merely a tool employed to witness and learn about past practices but it has turned into a medium through which the past is staged and felt. This means that visitors' priorities may now be rather different. As the anthropologist Hjemdahl (2002, 116) found in her research about an open-air museum in Norway, 'dirty butter, logs, bonfires and pancakes with honey are com- pletely uninteresting in terms of objects of the past – yet the grime, toil, smoke and stickiness nevertheless give rise to dreams and thoughts about life in another era'.

Arguably, at Lejre, too, perceptions and experiences of the material culture in Lethra appear to have become more important than the skills required for their man- ufacture and proper use. The houses have turned into stage-sets in front of which the prehistoric past is performed by families in suitable costumes (Steenstrup 1999, 56). Whereas back in the 1970s, the prehistoric families wore modern sweaters and rubber boots (Holten, personal communication, March 11, 2013), now it is deemed essential that they wear garments considered appropriate for the Iron Age. The introductory sessions for the prehistoric families both in spring and on the first day during 'our' week were filled with information about the practical dos and don'ts, while onstage in Lethra. Historical information, on the other hand, remained anec- dotal and linked to permissible behaviour, for example, when the question 'did they have wine in the Iron Age?' was addressed by combining information about archae- ological evidence for alcoholic drinks with expectations of the prehistoric adults during opening hours. On the introductory day in spring, the responsible staff mem- ber recommended selected archaeological literature about Danish prehistory but added half-jokingly that it was 'for the nerds' among us. However, it needs to be said too that the Centre currently employs five full-time archaeologists. There is also no doubt that some of the prehistoric families I met were genuinely interested in prehistory. Occasionally, they were more than willing to conduct their own little experiments about prehistoric living conditions, for example concerning the manufacture of simple leather shoes (Schou 2011).

Material culture is highly significant in the village, insofar as it evokes a theatri- cal scene, thus illustrating and prompting stories and their underlying plots. The Land of Legends management tells stories about objects to the prehistoric families and to the visitors, for example on information boards and during guided tours. The families in turn tell stories to the visitors using the props they have ready to hand. For example, when I employed my modern outdoor knife to carve an ad hoc bow for Tom, after vaguely remembering what I had played with as a child (Figure 1), the resulting weapon and its amazing capacity to distribute flying twigs around the village and among the geese initiated several conversations with an interested audi- ence of visitors who clearly admired our survival skills. The visitors in their turn also tell stories to the families, for example about their holidays in Africa where they saw similar objects in use. Finally, the families, after returning to their ordinary lives in the present, tell stories to their friends and relatives (or, as in the case of

Figure 1. The modern time travellers' tools of the trade after returning home from the Iron Age: a mix of modern technology bought on the internet (our knives), poorly executed home-made imitations (our dried shoes) and pure childhood fantasy (Tom's bow and arrows). Photograph: Cornelius Holtorf 2011.

this paper, to their colleagues and students) about the past they experienced. Irrespective of whether the account is given in person or using media such as facebook, I saw it several times supported by references to the prehistoric gear they took home (and this is true in the present case too, see Figure 1).

The prehistoric families have increasingly been considered by the Centre as paying guests who are seeking that special holiday experience, often concluding that Lejre is offering just that: a themed camping site. Significantly, the formal handbook for the prehistoric families prefaces its list of activities suitable for children and adults living in the Iron Age by stating that 'You are here of course in order to spend your holidays together with your family; except for preparing food, keeping the fire going, informing visitors and some relaxing you will not have to work very much' (Sagnlandet Lejre 2010, 8, my translation). One of the prehistoric families I met later described the appeal of their holiday experience, and the reason why they returned one year later, by emphasising the peacefulness and sense of quality time for the entire family resulting from a week spent to a large part around an open fire, talking and gazing into the flames. In the media too, the prehistoric families are discussed in the travel section: one page Thailand, the next page Iron Age (Bleach 2010). The demand for this particular package holiday is high and few of those selected to live in the past are taken aback when they realise that they are paying in parts for the privilege of performing for other paying guests.

Discussion

The transformation of the village of Lethra from a scientific field station to a theme park, go hand in hand with a changing engagement of the visitors and families with material culture. As I have outlined earlier, to some extent material culture has turned into a central part of human embodied experience in the present, rather than a tool to gain cerebral insights about the past. At the same time, the objects present at the site have ceased to be perceived predominantly as working models to test abstract hypotheses about prehistoric living conditions and instead function as a stage-set facilitating contemporary experiences and story-telling. Although it is unclear to what extent visitors and families already previously subverted the ambition of the Centre to impress through experimental archaeology, practical demonstrations and educational programmes, and instead enjoyed their embodied experiences in a themed environment, it is certainly evident that the emphasis has changed in the language being used by the Centre (compare Hansen 1964 with Land of Legends 2009 and Holten 2010) and to some extent also in the expectations of the families (Steenstrup 1999, 29–32).

These discernible trends have some important implications for a number of issues that lie at the heart of any archaeological open-air museum and are even significant for other forms of re-enactment even for cultural heritage sites, at large (see Melotti 2011). In the following, I wish to discuss a few consequences and implications of my observations about life at Lethra regarding the nature of authenticity and how the past 'comes to life'.

The nature of authenticity

Regarding the nature of authenticity, my experiences from Lethra exemplify an important shift in our understanding of how authenticity is negotiated between objects, experts and audiences. Whereas, objects at Lejre as elsewhere have long been authenticated *by* experts *for* audiences based on the assumption that authenticity is inherent in an object or a certain technology, but requires an expert to verify and describe it adequately; alternative views see the objects' authenticity as the outcome of a continuous negotiation of particular object qualities within and among audiences (Crang 1996; Holtorf 2013). The case of Lethra supports this alternative view (Figure 2).

The prehistoric families have gone through an introduction-day during spring and received extensive written documentation containing much expert knowledge about Lethra. However, for many, the particular appeal of their experience does not derive from acquiring authoritative insight and subsequently living it, as it were. Instead, they emphasise aspects that are reminiscent of their own previous camping experiences: the peacefulness and magical atmosphere of the place; the joint outdoor activities during the day; the somewhat exotic food, clothes and shoe-wear; the generally strong personal experiences; and the bonds they renew or create

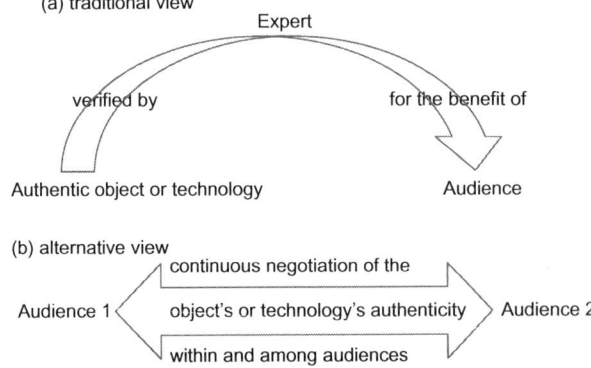

Figure 2. The changing nature of authenticity.

within their own families and with the families in the other houses (Steenstrup 1999, Chaps. 6–7; Bleach 2010). What in retrospect more than anything else appears to epitomise for visitors and families alike from the authentic experience of the Iron Age village of Lethra is the smoke of the open fire. Although you do not notice it on site, the smell will stick to your clothes and travel with you for hours after you have left Lethra prompting memories of living in another era (Hjemdahl 2002, 116).

My observations suggest that the visitors' evident experience of authenticity of the village is not to a particularly large extent reliant on expert knowledge and veri-fication of the reconstructions. In my experience, it is clear to visitors that the Land of Legends is scientifically orientated and that there is detailed expert knowledge available to visitors, for example on information boards throughout the site, from employees (often students of archaeology) who join and assist the prehistoric fami-lies during opening hours and of course in the book shop. However, it quickly became evident to me that although many visitors dutifully looked at the boards and read some of them and often ask questions both to the employees and to the prehistoric families, their appreciation of the village appears to rest mainly on the extent to which they are able to feel 'as if' they are in prehistory (cf. Beardsworth and Bryman 1999). For that quasification to take place, the houses have to provide a suggestive stage-set, the objects present on site need to function as props prompt-ing certain stories and behaviour and most importantly, the actors on stage need to offer plots that engage the visitors. When the visitors begin to understand prehistory with all their senses and through their own bodies, they effectively perceive what has been called 'performative authenticity', that is an empathetic understanding of something 'other' through bodily experiences (Knudsen and Waade 2010).

The objects visible in Lethra are all copies, models or imitations, yet that does not diminish but rather increase their value, insofar as all are free to handle and use them (see Hjemdahl 2002; Kalshoven 2012, Chaps. 4–5). Accordingly, the authen-ticity of the village is not contained somehow inside the objects and technologies on display and therefore, best understood by knowledgeable experts, but it resides largely in how the actors on a suggestive stage-set use their props to tell and per-form engaging stories. Visitors experience this authenticity especially when they are temporarily joining the actors on that stage (Figure 3). Among the props most suit-able to tell stories are the 'Iron Age' clothes and shoes the families are wearing, the tools they are using (like Tom's bow) and the pots and dishes they use during meal times. The picture of the situation emerging is thus not so different from the staged photographs taken a century ago, which employed many evocative props for depict-ing prehistoric scenes of life (see e.g. Schöbel 2004, Figures 15.1 and 15.2).

Another kind of 'Iron Age' authenticity derives from the visitors' meetings and conversations with the prehistoric families. The visitors to Lethra were very keen to hear where each of us was coming from, how long we were staying and why we were here. Visitors typically asked what we were eating, whether the clothes were scratching on the skin, whether we were freezing in the houses, which beds we each were sleeping in and whether they were soft enough (Sagnlandet Lejre 2010, 9). However, what I understood they meant was that they would like to hear *our* Iron Age stories rather than stories about the Iron Age that no longer is. This became very notable when Tom was wearing a very modern bandage over his thumb after he had injured himself and many visitors enquired about this, visibly full of empathy and interest in *just that* side of Iron Age life. I also remember

Figure 3. Being in Lethra. Classic view of the full-size model of the Iron Age village at Lejre. Come closer as the performance is about to start and you are going to be in it! Photograph: Cornelius Holtorf 2011.

vividly how visitors from the Netherlands, New Zealand and the UK lightened up when they noticed that my son and I were not Danish either and more than happy to talk to them in English. In the eyes of the visitors, somehow, meeting the time-travelling families authenticated the village and its objects rather than vice versa. Even at other sites, researchers found that the conversations visitors had with contemporary time travellers posing as ancient inhabitants are the most memorable part of any visit (Svendsen 2010, 54). Insofar as such encounters and associated story-telling directly affect the visitors and express emotional relations, they are being touched by a different kind of performed authenticity, one that arises from a particular affect inside themselves and that connects to the world at large, not to prehistory (Knudsen and Waade 2010).

How the past comes to life

I have argued that at Lethra we can discern a shift over time, from a concern with accurate material representations of a living reality in another age ('these are houses and tools like those they used in the Iron Age') to the intention of the Land of Legends to offer living presentations of a material reality created in our own age ('these are the ancient-looking houses and tools we are renting out during the holidays'). The experts' ability to create accurate representations of the Iron Age, thus loses in significance as they are charged with facilitating for both the families and the visitors alike embodied experiences in which material culture that is vaguely associated with the prehistoric past – like Tom's bow – serves to evoke some sense of presence of the past. Although competent regarding prehistory, archaeologists educated at the Universities are at present not necessarily be best equipped to create such holistic experiences (see also Daugbjerg, n.d., 15).

Creating a sense of presence is an essential prerequisite for audiences to delve temporarily into another reality including staged performances (e.g. actors in plays, animals in zoos, Disney theme parks) and virtual realities (e.g. games, flight simulators, educational models). Many heritage attractions and, especially, open-air museums are seeking to create this sense of presence of the past. For visitors to Lethra, prehistoric families can bring the past to live in a particularly vivid way, but how is this experience created? In the previous section, I discussed how the experience of authenticity emerges within and among audiences. Here, I wish to extend this discussion to draw some lessons for the creation of a sense of presence of the past. Both notions are related insofar as they mutually reinforce each other.

Presence is the perception of non-mediation (or immediacy). The extent to which you feel 'being in the past' will depend on a number of factors that contribute to creating that perception of non-mediation and immediacy between the audience and the past (Lombard and Ditton 1997; Kansteiner 2005). Given that the operating term here is audience perception, it will not be surprising that inherent material properties of objects which are the result of past human behaviour and require experts for identification and accurate description do not play the main part. Instead, decisive for evoking a sense of presence of the past is the extent to which

(1) the past reality presented is consistent and understandable,
(2) audiences are familiar with the medium and willing to suspend any disbelief,
(3) the audience's senses are persuaded through rich and vivid impressions,
(4) some of the audience's pre-understandings and expectations are matched and
(5) audiences are involved and engaged in a meaningful way (adapted from Lombard and Ditton 1997).

These criteria can easily be exemplified at Lethra, and this accounts for the strength and quality of the audience's experience of being in the Iron Age. Iron Age life is certainly relatively consistent, especially, during the Land of Legend's opening hours (10 am–5 pm) when the prehistoric families are on stage and instructed to keep up appearances. Having said that, there are many modern objects in the village which visitors never see – not just various fire and first-aid equipment but also the inhabitants' sleeping bags, modern shoes, swim vests, secret food supplies both of individual families (e.g. sweets for the children, cigarettes, beer and wine for adults) and for the entire group (e.g. milk cartons, coffee in thermos), an electric socket, a water cooker, cameras, various modern tools incl. steel knives, toilet supplies, among other items (see also Steenstrup 1999, 60–64). Since all this is hidden, the Iron Age remains consistent and therefore, understandable. Broadly speaking, contemporary audiences are also familiar with the medium of full-size models and the concept of living history, so that the question of whether or not the houses are two millennia old or why the families are wearing those ancient-looking clothes does not arise and it is relatively easy for many to suspend disbelief. Rich and vivid experiences contribute to creating a sense of immersion into a different reality. As in theme parks, Lethra offers much detail including features of the natural building materials used and in the flora and fauna in which it is enmeshed.

The Iron Age is also something which the audience is already familiar with, not only from school education but also from TV documentaries and popular culture such as Asterix and Obelix. Insofar as Lethra, therefore, matches some of the audience's expectations of an Iron Age village, for example by being recognised as representing 'Asterix time', it becomes credible as an Iron Age village (see Gustafsson 2002, 166–169; Hjemdahl 2002, 117). This pre-existing familiarity based on conventional representations makes it also easier to know how to behave in the Iron Age village. Audiences are pre-programmed in understanding that the Iron Age village is about certain basic routines of daily life (and primarily not about, say, warfare, industrial labour or religious worship). The families are easily instructed and engaged in the various necessary tasks and even visitors happily get involved as and when possible, so that both, although to a different extent, can feel at home in the Iron Age village and perceive the presence of the past. Once this sense of presence is established, audiences are ready also for astonishing surprises that challenge other expectations.

Conclusions: beyond the Iron Age

The time-travellers tools of the trade have been transformed drastically over the past few decades. At the example of the full-size model of an Iron Age village in the Land of Legends Lejre, known as Lethra, I argue that the role material culture plays in facilitating a sense of being in the Iron Age has been changing. Initially, objects imitating ancient tools and structures, employed in a range of re-enacted technologies, were predominantly seen as scientific and didactic devices for learning more about prehistoric living conditions. The emphasis was on accuracy and tightly controlled conditions, with a focus on gaining abstract and cerebral understanding of the past. Ultimately, it was down to archaeological and other experts to guarantee and explain the historical accuracy that was visible in the copies, models and imitations visible in Lethra. Subsequently, the structures and objects on site turned increasingly into a stage-set and props with the function of providing audiences with holistic experiences that would evoke a sense of presence of a generic prehistoric past. The emphasis now was on creative imagination and quasification, with a focus on story-telling and performance, i.e. on intangible dimensions. The quality of the experience was ultimately down to the visitor's own ability to suspend disbelief and let themselves in for an embodied encounter with a different time and its inhabitants. The role of the experts changed to facilitating this experience for the visitors. This evident transformation applies in principle, not only to the many ordinary visitors of the Land of Legends but also to the prehistoric families inhabiting Lethra during the summer months; although, there will inevitably be some variation between different individuals and groups of people (which was however not the subject of this study).

In concluding, I wish to point to a couple of potentially important trends for cultural heritage in our age that arises from my study. They deserve to be studied in more detail and from a larger, comparative perspective in the future. Firstly, in line with the transformation of the role of material culture just described, we can see a trend towards temporalities that are embodied rather than abstract. Whereas, conventionally, heritage temporalities encompass fixed points on our linear timescale relating to the historic time being represented, the time associated with the site as heritage and the time of the visit (Jamal and Hill 2004); at Lethra an altogether different kind of temporality complements this picture. Here, different periods were spatially separated to the extent that the prehistoric families belonging to a relatively vague 'Asterix time' on the conventional timescale were at the same time given very clear instructions not to leave the specific area designated to the Iron Age and possibly appear in their Iron Age garments in the contemporary visitor centre or among the nineteenth century farm buildings on the other side of the Land of Legends (Sagnlandet Lejre 2010, 10). And if, for some reason, we had to go during opening hours to the modern kitchen and bathroom facilities or the electric dryer, we were to use a hidden path preventing us from passing through the Viking Age. As a result, the only minor subversion of the system that we prehistoric families managed to master during our weeklong stay was encouraging Tom to get some bread and waffles 'from the nineteenth century' (and its friendly inhabitants) after our own bread-baking efforts had failed. Significantly, this spatial digression seemed far more subversive than the sudden presence of the wrong type of food in the Iron Age. Even archaeological dates and periods had thus become transformed from abstract chronographical concepts associated with particular objects to palpable chronotopes, where clearly delineated areas were associated with embodied performances of vaguely defined and creatively imagined pasts.

Secondly, a previously very notable emphasis in archaeological heritage attractions on tangible past technologies, techniques and craft, skilfully investigated by experimental archaeology appears to give way to an emphasis on intangible narratives loosely associated with various objects. In Lethra, Tom's bow was not significant for how it was made and how it can be used, but for the contribution it made to the larger stories being told by visitors and families about past and present. The object qualities operative here were not any physical characteristics, but the potential to act as a potent prop on stage and thus to contribute to evoking a holistic sense of presence of the past. In that sense, objects become subjects: they speak to us as we use them or see them in use (Hjemdahl 2002, 116).

It is easy to be critical about some of these developments, but in this paper I have tried not to give in to the temptation of judging the outcome of a process of change by the standards of its starting point. Instead, I have been trying to understand the character of time travelling to the Iron Age at Lejre for what it is (now), rather than for what it is not (anymore). In Lethra, we appear to have moved on from mostly tangible re-enactments of prehistoric living conditions to largely intangible enactments of what it could mean to live in the past. In this development, we may see a glimpse of the future of heritage experiences.

Acknowledgements

I am grateful for being invited to this selection of papers and the conference session in 2012 on which it is based. I am also very grateful for the week in 2011, which I was able to spend in Lethra as 'prehistoric family', and to Tom, the other prehistoric families and the staff for making it so enjoyable. I would like to thank especially Lars Holten, Director and Henrik Schilling, then Head of Communication, at Land of Legends Lejre for their interest and active support of this research by offering their time for advice and making internal documents available. Mads Daugbjerg sent me detailed comments at an early stage and allowed me to cite from his unpublished paper. Erika Cederholm Andersson, Michaela Fenske, David Lowenthal, Bodil Petersson, Marianne Rasmussen, Stefanie Samida and one prehistoric family all sent me valuable comments and suggestions after reading a first draft. Some of them also made important unpublished work available to me. Finally, I wish to acknowledge the constructive criticism received during the editing process from the issue's editors, two anonymous referees and Laurajane Smith.

References

Beardsworth, A., and A. Bryman. 1999. "Late Modernity and the Dynamics of Quasification: The Case of the Themed Restaurant." *The Sociological Review* 47: 228–257.

Bleach, S. 2010. "Time Travel." *The Sunday Times: Travel Section*, January 31, 22–23.

Crang, M. 1996. "Magic Kingdom or a Quixotic Quest for Authenticity?" *Annals of Tourism Research* 23 (2): 415–431.

Daugbjerg, M. n.d. *Being There. Historical Re-enactment as Experience and/or Experiment.* Unpublished manuscript.

Dreschke, A. 2010. "Die Stämme von Köln (Tribes of Cologne)." Documentary Film, DVD. Germany, 89 min. Distribution: Realfiction Filmverleih.

Drieschner, C. 2005. "Living history als Freizeitbeschäftigung – Der Wikingerverein „Opinn Skjold e.V. " in Schleswig." *Kieler Blätter zur Volkskunde* 37: 31–61.

Fenske, M. 2007. "Geschichte, wie sie Euch gefällt – Historische Doku-Soaps als spätmoderne Handlungs-, Diskussions- und Erlebnisräume." In *Historizität. Vom Umgang mit Geschichte*, edited by A. Hartmann, S. Meyer, and R.-E. Mohrmann, 85–105. Münster: Waxmann.

Gustafsson, L. 2002. *Den förtrollande zonen. Lekar med tid, rum och identitet under Medeltidsveckan på Gotland.* Nora: Nya Doxa.

Hansen, H.-O. 1964. *Mand og hus.* Copenhagen: Rhodos.

Hewison, R. 1987. *The Heritage Industry. Britain in a Climate of Decline.* London: Methuen.

Hjemdahl, K. M. 2002. "History as a Cultural Playground." *Ethnologhia Europaea* 32 (2): 105–124.

Holten, L. 2010. *Sagnlandet Lejre: Time Travel as Strategy.* Unpublished presentation, Lejre, June 15.

Holtorf, C. 2007. "Time Travel: A New Perspective on the Distant Past." In *On the Road. Studies in Honour of Lars Larsson*, edited by B. Hårdh, K. Jennbert, and D. Olausson, 127–132. Stockholm: Almqvist & Wiksell.

Holtorf, C. 2010. "On the Possibility of Time Travel." *Lund Archaeological Review* 15–16 (2009–2010): 31–41.

Holtorf, C. 2012. "The Past as Carnival. Review Article of A. Dreschke (dir.) 2010, Die Stämme von Köln. DVD, 89 min." *Time and Mind* 5 (2): 195–202.

Holtorf, C. 2013. "On Pastness: A Reconsideration of Materiality in Archaeological Object Authenticity." *Anthropological Quarterly* 86 (2): 427–444.

Holtorf, C., and B. Petersson, eds. 2010. "The Archaeology of Time Travel." *Lund Archaeological Review* 15–16 (2009–2010): 27–98.

Jamal, T., and S. Hill. 2004. "Developing a Framework for Indicators of Authenticity: The Place and Space of Cultural and Heritage Tourism." *Asia Pacific Journal of Tourism Research* 9 (4): 353–371.

Kalshoven, P. T. 2012. *Crafting the Indian. Knowledge, Desire and Play in Indianist Reenactment.* New York: Berghahn.

Kansteiner, W. 2005. "Alternate Worlds and Invented Communities. History and Historical Consciousness in the Age of Interactive Media." In *Manifestos for History*, edited by K. Jenkins, S. Morgan, and A. Munslow, 131–148. London: Routledge.

Keefer, E., ed. 2006. *Lebendige Vergangenheit. Vom Experiment zur Zeitreise.* Stuttgart: Theiss.

Knudsen, B. T., and A. M. Waade. 2010. "Performative Authenticity in Tourism and Spatial Experience: Rethinking the Relation between Travel, Place and Emotion." In *Re-investing Authenticity. Tourism, Place and Emotions*, edited by B. T. Knudsen and A. M. Waade, 1–19. Bristol: Channel View.

Kristiansen, K. 2001. "Resor i tiden." In *På resande fot*, edited by ETOUR, 144–153. Stockholm: Sellin.

Land of Legends. 2009. *Velkommen i Sagnlandet Lejre* [Slightly Different English Version Entitled Welcome to the Land of Legends Lejre]. Unpublished press information distributed over the site's homepage (no longer accessible now).

Land of Legends. n.d. (a) *Behind the Scenes*. Accessed March 10, 2013. http://www.sagnlandet.dk/Behind-the-scenes.449.0.html.

Land of Legends. n.d. (b) *Mission*. Accessed March 10, 2013. http://www.sagnlandet.dk/Mission.274.0.html.

Lombard, M., and T. Ditton. 1997. "At the Heart of it all. The Concept of Presence." *Journal of Computer-Mediated Communication* 3 (2). Accessed March 10, 2013. http://jcmc.indiana.edu/vol3/issue2/lombard.html.

Lowenthal, D. 2013. *The Past is a Foreign Country – Revisited*. Cambridge: Cambridge University Press.

Meldgaard, M., and M. Rasmussen, eds. 1994. "Historisk-Arkæologisk Forsøgscenter i Lejre. 30 års forsøg med fortiden." *Naturens Verden* 4–5: 121–176.

Melotti, M. 2011. *The Pastic Venuses: Archaeological Tourism in Post-modern Society*. Newcastle upon Tyne: Cambridge Scholars.

Paardekooper, R. 2006. "Interview: Sensing History with Hans-Ole Hansen." *EuroREA* 3/2006. Accessed March 10, 2013. http://journal.exarc.net/eurorea-3-2006/mm/interview-sensing-history-hans-ole-hansen.

Petersson, B. 2003. *Föreställningar om det förflutna. Arkeologi och rekonstruktion*. Lund: Nordic Academic Press.

Petersson, B., and L.-E. Narmo. 2011. "A Journey in Time." In *Experimental Archaeology. Between Enlightenment and Experience*, edited by B. Petersson and L. E. Narmo, 27–48. Lund: Department of Archaeology and Ancient History, University of Lund.

Rasmussen, M. 2011. "Under the Same Roof. Experimental Research and Interpretation with Examples from the Construction of House Models." In *Experimental Archaeology. Between Enlightenment and Experience*, edited by B. Petersson and L. E. Narmo, 147–166. Lund: Department of Archaeology and Ancient History, University of Lund.

Sagnlandet Lejre. 2010. *Fortidsfamilie i jernalderlandsbyen Lethra. En nyttig håndbog til jeres ophold i fortiden*. Revised June, 2010. Unpublished Handbook for Prehistoric Families. Lejre.

Samida, S. n.d. *Moderne Zeitreisen oder Die performative Aneignung vergangener Lebenswelten*. Unpublished manuscript.

Schöbel, G. 2004. "Lake-dwelling Museums. Academic Research and Public Information." In *Living on the Lake in Prehistoric Europe. 150 Years of Lake-dwelling Research*, edited by F. Menotti, 221–236. London: Routledge.

Schöbel, G. 2010. "Archäologische Museen in Deutschland – Traditionen, Situationen und Herausforderungen." *Archäologisches Nachrichtenblatt* 15 (2): 202–215.

Schou, V. 2011. *Jernaldersko til brug under ophold i Lethra*. Accessed March 10, 2013. http://visc.dk/projekter?t=148.

Steenstrup, J. 1999. "Jernalderen – en legeplads i nutiden. Et studie af nutidige familier i en rekonstrueret jernalderby." Specialerække no. 137, Masters thesis, University of Copenhagen, Dept. of Anthropology.

Svendsen, A. R. 2010. "Learning through Experience. A Study of Visitors' Experiences and Learning at Foteviken Archaeological Open-air Museum." *EuroREA* 7/2010: 51–54.

Zipsane, H. 2012. *Jamtli is Going Crazy! Entrance Fee up 120 Percent! – People Want Quality and They are Willing to Pay for it*. Manuscript, 8. Östersund: NCK. Accessed May 25, 2013. http://www.nckultur.org/index.php/oevriga-publikationer.

Drought and Rain: re-creations in Vietnamese, cross-border heritage

Rivka Syd Eisner

Department of Culture and Society, Aarhus University, Denmark

The *Drought and Rain* dance trilogy, by Vietnamese–French choreographer Ea Sola, evokes memory, history and everyday practices through song, stylised gesture and stark, graceful images. The performances aim not to represent ancient and wartime Vietnamese pasts as much as call attention to the ways in which the present and past invigorate and co-create each other. The unsettled, recursive and processual nature of Ea Sola's performances suggest it is necessary to periodically re-encounter the continuing legacies of violence. The performances enact a different form of historical (re)productivity, not predicated on a linear materialism, but based on processes of temporal turn and re-turn. I employ the most recent performance in the series, *Drought and Rain 2011,* as both subject and lens for exploring the unfinished dynamics of memory–history, and as a site and practice of cultural heritage. Embodying a hybrid mix of multiple re-performance categories, the *Drought and Rain* performances stretch current notions of heritage and are cross-border in terms of culture, nationality, arts genre and aesthetics and political implication. Primary points of focus include: the non-originality of performance, the unfinished nature of the past, and the way in which the *Drought and Rain* performances propose a counter-memory of the future.

Introduction: *do they remember the centuries past?*

With poise and determination in her eyes, Đoàn Thị Kết, a Vietnamese woman in her eighties, takes the stage and begins to sing. When not performing with Company Ea Sola, Đoàn works as a farmer in the rural rice fields of northern Vietnam. She first set foot on the professional dance stage in 1995, at the world premier performance of *Drought and Rain.*[1] Now more than a decade and a half later she again finds herself performing in a European city far away from home, this time in *Drought and Rain 2011.* Framing the dance–drama about to unfold, Đoàn looks out to the audience and tells us in sung Vietnamese 'This epic dance – "Drought and Rain"/Recounts the history of thousands of destinies'. The look on her face is energised and concentrated, her body poised for action like a coiled spring. She continues, keeping the suspense-filled air ripe with anticipation:

On the land [Vietnam], rich with alluvial deposits wedded to blood.
My ancestors for centuries opened up our pathways.
This epic dance – 'Drought and Rain'.
Recounts the history of thousands of destinies.
And this is what the poem said:
(*voices reply:* what did it say?)
The present generation, do they remember the centuries past?[2]

Đoàn's verses are drawn from the opening prologue of *Drought and Rain 2011,* by Vietnamese–French choreographer Ea Sola, which premiered on 27 June 2011 at the Napoli Teatro Festival in Naples, Italy. I viewed the performance a few months later at the King's Theatre during the Edinburgh International Festival on 1–2 September 2011.

Drought and Rain 2011 is a lyrical, contemporary epic poem, danced, sung and set to music by over twenty Vietnamese performers. The performance is a redoubled re-enactment. On one level, it is a re-performance of embodied traditions, historical events and personal/cultural memories – most centrally those of rural Vietnamese women, like Đoàn's, everyday experiences and memories of her country's mythic history and of the Vietnamese–American war. It is also an avant-garde chronicle of Ea Sola's process of working through and (re)encountering her own memories of war and its aftermath. Additionally, as the name implies, *Drought and Rain 2011* is also a re-do performance. It is the third iteration of Ea Sola's *Drought and Rain* series, preceded by *Drought and Rain* (1995) and *Drought and Rain: Vol. 2* (2005).

The three performances aim not to represent ancient and wartime pasts as much as call attention to the ways in which the present and past continue to invigorate and co-create each other. Ea Sola's aesthetics of temporal bricolage make the performances historically instable – they shift, they t-a-k-e their t-i-m-e, they rupture, repeat, double and double-back, refusing a linear plotline. As a series, they also defy linear developmental change, instead relating to each other through citational, constellating associations, incorporating new features and different dancers with each incarnation of the dance. The unsettled, recursive nature of Ea Sola's performances suggests it is necessary to periodically re-encounter the continuing legacies of violent pasts. Her work illuminates and enacts a different form of historical (re)productivity, not predicated on a linear materialism, but based on processes of temporal turn and re-turn.

This essay engages with the multiple layers of re-enactment and re-performance at play within *Drought and Rain 2011* and, to a lesser degree, its two preceding variations. I am especially interested in the *Drought and Rain* trilogy's play with re-enactment within and across multiple performance contexts – such as everyday life performance, cultural performance and aesthetic performance – and how this dynamic mix complicates our understanding of both re-performance and heritage. The *Drought and Rain* dances offer a particularly complex example of re-enactment in part because they simultaneously (1) transpose everyday life gestures into an aesthetic performance context as well as (2) transfer gestures and artistic traditions from one aesthetic performance to another. While heritage discourses tend to understand the latter as a form of traditional cultural inheritance, the former category largely falls outside its purview. Thus, with both forms of re-performance at play, works such as Ea Sola's *Drought and Rain* series present a varied and mixed, hybrid category of performance that exceeds and exists outside of what is commonly understood as heritage.

Adding to the complexity, the re-performed pasts and memories in *Drought and Rain 2011* are both transnational and deeply connected to Vietnamese traditions and temporalities. The performance plays with and weaves together history, myth, memory, everyday gesture, gender stereotypes, affective encounters between performers and observers and contemporary and 'traditional' art forms. Considering this hybridity, how might these mythopoetic performances be understood as heritage? More broadly, how might performance's notorious non-originality (its foundation in mimetic 'play' and re-citation), as seen in the *Drought and Rain* series, help re-theorise heritage beyond 'distinction[s] between truthful models [or originals] and fictional representations' (Diamond 1996, 1)? I wish to consider how thinking of the three *Drought and Rain* performances as cultural heritage might expand our understanding of what heritage is or can be. Engaging these questions requires exploration of what Rebecca Schneider calls the 'persistent pressure of the re-do, and its indeterminate tangle between the done, the re-done, and the not yet done' with a focus on embodied practice and the intersubjective, affective registers of Ea Sola's re-enactments (2011, 110).

I employ *Drought and Rain 2011* as both subject and lens for exploring the multi-faceted 'performative remains' of memory-history, and as a potential site and practice of cultural heritage (Schneider 2011, 19). To do this, I begin with a short discussion of re-enacted performances and then give some background on the *Drought and Rain* series, addressing how they came about as well as some of the histories, memories and politics the performances embody and convey. This leads to the subject of heritage and (re)performance, and what it means to consider the *Drought and Rain* performances as 'intangible cultural heritage', or *dialogic* cultural heritage. Finally, I highlight four provisional, performance-centred dynamics of heritage re-enactment that may be of value to heritage studies: heritage re-enactment can (1) 'preserve' through performative repetition, (2) promote affective, interkinaesthetic correspondence, (3) practice cross-border culture and communication and (4) help condition change/possibility for futures-in-the-making. Throughout the discussion I address the non-originality of performance, the unfinished nature of the past, and the way in which the *Drought and Rain* performances propose a counter-memory of the future.

(Re)making the old new again

Ea Sola's *Drought and Rain 2011* begins much like her fist *Drought and Rain* performance, in quiet, almost breathless, stillness. On the opening night of the performance, I sit in the audience of the King's Theatre in downtown Edinburgh, Scotland. I have seen Ea Sola's other *Drought and Rain* performances before: the first version from 1995 many times on DVD, and the second iteration, *Drought and Rain Vol. 2,* in 2006 in the city of Hue, Vietnam, and then again in the USA at the University of North Carolina at Chapel Hill later that same year. Waiting for the performance to unfold, anticipating the new and unknown but also something familiar, I know to expect 'the double, the second, the clone, the uncanny, the *againness* of (re)enactment' (Schneider 2011, 6).

As the stage lights come up, black and white tracings of misty mountaintops depicting landscapes in northern Vietnam come into view. This is the same scene audiences first witnessed in the 1995 version. Scrims veil the floor-to-ceiling ink paintings, making the scene all the more mediated and mysterious as the barely moving outlines of the dancers come into focus below. The performers creep forward holding life-size paper cutouts of famous figures from Vietnamese history. Some of the figures are historically 'real', while others are more mythic, but all are mythologised.[3] The dancers approach so slowly, at first it is difficult to discern the women performers from the cutout figures they hold and animate (see Figure 1). Drumming begins softly and builds to a crescendo as the women come into full view. After a few moments, the stage goes dark. This scene is replicated almost exactly the same as the first *Drought and Rain,* but then something new happens.

A trail of soft, filtered light rises on a lone silhouette, the shrouded outline of an anonymous individual. The shadowed being is wrapped in a clear plastic rain jacket and traditional conical hat (*Nón lá*), moving slowly, so slowly, across the stage – she is, it is, most certainly a ghost. The ghost, the *revenant,* is the indeterminate time traveller, beckoning us to follow her, and foreshadowing – along with the blending of live and drawn figures, historical and mythic – that this performance will not be abiding by a familiar, linear, progress-oriented sense of time or truth. I wonder as I watch and wait for more: Why has this ghost, and this performance, returned? What does it mean for this performance, these movements, songs, gestures and memories to return and re-surface again on European stages?

The short answer as to why this performance has returned again is that *Drought and Rain 2011* was commissioned as part of the Edinburgh International Festival.

Figure 1. Opening scene from *Drought and Rain 2011.* Photograph reprinted with permission from Company Ea Sola.

In line with current trends of 'reenacting precedent art' in the fields of performance art, dance and theatre, Ea Sola was asked to create a repeat performance of her first internationally acclaimed dance from 1995, *Drought and Rain* (Schneider 2011, 28). Richard Schechner writes critically of this fashion of 'redoing avant-garde classics,' a category into which *Drought and Rain 2011* could arguably fall, calling the phenomenon part of the current 'conservative avant-garde generating its own repetitions,' a practice that he views as overwhelmingly nostalgic, politically ineffectual or ambivalent and brand-seeking (2010, 905).

Schneider, and others such as Chalmers (2008) and Morgan (2010) are also intrigued by this re-performance trend. Like Schechner, Schneider calls attention to the ironies of Marina Abramović's recent efforts to canonise herself and copyright her works where once she and others creating performance art in the 1960s and 1970s declared their acts irreproducible and anti-canonical by their very nature and defining intentions (2011, 4–6, 28). However, Schneider, Chalmers and Morgan are less cynical than Schechner. Chalmers, drawing on the earlier work of Philip Auslander (2002), considers the changing meanings of authenticity figured through re-performance and sees the trend as a waning baby boomer era 'nostalgic process of historicization and sacralization' (2008, 23). But, she says, the rise of re-performance shows how authenticity is returning 'as a performative repetition rather than as a mere reproduction' (2008, 38). Morgan also notes how Abramović's earlier 2005 Guggenheim show *Seven Easy Pieces* 're-performed and re-interpreted' her work and the works of others, taking 'considerable liberties in terms of how she re-staged the various events' (2010, 11).

Schneider, Chalmers and Morgan do not share Schechner's lament about the 'lost opportunities' of precedent art repetitions, preferring to make closer, nuanced examinations of each particular re-enactment to see what may be (re)taking place (2010, 911). Instead they ask, what do these repetitions reveal about our investments in the 'real', the 'original', 'authenticity', material remains, archives and linear notions of time that do not always seem to hold? They each see vital ways in which different forms of re-enactment performance – those that aim for mimetic perfection as well as those that consciously re-interpret, those within the 'high arts' and those within popular/amateur practice – may help enable dialogue, questions and critical awareness. As Morgan expresses, building on Krauss (1999), 'performance art is less about limiting itself to a single course of ideology than opening up new thresholds of psychological, narrative, and interactive content' (2010, 5) such that the continuing vitality of re-performance is dependent upon its re-contextualisation 'within the ongoing present' (2). Schneider suggests that re-enactments do, and moreover must, continue to recur because 'historical events, like wars, are never discretely completed, but carry forth in embodied cycles of memory that do not delimit the remembered to the past' (2011, 32). Thus, the lengthier and potentially more complicated answer as to why another *Drought and Rain* – and why this re-enactment might be an important site and practice of heritage – perhaps lies in the deeper political investments of avant-garde art and in the ever-unfinished condition of 'war's performative remains' (Schneider 2011, 19).

*Drought*s *and Rain*s: a dance trilogy

Having been forced to flee Vietnam for France during the final years of the Vietnamese–American War in the early 1970s, Ea Sola sought out her first chance to return. Her opportunity came in 1990, soon after Vietnam began reopening its borders as part of the country's new economic policies (Đổi mới) initiated in 1986. Upon return, Ea Sola decided to live in the rural northern countryside to carry out what she describes as a kind of anthropological study of Vietnamese tradition, history and culture, learning with and from the local people, and in particular the older women. She shared meals with the women and listened to their stories, learning about their everyday labour, wartime memories, cultural knowledges, as well as the hardships and triumphs that comprised the women's lives. The first *Drought and Rain* performance grew out of Ea Sola's friendship with these women.[4]

Ea Sola worked intensively with the women to develop a dance made out of symbolic gestures and embodied images drawn from their personal and shared experiences of surviving through decades of colonial violence and war with France, imperial war with the USA, and years of post-war struggle. Describing her rehearsal process, Ea Sola explains that she wishes for the performers to 'discover themselves through the work and through the subject matter. I don't want the dancer to interpret a character. I want the dancer to be a consciousness in himself [*sic*]' (*Việt Nam News* 2011). The resulting *Drought and Rain* performance was not a literal rendering of the women's memories and life stories, but a combination of what Nathan Stucky has called 'natural performance' or the 're/performance of ordinary interaction' and a more Brechtian-inspired embodied condensation of the affective registers of their personal and shared pasts (1993, 168).

Drought and Rain premiered in 1995 to great international acclaim. Audiences were captivated not only by the unique and moving poetics of the dance, but also by the opportunity to catch one of the first glimpses of Vietnamese culture in the post-war era. One of the most intriguing elements was that Ea Sola's dance was performed by the older women themselves, not by professional dancers. As survivors of the American War, most of the women were in their 60s or 70s, as well as some in their 80s. The fact that the women were 'ordinary people' appealed to western audiences desires to witness and consume 'authentic' Vietnamese culture. The dance was authentic, or genuine, in that it was a sincere and powerful way of grappling with war's continuing aftermath, the persistence of human spirit and tradition, and the important effort to forge new cross-cultural dialogues.[5]

However, as an avant-garde work, the performance never sought to be authentic in the sense of re-presenting 'realistic' depictions or anything like 'pure' and untainted cultural traditions. As with both successive performances, the first *Drought and Rain* was, to use Paul Rae's fitting phrase, 'agricultural' in the sense that it combined a multiplicity of cultural traditions and practices: contemporary dance aesthetics with satirical Vietnamese sung drama (*Hát chèo*) elements, twentieth century wartime memory with mythic histories, ritualised gestures with modern-day objects and affects (2002). Ea Sola's dance rendered commonly held binaries, such as old vs. new, east vs. west, and 'high' vs. 'low' arts, obsolete categories of witness and appraisal. The performance enacted a new form of transcultural, aggregative temporal hybridity without becoming ahistorical or homogenously multi-cultural. Instead, audiences were invited to encounter the performance through affective correspondence with the dancers and their collectively expressed memories, opening viewers' to embodied forms of knowing through intersubjective 'kinesthetic awareness/imitation', more suggestive and evocative than definitive (Thrift 2008, 237).

Ten years past before *Drought and Rain Vol. 2* took the stage (again) in 2005. In the aftermath of 11 September 2001, and the USA's subsequent 'war on terror', Ea Sola felt compelled to re-visit the dance, to continue her personal exploration and cross-border conversation about war, memory and social responsibility with her dancers and with international audiences. *Drought and Rain Vol. 2* is clearly part of the series, yet has less in common with first and third versions. Most strikingly, the dancers in *Drought and Rain Vol. 2* were young professional, classically trained dancers from the Hanoi Ballet Opera. Whereas, the first *Drought and Rain* focused primarily on Vietnam, the second iteration used the legacies of war in Vietnam as a springboard for exploring post-war individuals' relationships and responsibilities to violence currently taking place elsewhere in the world. As *Drought and Rain Vol. 2* makes clear, the three performances engage the memory of war in Vietnam but are also about our responses to human violence within current contexts.

When Ea Sola set out to (re)make *Drought and Rain 2011,* most of the women from the first performance were in their 80s and 90s and too old to carry out the necessary performance work. Several had died. Just two dancers from the first performance, Ngô Thị Cát and Đoàn Thị Kết, joined *Drought and Rain 2011.* The other dancers, aged 58–75, are from 'a slightly younger generation whose experiences are different,' Ea Sola explains, '[t]hey did not fight [in the Vietnamese-American War], though they have memories of going to the front and singing to console the wounded. It seemed a beautiful image: instead of carrying guns, these women brought songs' (Hickling 2011).

The older women from the first performance are not as much re-placed as they are layered within and re-presenced by the younger dancers of *Drought and Rain 2011.* Drawing on Adrienne Rich, Schneider writes, '[e]ntering, or reenacting, an event or a set of acts (acts of art or acts of war),' and in this case of *Drought and Rain* both together, 'may be [...] an act of survival, of keeping alive *as* passing on (in the multiple sense of the phrase "to pass")' (2011, 7). *Drought and Rain 2011* and its earlier variations are acts of survival, possibly for Ea Sola, the performers, some audience members, cultural traditions, and countless unknown others who have already 'passed'. These performances are also acts of ethical relations; they are imbued with the imperative of 'passing on' the memory, the heritage and inheritance, of war's destructive forces across cultures and to successive generations. These acts of trans-generational as well as trans-cultural passing on, for survival and for social ethics, are what make the *Drought and Rain* performances an important form of dialogic, cross-border heritage, a point to which I will return later.

All three *Drought and Rain* performances share one central, powerful and connecting gesture. The culminating moment in each performance occurs when the dancers stand together in a row and stare out across the theatre space in complete stillness, holding pictures out for the audience to witness. In the first *Drought and Rain,* the older women take photographs, of relatives and friends killed during the Vietnamese–American war, out of their shirt pockets and hold them out to the viewers (see Figure 2). These photographs are in the style of those traditionally placed on ancestral altars in Vietnamese family homes. Ea Sola borrows this traditional practice, adapts it to the dance, and in so doing redoubles and remakes its meanings in order to both honour the dead and translate awareness of Vietnamese wartime losses for foreign viewers. In *Drought and Rain Vol. 2,* the young dancers also hold out pictures of people for the audience to witness. This time the images are

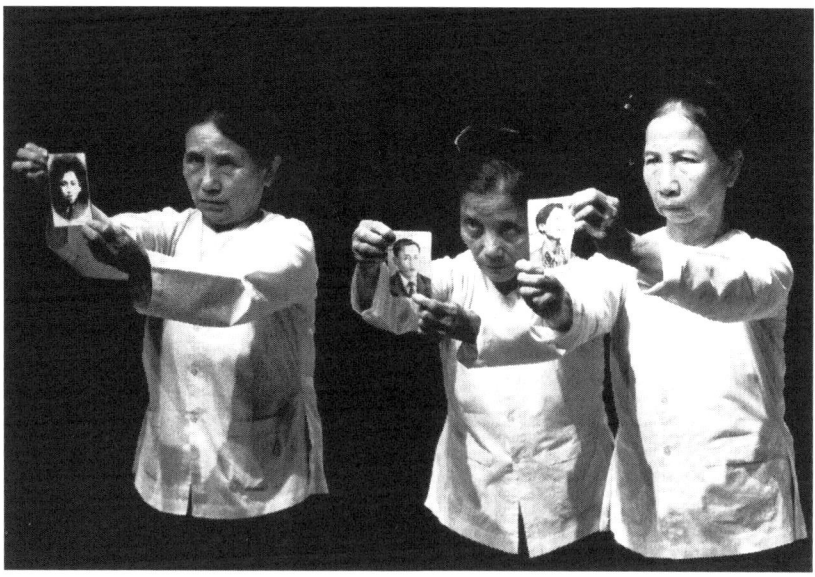

Figure 2. The women hold up photos of those who died during the war in the first *Drought and Rain* (1995). Photograph reprinted with permission from Company Ea Sola.

Figure 3. The young dancers from *Drought and Rain Vol. 2* (2005) show photographs to the audience. Photograph reprinted with permission from Company Ea Sola.

drawings of individuals from around the world who were recently killed in violent conflict (see Figure 3).

The third re-enactment of this gesture in *Drought and Rain 2011* is virtually the same as in the first performance except that different women hold the photographs. Each picture of a lost loved one stands in for hundreds of thousands of others. As the dancers stare out at the audience, one feels a current of what Susan Foster calls 'interkinesthetic connectivity', a mutually-charged affective exchange between performers and audience (2008, 46). The dancers stand motionless, the drums have gone silent, and we in the audience are also stilled. In this moment, each time I see the performance, I find myself holding my breath as if time is momentarily stopped. But this stillness, in all three performances, is very much alive. Those in the audience witness the simultaneous liveliness and deadness (photographs of the living after they have died) of those whose lives have passed and are, through re-enactment and audience witnessing, *still* passing (Schneider 2011).

These dances evoke and communicate war's affective legacies, but they are not transparent in their expressivity (Desmond 1997). The memories and experiences they re-enact are complex, multiple, oblique and evolving. Through the use of repeated gesture, one senses the layeredness, banality and obsessive tendencies of memory along with stylised performativities of violence that enable and produce contexts for the next violent acts (Anderson and Menon 2009, 6). Repetition, coupled with the performance's fits and starts, and deliberate slowness, puts viewers in a different relationship with time, perhaps evoking the realities of 'times of war', wherein protracted everyday banalities and eruptive, insurgent traumas coexist uncomfortably.

Audience members, particularly reviewers writing about *Drought and Rain 2011*, appear to have the most difficulty with Ea Sola's use of repetition and slowness.[6] One commentator expresses 'it is a slow-paced work, with too much repetition' (Anderson 2011). While another says there was a 'lack of momentum', and that the performance 'reflects this sense of the power of stillness, but [...] it is used far too frequently to have any real effect' (Whitham 2011). These and other similar criticisms seem to suggest that some viewers are unwilling or unable to encounter the performance on its own terms: with openness to the sometimes uncomfortable but potentially illuminating affective awareness of intentional, excessive repetition and slowness. Perhaps, as Auslander expresses, this is partly because 'audiences now expect live performances to resemble mediatized ones' where the preference is for experience to be increasingly sped up rather than slowed down (2002, 25). These qualities of slowness and repetition strangely overwhelm the senses and emotions by being, as evident in the above critics' comments, at once 'too much' and 'not enough'.

In reviewing audience responses from all three *Drought and Rain* performances, it is clear that most people have strong feelings about the work. In general, commentators either find the performances powerful, moving and original or they dislike them because of their slowness, repetition and oblique rather than literal reference to the war. Overall, international responses to the first *Drought and Rain* were most favourable, perhaps because at this time Ea Sola was a newcomer to the global arena of contemporary dance, Vietnam was just beginning to reopen its borders, the older women were survivors of war, and because, as Chalmers suggests, the 1990s were a time when the 1960s generation became more acutely concerned about its 'generational legacy' (2008, 35). *Drought and Rain Vol. 2* received the harshest critiques, most often for its unsettling frenetic and abstract movement sequences. Responses to *Drought and Rain 2011,* while divided, tend to be more complementary and similar to those from the 1995 version. Experiencing each of the three *Drought and Rain* performances, albeit the first one on DVD, as well as a number of Ea Sola's other works, has sensitised me to the subtly accumulative, perception-altering power of repetition and slowness. Familiarity with the works helps me chart common, repeated threads of meaning between the three performances (for example, the recurring photograph gesture, the use of eyes and looking, etc.) as well as encounter each performance on its own temporal, aesthetic and (non)narrative grounds without imposing particular expectations for what a dance addressing memory of the Vietnamese–American War 'should' entail.

The *Drought and Rain* performances embody the uncertainties and unfinishedness of difficult pasts that are still passing. Rather than leaving the performance with anything like a clear or full 'understanding' of what surviving war was like for Vietnamese women, the performance instils the feeling that one has but glimpsed unsettling worlds of experience and memory to which one will ever only have partial access. The dance's uncertainty and indeterminacy may be frustrating to some viewers, but this partial view is important in that it resists full apprehension and deflects feelings of ownership over other's pasts (overidentification and universalisation). In this sense, the performance potentially helps foster a more ethical practice of witnessing 'beyond recognition' (Oliver 2001). Within this context of partial, affective witnessing and knowing, how might *Drought and Rain 2011* and its prior performances be understood as heritage? Whose heritage?

Intangible cultural heritage and/as the performed copy

The term heritage 'has been associated traditionally with that which is inherited or handed on from one generation to the next', such that 'heritage is the contemporary use of the past, including both its interpretation and representation' (Smith 2003, 82). The *Drought and Rain* performances fit well within Melanie K. Smith's broad reading of heritage: as the interpretation and re-enactment of memory (of war, loss and survival) and long-standing beliefs and practices (of village culture and everyday life, Vietnamese art forms, mythic histories), transferred across generations, re-contextualised and remade within the present. The dances perform Vietnamese heritage and poetically express knowledges of which most non-Vietnamese may only have limited cultural access. As a hybrid cultural creation, expressing Vietnamese and transnational conditions of the war and its aftermath, the performances also evoke the heritage of the USA's imperial ambitions and destructive forces as well as a more far-reaching geopolitical call for nations, individuals and global society to learn from the past in the effort to mitigate future violence. The heritage performed in the *Drought and Rain* series is Vietnamese, and in different ways American, and in still additional ways it re-enacts a global inheritance.

Under official categories of heritage, as a performance of embodied knowledges and practices, the *Drought and Rain* trilogy would likely fall within the classification of 'intangible cultural heritage',[7] According to the 2003 UNESCO (United Nations Educational, Science and Cultural Organisation) parameters, intangible cultural heritage refers to:

> the practices, representations, expressions, knowledge, skills – as well as the instruments, objects, artefacts and cultural spaces associated therewith – that communities, groups and, in some cases, individuals recognise as part of their cultural heritage. This intangible cultural heritage, transmitted from generation to generation, is recreated by communities and groups in response to their environments, their interaction with nature and their history, and provides them with a sense of identity and continuity, thus promoting respect for cultural diversity and human creativity. (UNESCO 2003, Article 2.1)

127

As Ahmed (2006, 299) paraphrases, the Convention definition also includes 'oral traditions and expressions, language, performing arts, social practices, rituals, festive events and traditional craftsmanship'. At first glance, it seems the *Drought and Rain* performances would fulfil these requirements. The notion of performative change through 'recreation' is even included in the official declaration.

However, state and international institutions' interests in intangible cultural heritage are ostensibly grounded in the desire to preserve old or ancient, 'traditional' social and/or public practices that appear under threat of disappearance[8] rather than something like a contemporary dance, even when it draws on long-standing arts practices as in the case of the *Drought and Rain* performances.[9] Richard Kurin expresses that the UNESCO definition 'can encompass a broader range of activity than the framers assumed' and that the majority of 'experts who helped formulate the Convention assumed that intangible cultural heritage is traditional culture' (2004, 69). The focus on 'traditional' and threatened art forms is understandable and important. However, the underlying assumptions about what constitutes intangible cultural heritage, how it ought to be preserved and the narrow parameters of what ends up being recognised (Kurin 2004, 74), may perpetuate misconceptions about the perceived innate frailty of embodied practices (Bouchenaki 2004), overemphasise the idea of 'authentic' and pure art forms (Taylor 2008; Kenny 2009; Smith and Waterton 2009), and create categories where other forms of important and challenging heritage practice are left out of the discussion.

Insight into the problematics of heritage classification is offered by Barbara Kirshenblatt-Gimblett in her critique of UNESCO's continuing debate on how to categorise and 'secure' intangible cultural heritage that 'belongs' to or is co-created by multiple individuals and/or cultural groups (2006). The institution has difficulty escaping legally-based notions of single party/culture origination and ownership. When it does move beyond the single culture single heritage model, the inheritor becomes a vague and differently problematic universal 'humanity' (2006, 183–185). Both extremes do not allow enough space for complex, cross-cultural and cross-border, messy, contested and provisional forms of what could be called *dialogic cultural heritage*.[10] The *Drought and Rain* performances enact culturally specific as well as culturally dialogic global heritage. They are dialogic in the dual sense of performing agricultural aesthetics as well as putting into practice Ea Sola's desire that the performances help spark thought, conversation and communication – about the multiple legacies of violence that impinge upon local/global presents and futures – across borders of cultural and national difference.[11]

Regarding the 'intangible,' Diana Taylor also expresses, despite the inclusion of this category in internationally recognised definitions of heritage, there has been difficulty in persuading international bodies focused on preservation, such as UNESCO, of the key importance of practice, or performance (2008). She explains that 'the objectifying approach to the "intangible"' is at odds with 'the "here" and "now" of performance, the body memory of those performing, the meaning of the interaction between performers and participants/spectators' (2008, 94). The problem, it seems, is the very ontology of performance: enactment and re-enactment, the process of 'doing', and 're-doing', heritage. Despite the Convention's statement that intangible cultural heritage is transmitted across generations and 'is constantly recreated by communities and groups' (UNESCO 2003, Article 2.1), the 'authorised heritage discourse' (Smith 2006, 4) often implicitly assumes discrete cultural origins and/or 'authentic' tradition (Kenny 2009; Smith and Waterton 2009).

As Taylor argues in her discussion of what she calls the embodied knowledges and practices of the 'repertoire', (2003) it is crucial to recognise that '[t]he way to understand and preserve practice is through practice' (2008, 101). Unfortunately, she finds that UNESCO's definitions of intangible cultural heritage treat cultural practice as if it is temporary, vulnerable and caught in the past (2008, 99). This is problematic because it categorises cultural performance and embodied practice as historical relics, with the tendency to think of translating intangible cultural heritage into 'some manifestation of materiality' as the best way to preserve it (Bouchenaki 2004, 9). The challenge that performance brings to traditional renderings of heritage is that without change and exchange, embodied practices cease to exist and/or lose their meaningfulness within contemporary contexts. Embodied practices, or performances, do not live without re-enactment. Re-enactments always involve sameness and alteration within and between the 'doing' and the 'thing done' (Diamond 1996, 1). If heritage projects wish to include embodied practices and knowledges, nuanced understandings of re-enactment and the risky yet vital changes that come with each (re)new(ed) iteration are crucial. Heritage discourses appear to be moving in the direction of embracing the contingencies of practice in and as preservation (Hassard 2009; Skounti 2009; Smith and Akagawa 2009). However, as Laurajane Smith and Natsuko Akagawa contend, the 'jury [...] is still out on the degree to which this [conceptual] shift has actually occurred within international debates and practices' (2009, 2).

What does consideration of the *Drought and Rain* performances as cultural heritage do for our understanding of what heritage is or can be? Welcoming such hybrid performances, with all their untidy 're's' and repetitions, into conceptualisations of heritage would 'encourage a permeable understanding of history and change' and help highlight that what we name as heritage is messy, provisional and contested (Diamond 1996, 2). All of these qualities run counter to long-standing ideas about preserving authentic originals, a concept to which heritage often clings for definition and legitimacy. But in fact, performance is essential to the work of preservation in that it is only through activation and re-enlivening that the past, deemed heritage or not, endures (Diamond 1996; Pollock 1998; Taylor 2008; Schneider 2011; Eisner 2013). Mimesis, the foundation of performance, lacks definitive origins, but it does have history (Schneider 2000, 24). This history, rather than absolute origin, is vital to our understanding of heritage as active, moving and transforming. Schneider playfully points out that:

> mimesis makes all things slippery: the seeming original slips in and out of the ostensible copy, which slips around and through the original. Slippery, mimesis always gets away from us if we search for precision – especially if we seek an origin. (2000, 24)

The preservation of intangible cultural heritage is slippery business; it involves practices of copying copies as much or more than copying anything we might wish to call original (Schneider 2000).

Thinking of mimesis and transmission, Taylor uses dance to make her point about re-enactment and repertoires when she writes '[c]horeographers might draw from earlier repertoires to reenvision and reinvent new work that honours its predecessors even as it breaks new ground' (2008, 100). This is precisely what Ea

Figure 4. The dancers let down their hair near the end of *Drought and Rain 2011*. Photograph reprinted with permission from Company Ea Sola.

Sola's *Drought and Rain* performances *do* with, and as, heritage. The performances draw on memory and cultural tradition, reinvent its practices and meanings through re-enactment, incorporate contemporary elements, and create something new out of what has been done and re-done before. Re-enactment thus enables an alternative understanding of historical (re)productivity, one that is open to recursivity and recombination rather than determined by linear notions of development or set on 'freezing' (and potentially deadening) cultural traditions in the name of safeguarding 'cultural diversity or defending against cultural globalisation' (Kurin 2004, 74). When the women in *Drought and Rain 2011* let down their hair and whip their bodies about the stage near the end of the performance there can be no question that they, and the pasts they carry, are very much alive in the present (see Figure 4). The necessary repeating and/as reinventing of embodied practices highlights and reaffirms intangible cultural heritage as living and dialogic, where re-enactment is not immediately dismissed as the 'cheap copy', but valued as essential in the sustaining and passing on of vital embodied knowledges, practices and memories.

Toward a re-enacted, affective and dialogic, cross-border heritage

> The time to protest the war in Afghanistan is not over. The time to protest the war in Iraq is not over. The time to protest the war in Vietnam is not over [...] In fact, the time to protest war and its inevitable ties to industry, to capital, and to the drive to empire *is not, and is never, complete* [...] The time to protest is Now. It is Again. It is the necessary vigilance, the hard labour, of reiterating *Nunca Màs,* Never Again.
>
> Never, Again.
> And, now, again. (Schneider 2011, 186)

Schneider's claim that '[t]he time to protest the war in Vietnam is not over [...] The time to protest is Now. It is again', is apposite in expressing why *Drought and Rain* has recently re-emerged on European stages and why it is important for this performance, as a form of living-dialogic-global-heritage-as-protest, to be re-enacted again (186). Ea Sola specifically states that she understands her performances, the *Drought and Rain* series and others, as forms of protest (Eisner 2013). There are, as Schneider and Ea Sola powerfully contend, political imperatives to the againness of re-enacting the past, a past that is *still passing,* and that may in fact be/come our future.

Rephrasing Kierkegaard, Brian Massumi writes '[w]hereas memory as normally understood is a recollection of what has been, repetition is a recollection of what has not yet come – a memory of the future' (2010). While the seemingly discrete separation between memory and repetition is arguable, I do find compelling the suggestion that repetition, or re-enactment, has everything to do with futures-in-the-making. In Massumi's discussion of the US military, warfare readiness (in the form of repeated practices and utterances) is what I would call a *performativity of violence*: a repeated, self-contracting assurance of future wars-in-the-making. As Massumi and Schneider express, war and violence are ever incomplete, and so, counter-moves in the form of re-enacted protest, critique and dissent, must also continue indefinitely. Ea Sola's *Drought and Rain* series, as a re-enactment of Vietnamese, American, French and global heritage, is a counter-action to the unfinishedness of violence and the parallel, ongoing preparations for (more) war. Thinking with Massumi's formulation, Ea Sola's work of re-enactment acts as a *counter*-memory of the future. Ideally, as the *Drought and Rain* performances exemplify and as Schneider also contends, re-enactment of the heritage of war and violent pasts can, and in fact must, be used in the pursuit of conditioning futures with less (rather than more) suffering.

Drought and Rain 2011 and its prior variations help illuminate important qualities of re-enactment from which heritage studies and heritage preservation practices may benefit. The following is a provisional list of four performance-centred dynamics of heritage re-enactment. While I recognise that these qualities are not inherently 'good', I offer them in the spirit of their positive potentials:

(1) *Heritage re-enactment 'preserves', or sustains, through performative repetition*: The 're' of re-enactment is a necessary excess. It is integral to the process of handing down what is deemed valuable from one generation to the next. It is only through the duplicitous, predictable/unpredictable double that is never fully self-same that performance, through performative repetition, constitutes and (re)creates (Butler 1990). Put another way, the '[r]e' (of performance) acknowledges the pre-existing discursive field, the repetition – and the desire to repeat – within the performative present, while 'embody,' 'configure,' 'inscribe,' 'signify,' [and enact] assert the possibility of materialising something that exceeds our knowledge, that alters the shape of sites and imagines other as yet unsuspected modes of being (Diamond 1996, 2). Thus, the 're' of re-enactment performance, if added to Diamond's list, is in fact necessary in 'preserving,' or rather *sustaining,* heritage through time and space. Repetition, somewhat paradoxically, can be that which opens toward, rather than closes itself off from, difference. Operating by way of recursive (re)productivities, re-enactment has the capacity to open new knowledge through practicing, and exceeding, the known.

(2) *Heritage re-enactment promotes affective, interkinaesthetic correspondence*: Re-enactment is embodied and participatory, even if performer and audience

are one and the same. Through exchange of affective intensities or interkin-aesthetic connectivity, performers and audience members may generate greater awareness of self and other that is not necessarily reducible to the 'same feeling', but rather more like a resonating field of connexions. Foster claims we need not think of the interkinaesthetic as 'contamination to which we succumb, but instead, [...] as a basis for creating our social existence' (2008, 57). In other words, affect, or the 'intensities that pass body to body,' those 'visceral forces beneath, alongside, or generally *other than* conscious knowing, vital forces insisting beyond emotion' (Gregg and Seigworth 2010, 1) can be fundamental connecting tissues between people, passing through and across generations and borders of difference. Heritage re-enactment's reflexive and transitive affects have vital pedagogical potentials.

(3) *Heritage re-enactment practices cross-border culture and communication*: Hybrid re-enactments like the *Drought and Rain* series show it is possible to practice cross-border culture and aesthetics without becoming homogenised or claiming universal transcendence. The *Drought and Rain* series is an eclectic, provisional, contested and dialogic form of cultural heritage. The heritage the performances re-enact is Vietnamese, but not just Vietnamese. Due to the *Drought and Rain* series' mixed cultural, historical and political underpinnings, and the fact that the performances travel internationally, they initiate and enable important cross-border conversations and reflection (for example in post-show discussions and conversations, university classes, newspaper articles, etc.) that might not otherwise occur. In these ways, re-enactment helps heritage move, and translate, across borders.

(4) *Heritage re-enactment conditions change/possibility for futures-in-the-making*: as much as heritage projects concern themselves with the preservation of the past, they must also remain open to change. Repetition conditions the promise of change (Pollock 2005). This is not always a bad thing for heritage. Re-enactments like the *Drought and Rain* performances which are open to change, or even deliberately invested in it, can breathe new life into cultural practices, help sustain memory communities and enable people from diverse locations and walks of life to better understand particular and shared pasts, bear witness to continuing legacies of war and suffering, and hopefully, help intervene on present and future performativities of violence.

These four performance-centred dynamics of heritage re-enactment are not meant to be definitive, but rather to point towards the potential value in bringing varied and open notions of re-performance and re-enactment into play with conversations about heritage. Ea Sola's *Drought and Rain* series offers an especially complex rendering of re-enactment in that it simultaneously embodies the re-performance of everyday gestures as aesthetic performance while it also is the re-creation of one, or actually several, aesthetic performances into another. For the most part, heritage discourses can account for the latter as the transmission of traditional culture, but they have less to say about the former, where the legacies of everyday gesture – steeped with memory, history, ritual ceremony and the mundane yet facile functionality of long-standing habits – are transposed into aesthetic performance.

Ea Sola employs practices drawn from multiple cultural and national contexts, yet they are often not put to 'traditional' use. Her method of preservation is through re-combination and re-creation, engaging re-performance not as reproduction but as performative repetition (Chalmers 2008). Ea Sola's practice helps recast 'preservation' as *sustaining* traditions. Within the field of performance studies, much recent work on re-performance has focused on remakes of aesthetic performances (Chalmers 2008; Morgan 2010; Schechner 2010; Schneider 2011), historical re-enactments (Schneider 2011), re-telling memory narratives (Pollock 2005; Eisner 2012) or aesthetic performances that engage everyday activities (Stucky 1993; Morgan 2010). However, not enough attention has been given to the hybridity within re-performance. Re-performances like Ea Sola's *Drought and Rain* series, present complex, aggregative forms of re-enactment – aesthetic performance, social and cultural performance, everyday life performance, historical and memory performance – within a single (re)staged event. Closer examination of the different categories of re-enactment, and the layeredness and composite nature of re-performances can help us identify multiple variants of performance politics bound up in each re-staging, as well as question our assumptions about preservation and archiving, the 'origins' of memory, history, tradition and what we understand, inherit and hope to pass on as heritage.

Conclusion

Dance critic Thomas Hanh has said Ea Sola is 'akin to a NGO in arts' who 'defends Vietnam's cultural heritage against the extinction of memory brought about by globalisation' (n.d.). However, she has never been what one might think of as a typical 'tradition bearer'. Ea Sola facilitates the transfer of knowledges, practices and traditions diachronically across generations but also synchronically between individuals, groups, cultures and nations. Her work draws on and brings together embodied practices from multiple cultural and national lineages and she does not shy away from re-making and re-contextualising these art forms and aesthetic philosophies. The degree to which individuals or groups in Vietnam feel a 'sense of identity and continuity' in relation to the *Drought and Rain* performances is unclear, although people may more readily identify with histories and art forms that are used and referenced in the performance (UNESCO 2003, Article 2.1). Yet, despite the way these performances resist easy categorisation, as re-performance and heritage, they embody forms of inheritance, Vietnamese and global, that are valuable and important to sustain.

Ea Sola's *Drought and Rain* series helps illuminate various forms of re-enactment: re-performance of memory and history, everyday life practices, social and cultural performance, and prior aesthetic performances and traditions. Heritage discourses understand the transfer of aesthetic performance and cultural tradition as a form of cross-generational tradition, but when multiple kinds of re-performances are happening at once, and when there are a number of different cultural and national practices involved in the creation of a contemporary, avant-garde work, as in the case of *Drought and Rain,* these performances often fall outside traditional readings of heritage. My argument is that there should be space for understanding hybrid re-performances like the *Drought and Rain* series as heritage. Not only does *Drought and Rain* help sustain Vietnamese art forms and memories, these performances also translate knowledges and pasts across cultural and national borders, encouraging greater understanding and respect, promoting dialogue and continuing reflection and political critique.

Figure 5.   The young woman dances alone on stage with a marionette-like doll in *Drought and Rain 2011*. Photograph reprinted with permission from Company Ea Sola.

Recalling Đoàn's question from the beginning of *Drought and Rain 2011*, she asks: *the present generation, do they remember the centuries past?* The only partial response we in the audience receive is the recurring duet of a young woman, Nguyễn Thị Huyền, dancing with a life-size marionette-like doll. Perhaps Nguyễn too carries pieces of these ancient and more recent pasts as she imagines into her future (see Figure 5). We do not receive a clear or comforting answer. There is no guarantee that the present or ensuing generations do or will remember. This is why pasts must be told and re-told, re-enacted again and again. This is why *Drought and Rain* may, yet again, return.

Through their dialogic re-enactments of heritage the *Drought and Rain* performances remember and propose a counter-memory of the future – one that is uncertain and unfinished, but persistent. In the performances, the 'dancing body,' as 'the site of meaning in motion' is more than a useful metaphor for heritage as living, changing, affective and dialogic socio-cultural process (Desmond 1997, 20). It is the performing body, and the re-enacted renewal of heritage knowledges, practices and memories between bodies, that has the potential to move and (re)make futures.

Acknowledgements

The author would like to thank Ea Sola, So Kwok Wan and Dominique L'Huillier for their generous assistance. Many thanks also for the helpful comments from two anonymous reviewers and IJHS Editor Laurajane Smith, to Britta Timm Knudsen and Mads Daugbjerg for their insights and valuable feedback, as well as to the Danish Council for Independent Research|Humanities (FKK) for funding this research.

Notes

1. *Drought and Rain* (*Sécheresse et Pluie*) premiered at L'Hippodrome Scène Nationale in Douai, France in 1995.

2. This text, based on Ea Sola's dramaturgy and sung in Vietnamese, comes from the opening Prologue Song in the original libretto for *Drought and Rain 2011* and *Drought and Rain* (1995), which was written by esteemed literary figure Nguyễn Duy in collaboration with Ea Sola. The drum section was written by contemporary composer, and well-known *Chèo* musician, Nguyễn Xuân Sơn. This is Ea Sola's translation from the performance programme.

3. Some of the figures are anonymous, while others depict historical Vietnamese figures of mythic status such as famed fourteenth/fifteenth century scholar and military strategist Nguyễn Trãi, the heroic rebel fighters and sisters Hai Bà Trưng ('Hai Bà' means 'two ladies'), the tenth century emperor credited with unifying Vietnam after Chinese rule Đinh Tiên Hoàng, eighteenth century emperor and military hero Nguyễn Huệ, anti-colonial rebel Hoàng Hoa Thám, and the nationalist intellectual Phan Bội Châu.

4. Đoàn Thị Kết, mentioned at the beginning of this article, was one of the women Ea Sola met and worked with in Vietnam in the early 1990s.

5. See Knudsen's helpful distinction between 'authenticity' as experienced feeling and 'genuineness,' as 'the object's character of being a genuine trace' (2006, 10–11). Knudsen relates genuineness to specific places or objects, but I use it here to describe the sense of sincerity bound up in the performance and in Ea Sola's social efforts.

6. Here I am referencing reviews of the *Drought and Rain 2011* performances that took place in Edinburgh and London (e.g. reviews from *The Scotsman, The Guardian, The Independent, and The Telegraph*).

7. Although I use the term intangible cultural heritage to engage with current heritage discussions, I agree with many other scholars who contend that the various UNESCO categories of heritage (e.g. intangible, tangible, cultural, and natural) are problematic and reflect normative Euro-American assumptions (Kirshenblatt-Gimblett 2004; Kurin 2004; Smith and Akagawa 2009; Smith and Waterton 2009; Harrison 2013).

8. The UNESCO Convention for the Safeguarding of the Intangible Cultural Heritage creates two lists, (1) The Representative List of the Intangible Cultural Heritage of Humanity, and (2) The List of Intangible Cultural Heritage in Need of Urgent Safeguarding (UNESCO 2003, Article 16–17). The latter list specifies the need for urgent protections, but repeated reference to 'safeguarding' is present throughout the Convention and is clearly considered a central focus.

9. As many scholars have stressed, the increasing commodification of heritage requires consideration of the heritage industry, particularly the growing field of heritage tourism and experience economies (Kirshenblatt-Gimblett 1998, 2006; Smith 2003; Taylor 2008; Hitchcock, King, and Parnwell 2010; Knudsen and Waade 2010). One interesting aspect in considering the *Drought and Rain* performances within the heritage economy, is that they operate somewhat in the reverse of heritage tourism: instead of tourists travelling to a particular location to spectate, the heritage performance travels.

10. What I mean by 'dialogic' is akin to Rodney Harrison's proposal (2013), with the inclusion of mixed and multiple cultural practices. The UNESCO website on intangible cultural heritage states that heritage practices can help promote cross-cultural dialogue and respect (n.d.). The point I wish to make is inclusive of these claims and also extends the possibility of considering some intangible cultural heritage itself as dialogic in its form, construction, processes, relationship to time, and/or the individuals, communities, and transnational cultures involved.

11. A striking example of how the performances enabled cross-cultural, cross-border dialogue that would not otherwise have taken place, occurred after a US performance of *Drought and Rain* in 1995. To their surprise, the full cast was invited by General Westmoreland and his wife to have lunch at their home. Thus, twenty years after the official end of the war, the *Drought and Rain* performers ended up sharing a meal and conversation with the top commander of the US military operations in Vietnam during the war's most violent years.

References

Ahmad, Yahaya. 2006. "The Scope and Definitions of Heritage: From Tangible to Intangible." *International Journal of Heritage Studies* 12 (3): 292–300.

Anderson, Zoë. 2011. "Drought and Rain, Sadlers Wells, London." *The Independent*, September 28. Accessed April 9, 2013. http://www.independent.co.uk/arts-entertainment/theatre-dance/reviews/drought-and-rain-sadlers-wells-london-2361880.html

Anderson, Patrick, and Jisha Menon. 2009. "Introduction: Violence Performed." In *Violence Performed: Local Roots and Global Routes of Conflict*, edited by Patrick Anderson and Jisha Menon, 1–14. New York: Palgrave Macmillan.

Auslander, Philip. 2002. *Liveness: Performance in a Mediated Culture*. London: Routledge.

Bouchenaki, Mounir. 2004. "Editorial." *Museum International* 56 (1–2): 6–10.

Butler, Judith. 1990. *Gender Trouble: Feminism and the Subversion of Identity*. New York: Routledge.

Chalmers, Jessica. 2008. "Marina Abramović and the Re-performance of Authenticity." *Journal of Dramatic Theory and Criticism* 2 (Spring): 23–39.

'Culture Vulture.' 2011. *Việt Nam News*, last modified September 1. Accessed April 9, 2013. http://:vietnamnews.vnagency.com.vn/Pages/PrintView.aspx?ArticleID=214965

Desmond, Jane C. 1997. "Introduction." In *Meaning in Motion: New Cultural Studies of Dance*, edited by Jane C. Desmond, 1–25. Durham, NC: Duke University Press.

Diamond, Elin. 1996. "Introduction." In *Performance and Cultural Politics*, edited by Elin Diamond, 1–12. New York: Routledge.

Eisner, Rivka Syd. 2012. "Performing Pain-taking and Ghostly Remembering in Vietnam." *TDR: The Drama Review* 56 (3): 58–81.

Eisner, Rivka Syd. 2013. "Living Archives as Interventions in Ea Sola's *Forgotten Fields*." In *Performing Archives/Archives of Performance*, edited by Gunhild Borggreen and Rune Gade. Copenhagen: Museum Tusculanum Press.

Foster, Susan L. 2008. "Movement's Contagion: The Kinesthetic Impact of Performance." In *The Cambridge Companion to Performance Studies*, edited by Tracy C. Davis, 46–59. Cambridge: Cambridge University Press.

Gregg, Melissa, and Gregory J. Seigworth. 2010. "An Inventory of Shimmers." In *The Affect Theory Reader*, edited by Melissa Gregg and Gregory J. Seigworth, 1–25. Durham, NC: Duke University Press.

Hanh, Thomas. n.d. "Ea Sola – Harmony Between Body, Soul and Expression." Accessed February 14, 2013. http://www.gtlive.nl/producties/prod_thewhitebody.html.

Harrison, Rodney. 2013. *Heritage: Critical Approaches*. New York: Routledge.

Hassard, Frank. 2009. "Intangible Heritage in the United Kingdom: The Dark Side of Enlightenment?" In *Intangible Heritage*, edited by Laurajan Smith and Natsuko Akagawa, 270–288. New York: Routledge.

Hickling, Alfred. 2011. "Ea Sola: 'I am not an intellectual, I come from the forest'." *The Guardian*, August 25. Accessed September 1, 2011. http://www.guardian.co.uk/music/2011/aug/25/ea-sola-drought-and-rain-vietnam-war/print.

Hitchcock, Michael, Victor T. King, and Michael Parnwell. 2010. *Heritage Tourism in Southeast Asia*. Copenhagen: NIAS Press.

Kenny, Mary Lorena. 2009. "Deeply Rooted in the Present: Making Heritage in Brazilian Quilombos." In *Intangible Heritage*, edited by Laurajane Smith and Natsuko Akagawa, 151–168. New York: Routledge.

Kirshenblatt-Gimblett, Barbara. 1998. *Destination Culture: Tourism, Museums, and Heritage*. Berkeley: University of California Press.

Kirshenblatt-Gimblett, Barbara. 2004. "Intangible Heritage as Metacultural Production." *Museum International* 56 (1–2): 52–65.

Kirshenblatt-Gimblett, Barbara. 2006. "World Heritage and Cultural Economics." In *Museum Frictions: Public Cultures/Global Transformations*, edited by Ivan Karp, Corinne A. Kratz, Lynn Szwaja, and Tomás Ybarra-Fraust, 161–575. Durham, NC: Duke University Press.

Knudsen, Britta Timm. 2006. "Emotional Geography: Authenticity, Embodiment, and Cultural Heritage." *Ethnologia Europaea* 36 (2): 5–15.

Knudsen, Britta Timm, and Anne Marit Waade, eds. 2010. *Re-Investing Authenticity: Tourism, Place and Emotions*. Bristol: Channel View Publications.

Krauss, Rosalind. 2000. *A Voyage on the North Sea: Art in the Age of the Post-medium Condition*. London: Thames and Hudson.

Kurin, Richard. 2004. "Safeguarding Intangible Cultural Heritage in the 2003 UNESCO Convention: A Critical Appraisal." *Museum International* 56 (1–2): 66–76.

Massumi, Brian. 2010. "Perception Attack: Brief on War Time." *Theory & Event* 13 (3). Accessed February 15, 2012. http://muse.jhu.edu.ez.statsbiblioteket.dk:2048/journals/theory_and_event/v013/13.3.massumi.html

Morgan, Robert C. 2010. "Thoughts on Re-performance, Experience, and Archivism." *PAJ: A Journal of Performance and Art* 32 (3): 1–15.

Oliver, Kelly. 2001. *Witnessing Beyond Recognition*. Minneapolis, MN: University of Minnesota Press.

Pollock, Della. 1998. "Introduction: Making History Go." In *Exceptional Spaces: Essays in Performance and History*, edited by Della Pollock, 1–45. Chapel Hill, NC: University of North Carolina Press.

Pollock, Della. 2005. "Introduction: Remembering." In *Remembering: Oral History Performance*, edited by Della Pollock, 1–17. New York: Palgrave Macmillan.

Rae, Paul. 2002. "On Applause." Unpublished seminar paper, Middlesex University, UK.

Schechner, Richard. 2010. "The Conservative Avant-garde." *New Literary History* 41: 895–913.

Schneider, Rebecca. 2000. "On Taking the Blind in Hand." *Contemporary Theatre Review* 10 (3): 23–38.

Schneider, Rebecca. 2011. *Performing Remains: Art and War in Times of Theatrical Reenactment*. New York: Routledge.

Skounti, Ahmed. 2009. "The Authentic Illusion: Humanity's Intangible Cultural Heritage, the Moroccan Experience." In *Intangible Heritage*, edited by Laurajane Smith and Natsuko Akagawa, 74–92. New York: Routledge.

Smith, Melanie K. 2003. *Issues in Cultural Tourism Studies*. London: Routledge.

Smith, Laurajane. 2006. *Uses of Heritage*. London: Routledge.

Smith, Laurajane, and Natsuko Akagawa. 2009. "Introduction." In *Intangible Cultural Heritage*, edited by Laurajane Smith and Natsuko Akagawa, 1–9. New York: Routledge.

Smith, Laurajane, and Emma Waterton. 2009. "'The envy of the world?': Intangible Heritage in England." In *Intangible Heritage*, edited by Laurajane Smith and Natsuko Akagawa, 289–302. New York: Routledge.

Stucky, Nathan. 1993. "Toward an Aesthetics of Natural Performance." *Text and Performance Quarterly* 13: 168–180.

Taylor, Diana. 2003. *The Archive and the Repertoire: Performing Cultural Memory in the Americas*. Durham, NC: Duke University Press.

Taylor, Diana. 2008. "Performance and Intangible Cultural Heritage." In *The Cambridge Companion to Performance Studies*, edited by Tracy C. Davis, 91–94. Cambridge: Cambridge University Press.

Thrift, Nigel J. 2008. *Non-Representational Theory: Space, Politics, Affect*. New York: Routledge.

UNESCO (United Nations Educational, Scientific and Cultural Organization). 17 October 2003. "Convention for the Safeguarding of the Intangible Cultural Heritage." 32nd Session of the General Conference, 1–14, Paris. Accessed January 5, 2013. http://unesdoc.unesco.org/images/0013/001325/132540e.pdf

UNESCO (United Nations Educational, Scientific and Cultural Organization) n.d. "What is Intangible Cultural Heritage?" Accessed April 9, 2013. http://www.unesco.org/culture/ich/index.php?pg=00002

Whitham, Caroline. 2011. "Edinburgh Festivals: Drought and Rain (re-creation 2011)." *Edinburgh Festivals Magazine,* September 1. Accessed March 14, 2012. http://edfestmag.co.uk/international/dance/2070-201109droughtandrain

Index

Note: page numbers in italic type refer to Figures; those followed by 'n' and another number refer to Notes.

INDEX